ParishWor

Tips and Templates to Revitalize Your Church

Ward McCance

COMPLEMENTS OF THE PROGRAMME OFFICE

Stewardship resources, additional copies of this book, and direct assistance are available to those looking to expand the stewardship ministry in their parish. For further information, please contact:

Steven V. Matthews, Stewardship Officer
Telephone: (514) 843-6577, ex 256
smatthews@montreal.anglican.ca

ABC Publishing
ANGLICAN BOOK CENTRE

ABC Publishing
ANGLICAN BOOK CENTRE

From Scarcity to Abundance: A Complete Guide to Parish Stewardship *by David M. Ponting.* In this superbly practical and accessible resource for parish stewardship, David Ponting demystifies the process of nurturing a culture of stewardship, working with limited volunteer availability, year-round stewardship programs, and using effective tools and techniques such as Narrative Budgets, Planned Giving programs, and Capital Campaigns. *1-55126-438-2 $24.95*

Seeking the Seekers: Serving the Hidden Spiritual Quest *by Paul MacLean and Michael Thompson.* Who are the seekers? What are they searching for? Discover effective ways to reconnect with the lives of people and realize new energy in the local parish. "A brilliant addition to our wisdom about ... ministry today"—Loren B. Meade, founding president, The Alban Institute. *1-55126-308-4 $16.95*

Your Church Can Thrive: Making the Connections that Build Healthy Congregations *by Harold Percy.* Provides solid, easy to follow advice on how churches can understand the needs of their members, friends and family, visitors, and community—and also reach out to them. The central goal is to offer people new life in Christ. *1-55126-408-0 $17.95*

The Sanctuary: Preparing the Church for Worship *by Virginia Mainprize.* This valuable resource combines a history and description of vessels, vestments, and church furnishings with specific instructions for their care and use. Spiral-bound. *1-55126-096-4 $16.95*

Servers and Services: Instructions for Serving Anglican Liturgies *by Greig S. Dunn.* This best-selling manual offers clear instructions along with illustrations for simple or elaborate ceremonial for the BCP and BAS liturgies. Spiral-bound. *0-919891-41-1 $16.95*

ParishWorks

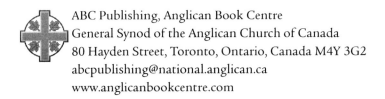

ABC Publishing, Anglican Book Centre
General Synod of the Anglican Church of Canada
80 Hayden Street, Toronto, Ontario, Canada M4Y 3G2
abcpublishing@national.anglican.ca
www.anglicanbookcentre.com

Text set in ITC Legacy
Cover and text design by Jane Thornton

Ward McCance is available on a consulting basis to help kick-start or evaluate your ParishWorks and program(s). He can be contacted through e-mail (parishworks@sympatico.ca).

Library and Archives Canada Cataloguing in Publication
McCance, Ward
    ParishWorks : tips and templates to revitalize your church / Ward McCance.
Includes index.

ISBN 1-55126-484-6
ISBN 978-1-55126-484-4

1. Church management. 2. Christian leadership. 3. Church renewal.
I. Title.
II. Title: Parish works.

BV600.3.M356 2007   254   C2007-900727-9

Printed in Canada

Table of Contents

Preface

Every church member brings skills to his or her parish. Working as a rector's warden, stewardship chairperson, and restoration project leader, I brought knowledge of financial management and process improvements from my careers in banking and information technology. While I helped make improvements in the works of my parish, it was not until I became involved with other parishes through diocesan assignments that I came to see how many struggle with the same problems, only to invent solutions already created elsewhere. Often, I found, parishes were reinventing the same wheels—and too many square ones. It seemed to me that parishes could benefit from each other's experiences—what works, what doesn't.

I shared these concerns with my diocesan bishop, the Rt. Rev. Colin Johnson, who suggested I create a resource to help parishes with their works. I followed up with ABC Publishing, Anglican Book Centre, and this publication is the result.

Now, I'd be the first to agree that not every suggestion in this book will be applicable to your parish, nor in the forms presented. However, I do believe that having a framework for parish position descriptions, forms, checklists, and program plans will help the members of any parish (large or small) move forward more effectively in improving their ParishWorks. All templates for this framework, provided in *ParishWorks*, are included on the enclosed CD in Microsoft Word format. Parishes can copy the templates to a computer, then edit them to suit their parish. In this way, parish teams do not have to start with a blank page when they begin a new parish program or process. Also, the information in the templates will help teams consider other aspects of their ParishWorks that they may not have considered, as well as give suggestions for what works in other parishes versus what doesn't, and why not. My hope is that you will read the book first, of course, so that you will appreciate the background information and tips about the tools before charging off to improve your ParishWorks.

You may feel you need to read only the chapter that relates to your current focus and can ignore the rest, but this may not be a good idea. Parish teams do not operate on their own. Their actions affect others, and vice versa. For example, one team may want to launch an outreach campaign. The campaign will affect the finances of the parish (Financial Management), and it will affect the stewardship aspects of the members (Congregation Development). The team will need to keep the parish's mission statement in mind as they create the outreach campaign (Mission Statement); the campaign will likely need volunteers to help run it (Volunteer Management); the team will need to effectively communicate the campaign goals and results to the congregation and community (Communications Management); and the team will likely need to include the worship team in their plans, for outreach Sunday services in the campaign (Worship Program Development). Once you have read and clearly appreciate the interconnections parish teams make, you are then best able to use the templates, armed with the necessary knowledge to make your parish programs and projects successful.

Even given the content of this book, you may need a helping hand at times. Sister parishes are a good start—another parish may have carried out the same initiative you are planning, and may have solved many unforseen problems you might come up against. Your diocesan office, too, will have resources to share. As well, I would be willing (on a consulting basis) to help kick-start or evaluate your ParishWorks and program(s). I can be contacted through e-mail (parishworks@sympatico.ca).

Regardless, you should never feel you are on your own. Few things are more daunting (especially for a volunteer) than doing something for the first time. Lean on your teams—lean on other teams and other parishes, because we are all in this together. No one has all the answers; but most of the answers you will need are only an ask away.

I hope this book gives you some ideas to help you with the works of your parish—so that you can show your members and your community how your ParishWorks.

Acknowledgements

One might consider a handbook about parish administration to be less thrilling than a suspense novel, yet in writing this book I found unexpected excitement considering what our parishes can be, with more planning, coaching, and celebrating. I hope you will find it helpful to move your parish beyond what you can imagine today.

While many parishes have contributed to the experiences that are the basis for the information in this book, I would particularly like to thank four people for their support.

First, I would like to thank Bishop Colin Johnson, Anglican Diocese of Toronto, for suggesting the project and for enabling experiences that led to the content in *ParishWorks*.

Second, I would like to thank the Rev. Jim Blackmore, St. George's Anglican Church, Pickering Village, Ontario, for having enough faith in these ideas to try them out at St. George's, and for more than 20 years of inspiration in the parish, helping to show what a relatively small parish can accomplish when given a vision.

Third, I would like to thank my daughter, the Rev. Heather McCance, Christ Church (Anglican), Holland Landing, Ontario, and St. James the Apostle Anglican Church, Sharon, Ontario, for showing me how parishes can grow in numbers and in passion, with inspired leadership.

And last but not least, I would like to thank my wife, Linda McCance, who got me refocused on our church, encouraged me throughout my parish administration assignments, and who tolerated my hours of keying on our PC to put these pages together.

Ward McCance
Cobourg, Ontario

Chapter 1

Introduction and ParishWorks Self-Assessment

Responsible Stewardship

In the Bible there are many lessons for us that focus on responsible steward-ship of our resources. Christ showed us several examples during his lifetime. Often church members find themselves looking for ways to apply these lessons in their lives, but do not know where to start.

During the next Sunday service, look around. Are the church building and parish hall well cared for? Are they places where newcomers would feel welcome?

When parishioners give at collection time, are they confident that their financial gifts will be put to the best use? Do they understand the costs of operating the parish? Are the destinations of outreach financial gifts well known and reaching those most in need?

During the exchange of the Peace, ask yourself, Are members of the parish well cared for? Do all know they are valued? Are their desires and passions known, and do the parish programs meet their needs? Are new-comers welcomed?

If any members of your parish are looking for opportunities to practise good stewardship, they won't need to look farther than the Sunday service. Parish assets—financial, physical, and most important, people—need to be looked after. Each has diverse needs that must be addressed with the proper skills and knowledge through the parish's leadership and team members. Many are volunteers, though, and may lack some of the knowledge and skills required.

When properly managed, these tasks and responsibilities can offer exciting opportunities for parish volunteers, if they are given sufficient understanding and support. Often there are potential volunteers just wait-ing to be asked, but they are not; or volunteers are asked but not given any guidelines to follow, and they back away.

This book attempts to bridge some of the knowledge and support gaps experienced in many parishes, and to give parish leaders a head start in up-grading parish administration, stewardship, and development so that the works of your parish will show your members and community that your *ParishWorks*.

You'll find (1) tips and best practices that have generated fresh ideas and leadership to help parishes grow in numbers and enthusiasm; and (2) working templates that have positively and methodically guided parish teams to run effective programs.

Application in Small and Large Parishes

Some how-to publications attempt a "one-size-fits-all" approach. This tends to be confusing because it helps some readers, but not others.

The tips, templates, and techniques described here have been adapted successfully in a range of parish sizes and settings: a small inner-city parish, a large suburban parish, and a small two-point rural parish, among others. The topics in each chapter will apply to your parish, regardless of its size. Each chapter includes a list of priorities for parishes with limited resources (that would be just about every one). A plan of action for small-, medium-, and large-scale parishes is also offered, with suggestions on how to adapt the information for different parish settings.

ParishWorks Self-Assessment

To see how your parish might best benefit from this handbook, and where to concentrate its efforts, complete the following checklist. You might also ask your parish leadership team, or perhaps the advisory board members, to complete the assessment. A template for the assessment form may be found on the enclosed CD in Microsoft Word format (see selfassessment.doc).

If your parish scores
- 0–2 Nos in a topic area, probably your parish is in good shape;
- 2–4 Nos, read on for practical ways to improve;
- 4+ Nos, read on and be prepared to make some rewarding changes.

Assets Management	Yes	No
1. Does the parish have a copy of its property survey and know its ownership status and restrictions?	____	____
2. Have the parish buildings been inspected within the last five years and have all inspection issues been taken care of?	____	____
3. If the parish rents any of its space, is there a rental agreement in place? Has it been approved by the diocese and has a legal opinion been sought?	____	____
4. Does the parish have a capital fund? Is there an annual budget for capital expenditures based on a list of costed improvements?	____	____
5. Does the parish have a sexton whose roles and responsibilities are outlined in a position description?	____	____
6. Is there an inventory of parishioners who can pitch in and carry out small repairs and improvements to the buildings, and are their services consistently utilized?	____	____
7. Does the parish market the availability of its building space to the community?	____	____
8. Has the parish utilized volunteer help as much as possible to clean parish buildings?	____	____

Congregation Development	Yes	No
1. Has a parish survey been carried out within the last year to obtain feedback about parish programs and to inventory the parishioners' passions?	____	____

2. Have the survey results been applied to change parish programs and improve how volunteers are used? _____ _____

3. Has the parish held volunteer appreciation events this year? _____ _____

4. Does the parish have a growth/marketing plan, with growth targets tracked each year? _____ _____

5. Does the parish advertise its programs and special events regularly? _____ _____

6. Does the parish participate in community events, and does it partner with service clubs and other churches in the community? _____ _____

7. Does the leadership team follow up regularly with absentee parishioners? _____ _____

8. Do parish programs match the passions of its parishioners? _____ _____

9. Does the parish have greeters at services (in addition to sidespeople) whose role is to welcome newcomers and parishioners who have been absent? _____ _____

Outreach

	Yes	No
1. Has the parish carried out a community needs analysis within the past two to three years, to determine any gaps in the safety net for those most in need?	_____	_____
2. Does the parish have a local outreach program based on helping those in need who might otherwise not receive assistance?	_____	_____
3. Does the parish integrate its local outreach program with those of the diocese and national church, so that all programs make sense to donors?	_____	_____

4. Does the parish arrange to have outreach beneficiaries visit the parish to share their good news stories? _____ _____

5. Does the parish thank its donors formally each year? _____ _____

6. Does the parish supplement its outreach program with homilies and lay addresses on good stewardship, including suggested givings? _____ _____

7. Does the parish have annual tours of local outreach facilities for parishioners? _____ _____

8. Does the parish partner with other local churches and service clubs to build more effective community outreach programs? _____ _____

Worship Development	Yes	No
1. Do lay volunteers help plan the worship themes and service structures?	_____	_____
2. Are worship themes planned for the year, and are these known to the parishioners in advance?	_____	_____
3. Does the parish vary its service structure, to recognize other Anglican forms used in other countries?	_____	_____
4. Do Sunday school and youth group curricula match the service themes?	_____	_____
5. Do the Sunday school and youth groups lead the service at least once a year?	_____	_____
6. Does the parish use its web site to deliver service content (e.g., service bulletin, sermon) to shut-ins?	_____	_____
7. Does the parish have an active pastoral care program that serves all shut-ins each week?	_____	_____

8. Does the parish have a variety of people delivering the service homily (e.g., guest rectors, parishioners) at least once a month? _____ _____

Financial Management	Yes	No

1. Does the parish have a balanced operating budget for the current year, including contingency? _____ _____

2. Does the parish have a yearly budget based on monthly actuals of past years, and are variances tracked accordingly? _____ _____

3. Does the parish have a treasurer whose roles and responsibilities are clearly outlined in a position description? _____ _____

4. Do the treasurer, wardens, and rector meet each month to review the past month's income and expenses, and any variances to the budget? _____ _____

5. Does the parish's chart of accounts segregate operating funds from capital and outreach? _____ _____

6. Do the various parish program teams maintain their own budget lines and report actuals each month? _____ _____

7. Is the GST-refundable being calculated correctly and remitted regularly? _____ _____

8. Are all expense transactions being co-signed by the wardens, and is the Sunday collection being counted and banked by two people? _____ _____

9. Are all paid staff up to date with their Canada Pension Plan, Employment Insurance, and other deductions, and has reporting been done correctly to the Canada Revenue Agency? _____ _____

"But Where Do We Start?"

The assessment questionnaire focuses on five key aspects of parish administration: assets management, congregation development, outreach, worship development, and financial management. From the results of the assessment a picture will emerge: the Yeses reflect a parish's mission statement and the unique passions of its members. The Nos may indicate that some aspects of parish administration are being neglected. In either case, improvement is often possible.

For example, one parish might see itself as a mission parish and concentrate its energy on outreach. In this case, the parish leadership team could consider chapter 8, Outreach Program Development, to see if they are being fully effective with their volunteers' energies and talents, and whether outreach beneficiaries are well served. The parish could also consider other important aspects of ParishWorks, to ensure that they are not focused on too few parish aspects to their detriment. Are they taking care, for instance, of their outreach volunteers (chapter 5, Volunteer Management)? Are they managing the donations and outreach disbursements properly (chapter 11, Financial Management)? Are they taking care of their church buildings (chapter 9, Parish Assets Management)? Is their worship program lively and varied (chapter 7, Worship Program Development)?

It may be helpful to arrange the five key aspects of parish administration into columns. In each column, list the work that *must* be done for that particular focal point, then the work that the parish *should* and *could* be doing. For example, under Worship Development, the musts would include Sunday services, Sunday school, choir—the basics. Below these, the shoulds might be worship themes, lay leadership, and youth services (see chapter 7, Worship Program Development). Then, considering parish priorities and the mission statement, the parish leadership team could decide for each column how far they *could* take their parish, given the resources available. The example below may also be found on the enclosed CD in Microsoft Word format (see priorities.doc).

Parish Improvement Priorities

Worship Development	Outreach Development	Financial Management	Assets Management	Congregation Development
Musts • regular services • Sunday school • youth program • Bible study • organist	**Musts** • information distribution • financial tracking • local program	**Musts** • monthly reporting • budget tracking • bank reconciliation • dual controls • fund-raising	**Musts** • sexton • maintenance list • inspections • capital fund	**Musts** • volunteer inventory • greeters • fellowship events • thank-you events
Shoulds • lay sermons	**Shoulds** • partnerships	**Shoulds** • monthly variances	**Shoulds** • building committee	**Shoulds** • marketing program
Coulds • theme services • kids' services • guest speakers • alternate forms	**Coulds** • sponsors • themes • needs assessments • stewardship	**Coulds** • trend analysis • stewardship • expense management • program budgets	**Coulds** • capital campaigns • rentals	**Coulds** • program development • visitations

Small parishes may find that they can skim only the top of the five columns—and that's fine. It is important that, given very limited resources, small parishes carefully review the chapters on each of the five aspects of ParishWorks to ensure that they are proceeding in the most effective ways possible, especially since their volunteers' time is at a premium. Small parishes, however, could also review the information in the other chapters for tips on how to make the works of the parish more meaningful. For example, a small parish may have an excellent fellowship program, but may not keep track of volunteer burnout (see chapter 5, Volunteer Management). While the parish leadership team may think it does not have time to consider a volunteer inventory and volunteer succession planning, they will find that, without them, their limited volunteer base will shrink, either in numbers or in the time that volunteers are willing to give. By neglecting to properly care for volunteers, a small parish will have difficulty just doing the basics—a failure spiral might result.

Although your parish may not carry out all the recommendations in this book next year (and it likely couldn't), the leadership team may find it helpful to learn what other parishes have done. In this way, if the parish's priorities change, the leadership team will know how to move in new directions. The suggestions in each chapter are intended for your parish's consideration. You may find, for example, having carried out an outreach needs analysis in your community (see chapter 8, Outreach Program Development), that you uncover a dire need that your parish is well-positioned to address. Often it is helpful for parishes to reassess their priorities and shake themselves up. It can be amazing to see what your parish can do, that you could not have asked for or imagined.

I hope you will enjoy this book. Relax as you go through it. Don't worry what your parish hasn't done. Instead, ask yourself what your parish might do, using some of the tips and techniques offered, to help lead the teams to success. And if the parish cannot do everything this year—there is always next year.

Chapter 2

The Parish Leadership Team

Before we explore the tips and templates for effective ParishWorks, we need to consider the various roles of the parish leadership, and how the team works together. If parish leaders are having difficulties with their responsibilities and communication, the parish will be unable to move forward.

Roles of the Wardens and the Rector

While each diocese's canons differ slightly, they tend to match in describing the duties of the wardens and the rector. The parish leadership team should be familiar with these descriptions; if not, they should review them and, if anything seems unclear, contact the diocesan office to obtain clarity.

Generally the two wardens are responsible for the parish finances and property, or buildings and land, while the rector has responsibility for the forms of worship used. This arrangement seems straightforward, but there are as many ways of managing these responsibilities as there are parishes. At one extreme, some wardens have been known to dominate the parish and relegate the rector to a "staff" position, limiting his or her role to the weekly sermon. At the other end of the spectrum, some rectors have chosen both wardens and have given them very little responsibility, except to sign (or in some cases, pre-sign) cheques. Clearly either of these extremes will be damaging to the parish and is not workable in the long run.

Technically the rector is paid by the parish to carry out its ministry leadership, but the canons are not intended to set up a staff–management relationship with the rector and wardens. While the canons specify that the rector will appoint one of the wardens, this does not mean the rector's warden "works for" the rector. Rather, both the wardens and the rector form the parish leadership team, with each contributing to help move the parish forward.

Ideally each should understand their role to be a position of trust. They are not expected to "take over" the affairs of the parish or lead the parish in all ways. In fact, this team needs to facilitate the distribution of various parish responsibilities to those parishioners who best suit the tasks. How much the congregation is engaged in its ParishWorks is a key measure of the effectiveness of its three leaders.

Trust begins with how the wardens and rector treat each other. Honesty, understanding, caring, and sharing are all attributes of a well-integrated leadership team. There is often more work to be done than there is time, and the effective distribution of tasks to each leader is necessary so that nothing slips between the cracks. Each of the three leaders also needs to be able to back up the other two, in case one is away or is swamped with other tasks. Sharing work in this way provides a good safety net for the parish.

The next step for the leadership team is to divide up the work of the parish, so that each will not be stepping on the others' toes. Though the canons need to be followed, there is ample room for flexibility, especially in cases where one leader has a passion for a specific parish responsibility that may "belong" to one of the others. The team should allocate the various responsibilities with respect to their skills and desires. For example, the rector is normally responsible for selecting, or approving the selection of, the music used during services. One of the wardens, though, may be particularly gifted in music, and may be a better choice than the rector. The rector, in turn, may have valuable experience in church-building restoration, for example, and might be the best person to oversee a restoration project, if he or she has the time and the interest.

While some flexibility may be desirable, two important canonical directives must always be followed:

1. Since the wardens are the legal officers of the parish corporation, their dual signatures on all financial transactions (e.g., cheques, contracts) are required. This duty cannot be shared by the rector.

2. The rector has been ordained and has been charged with the ministry of the parish by the diocesan bishop. This responsibility cannot be assumed by the wardens.

When in doubt, it is advisable for the team to contact the diocesan office to ensure that their responsibility-sharing model is acceptable. Once the model is established, the leadership team should publish their roles and responsibilities, and present these descriptions to the parish, making it clear who does what and why for the parish. The start of a good description for each role (rector and wardens) may be taken from the canons. To the basic roles, the team may add specific examples, as agreed among themselves. Example: the rector's warden may serve as the primary contact for the parish's buildings and property, and the people's warden may serve as the primary contact for the parish's financial affairs. Or the rector might be the primary contact for the parish's outreach program. And so on.

An example of a warden's position description follows. An electronic version in Microsoft Word format may be found on the enclosed CD (see warden.doc).

Position Description: People's Warden

Role

In accordance with the canons of the diocese, the people's warden is one of the two wardens of the parish corporation, and forms the legal identity of the parish. With the rector's warden and the parish rector, the people's warden is a member of the parish executive, and ensures that the parish operates according to the canons of the diocese and the legal requirements of the country, province, and municipality.

Along with the rector's warden, the people's warden ensures that the parish remains financially sound and that the assets of the parish are protected.

Responsibilities

The people's warden shares the following responsibilities with the rector's warden:

- signing authority for all legal documents of the parish, including cheques, contracts, and approvals;
- preparation of the parish's financial returns for the diocese, the Canada Revenue Agency, and any other regulatory bodies;
- care of the parish's buildings and property, including insurance, security, inspections, and corrective measures when indicated by health and safety issues;
- management of the financial accounts of the parish, ensuring that records are complete and correct, and audited yearly;
- collection at services, ensuring confidentiality, security, and accuracy of recordkeeping;

- creation of the parish's annual budget, tracking actual expenses each month, and taking corrective action as necessary; and
- management of staff hired by the parish.

In addition to the above responsibilities shared with the rector's warden, the people's warden is responsible for *(include here any additional responsibilities, as agreed by the rector's warden and the rector, such as those below)*:

- the parish's outreach program, ensuring that the donations collected reach the designated programs;
- chairing the parish's monthly advisory board meetings; and
- upkeep of the parish cemetery and the cemetery fund.

Duration

The people's warden is elected by the vestry for a term of one year.

Skills Required

- Knowledge of the canons and diocese/parish responsibilities;
- financial management, especially in income/expense reporting and chart of accounts management, as well as budgeting and variance reporting;
- staff management;
- knowledge of the property bylaws of the municipality; and
- *(list the skills required for the additional responsibilities outlined above)*.

Keep in mind that the distribution of parish leadership responsibilities does not mean assigning all work associated with that responsibility to the wardens or rector—rather, the wardens and rector will monitor those assigned to various tasks, to ensure that the work is done properly. For example, if the rector's warden agrees to have primary responsibility for parish buildings and property, this would be noted in his or her position description. In distributing the workload, however, the rector's warden would appoint, or have vestry elect, a parish sexton to oversee day-to-day upkeep of the buildings and property, perhaps aided by an assets management team. The rector's warden, in delegating this canonical responsibility to the sexton, would ensure that the buildings and property were being properly cared for.

Communicating and Working Together

All three members of the leadership team will be engaged with other work. The wardens may still be in the workforce, and will be focused on their careers and families. The rector may be busy with choir practices and diocesan meetings, or carrying out visitations. It is easy for the leadership team to drift apart for one to two weeks at a time, without being in touch.

To bridge these potential gaps, the team should meet every two weeks, or at least monthly, to discuss the affairs of the parish and to stay in accord among themselves. At a monthly wardens' meeting, the treasurer should compare the income and expenses of the previous month with the budget, and highlight any variances. This gives the leadership team the opportunity to take corrective action, as required. They may also wish to use the advisory board as a sounding board for corrective action ideas, before they make a final decision.

The parish income and expenses, while important, should not dominate the wardens' meeting. Once the financial situation has been reviewed, the treasurer should leave, and the leadership team then go on to deal with other parish matters. This might include any issues needing their attention or preparation for the upcoming advisory board meeting. Here is a suggested agenda:

Where are we?
- Treasurer's monthly update (20 mins).
- Congregational health/growth/newcomers (15 mins).
- Program team updates and issues, if any (15 mins).
- Other issues (10 mins).

What's coming up?
- Upcoming events and issues, if any (10 mins).
- Upcoming advisory board meeting preparation (15 mins).
- Upcoming absences and coverage (5 mins).
- Other business (5 mins).

While it is desirable for these one and a-half- to two-hour meetings to be focused and productive, they also offer a good way for the leadership team to get to know each other better and to understand any concerns, including those that may be felt but not voiced. To the extent possible, the rector and wardens should try to reach an understanding of each other, so that each has a fair idea of what the other two might do in a given situation, and may act accordingly—as a team.

Communicating and Working with the Parish

Often parish leadership teams do not communicate effectively with the parish members. Months may go by without the parish hearing from their wardens. Parish issues can simmer in the background without updates from the wardens or rector. The team may not respond consistently when asked about a parish event or issue. Many people assume that the "grapevine" or simple "osmosis" will keep everyone informed. This just does not happen, even in the smallest parish. Without good communication, parishioners are left to interpret events, and parish gossip may ensue. This builds division within the parish.

The parish executive team should see that the parish is as up to date on parish events, issues, and related decisions as its leadership. The communication plan for the year may vary, depending on what works best within the parish culture, but the team must proactively plan for the communication stream to happen monthly—or more frequently, as events dictate. Ideally leadership teams should map out their communication strategy at the start of each year. All of the following ideas may be adapted and mixed for best effect:

- wardens' addresses/updates during Sunday services;
- service bulletin updates from the wardens and rector;
- wardens' and rector's updates in the parish newsletter;
- wardens' and rector's monthly updates on the parish web site; and
- wardens' updates during fellowship events.

The wardens and rector need to take turns handling the parish updates. None of the team should be seen by the parish to be dominating.

The leadership team is as good as its parish volunteers. The team needs to foster its natural leaders, and support them when they run into roadblocks. They need to celebrate the various parish teams' successes, and thank them for a job well done. While much more may be said on this aspect of parish leadership (see chapter 5, Volunteer Management), the care and building of parish teams must come from the leadership itself. They are the respected leaders of the parish—if they do not help create and celebrate the parish's achievements, who will?

Chapter 3

The Parish Mission Statement

Let's say your parish has an effective leadership team. What's next? Do all of the parishioners go off, form committees, and direct their passions on behalf of the parish? In order for a parish to move forward in a focused, coordinated way, it must take one crucial step: the building of a parish mission statement.

Mission Statements versus Slogans

In the secular world, mission statements range from one-line slogans for marketing purposes (for instance, "committed to excellence") to more internally focused statements of corporate objectives and measurements for achievement (for instance, "We will grow our client base by 12% per year through a program of higher product quality and highly responsible client service, measured through annual client surveys").

In practice, slogans are just that: slogans. Typically they are open-ended and lack a plan for action and measurement. Many parishes, unfortunately, rely on slogan-type mission statements: "Welcoming all people with warmth and tradition" ... "A symbol of God's presence and love in the city" ... "To experience God; to grow spiritually and to ask questions."

Corporate mission statements, however, when carefully constructed, tend to focus management and employees on the key objectives of the organization, and the measurements that will be carried out to ensure success. How can using this kind of structure help create strong parish mission statements that are both purposeful and achievable?

Effective Parish Mission Statements

A well-developed parish mission statement will focus the parish on its role and objectives, which will direct all of its ParishWorks. This, in turn, will answer the "W" questions:

- **Who** (are we)?
- **What** (do we do)?
- **Where** (do we do what we do)?
- **Why** (do we do what we do)?

While not a "W" word, effective parish mission statements will include the question, **How** (do we do what we do)? This ensures that the parish has some way of monitoring its actions and programs, so that parishioners can measure their successes.

Another key "W" word is **When** (do we plan to do what we do)? At the end of each year, the parish should prepare a plan for the upcoming year, to map out what they intend to accomplish. These plans (see templates Congregation Development Plan, Outreach Development Plan, Assets Management Plan, and Financial Management Plan included in this book) define the Whens of the mission statement, year by year.

How might a parish include all of these aspects in its mission statement? Consider the mission statement from St. George's Anglican parish in Ajax, Ontario:

Following the example of Jesus Christ day by day, the members of St. George's parish family are called by God to Welcome, Worship, Learn, Care, and Grow in our church, in our communities of Ajax and Pickering, and beyond:

— We Welcome all adults, youth, and children with excitement, interest, and openness—treasuring our human diversity;
— We Worship in the Anglican tradition through a variety of liturgies;
— We Learn by seeking and serving Christ in all persons, loving our neighbours as ourselves;
— We Care for each other and for those in our communities in need—by sharing our time, compassion, and spiritual gifts; and
— We Grow in number and in human spirit, year by year.

In the first sentence of the above mission statement, the parish has defined **Who** they are *(the members of St. George's parish family)*, **What** they do *(Welcome, Worship, Learn, Care, and Grow)*, **Where** they do what they do *(in our communities of Ajax and Pickering, and beyond)*, and **Why** they do what they do *(following the example of Jesus Christ)*.

The parish has then defined some of the **How**s for their activities

(Welcome, Worship, Learn, Care, and Grow) in measurable terms. This structure makes for an effective parish mission statement. St. George's Anglican parish still uses a one-line slogan ("Come Grow With Us") on its Sunday bulletins and brochures as a brief parish identifier. The mission statement, though, is what really drives members and their ParishWorks forward.

Once the parish has developed a mission statement all have agreed to, each parish team (worship development, congregation development, outreach development, etc.) should use the statement to guide their program development plans. This way, each parish team will maintain focus on the objectives the parish has selected, and not get sidetracked or waste valuable volunteer time in unsupported initiatives.

Mission Statement Workshop

How does a parish build a meaningful mission statement? In practice, the most effective approach usually involves a small group of interested parishioners (say, the advisory board members) who spend one to one and a-half hours in a workshop developing the parish's mission statement. The team then circulates the draft mission statement to all parishioners, handing it out at consecutive Sunday services with a request for feedback. With respect to the feedback received after two to three weeks, the team amends the statement, then publishes it (again, as a Sunday service handout).

Some preparation is required for the workshop. Participants should surf other parishes' web sites to read a variety of mission statements. They should review the diocese's mission statement, keeping in mind that the parish's mission statement will complement the diocese's. Participants should also consider the "W" words, and come to the workshop with ideas of what their parish means to them for each "W" category.

One of the attendees might serve as the workshop facilitator. Ideally this person will be familiar with leading workshops, in which groups of people jointly develop a product. If the parish does not have a person with this experience, the diocesan office may provide a facilitator. There are pluses and minuses in inviting an "outsider" to facilitate: the pluses include having an expert, someone who has no bias as to the outcome, lead the team through the process. A minus might be that the facilitator may slow down the team as he or she becomes acquainted with the team and the parish. Outside facilitators also may impose process rules on the team which, if kept to a minimum, could be fine. The workshop, though, is a one-time event, with a short time-frame and a single goal. The team may become frustrated with a lot of process rules.

The facilitator should record the team's ideas, using a flip chart. Consider having one sheet per "W" word to capture ideas, then have the team string together key words to create a loose statement. Warning: the team could get sidetracked by fussing about the wording of the statement, rather than noting the key elements. The facilitator should avoid letting the team drift into an editorial-board type of session—fine-tuning can be done later, with the rest of the parishioners' help.

Once the "Ws" are built into a statement, the team could then list the Hows for each What, using one page for each. The facilitator would take the first What (*Welcome* in the St. George's Anglican Church mission statement), and have the team list the Hows before moving onto the next What. In the St. George's example, the team came up with *excitement, interest, and openness*, before moving on to their next What (*Worship*).

Once approved, the mission statement should be used often—on parish letterhead, Sunday bulletins, the parish's web site, banners, and advertising—to remind parishioners what their parish family is about, and to let the community and newcomers know what the parish stands for, and how it is making a difference.

Each parish team (outreach development, congregation development, worship development, etc.) should review the mission statement when making plans for the upcoming year to ensure that their ParishWorks move the parish in the direction the mission statement intends.

The parish's mission statement will help you know whether you are progressing in measurable ways. The statement should be used to direct the parish, keep everyone in sync, and give the parish reasons to celebrate successes along the way. You and your workshop team will know when you have it just right for your parish—all will take pride and share ownership in its creation. The pride will be contagious, as the mission statement grows with feedback from other parishioners. Once set, all will have a stake in its success.

Chapter 4

Congregation Development

Past Approaches

The parish's congregation is its most important asset. Often it is difficult to see that its members are highly valued and treasured. Through parish surveys, many parishioners have expressed a feeling that others do not seem to care whether they come or go. Of course, we all do care—but we are often not explicit enough in our actions and words to make this known.

Some parishes take the stance of "build it and they will come," and integrate newcomers into their midst as they show up, or not. When families stop attending services, often there is no follow-up: rather, parishioners just assume the family has a scheduling conflict or a sickness. As family absences extend, people are forgotten and eventually removed from the parish list. ***The parish's lack of follow-up seems to confirm the soundness of the family's decision to leave.***

The same apparent lack of caring may be widespread. Some parishes, for instance, use sign-up sheets to recruit volunteers. If you sign up, fine; if not, that seems to be okay too. Would you go out of your way to sign up if you felt that it did not matter either way? If not enough names appear, then parish events are cancelled—which discourages volunteers for future events. When parishioners do participate in developing parish events, there is often no formal thank-you process. Many parish events focus on fund-raising: sometimes it seems that is all we are interested in.

These unplanned, and unintentionally thoughtless, approaches speak volumes to parishioners. It is not surprising that many of our parish members feel valued only as a source of income, if at all. If the parish were an enterprise in the secular world, such approaches would soon put it out of business.

Clearly we need to value our congregation as our most important asset, and care for people accordingly. We can improve our congregation development approaches in dynamic ways, not only to build energy and excitement within existing members, but to grow in numbers and in achievements year by year.

The First Step: The Parish Survey

How can the value of a congregation be realized if we do not know, or only guess, what skills and gifts its members are willing to share with the parish? Here are some actual examples:

1. Tradespeople are contracted by the wardens to carry out building repairs, although several members of the congregation not only have the same skills, but are ready and willing to pitch in as volunteers. They are only waiting to be asked. In these situations, not only does the parish incur unnecessary expenses, but more importantly, when the skilled parishioners discover that "outsiders" were brought in to do work on *their* church that they could have done, many interpret this (incorrectly) as a snub. This situation has caused more than one family to leave parishes.

2. Parish leaders have discovered that certain parishioners have professional skills and have asked them to use those skills in the parish, not knowing that this is the last thing they want to do. They come to the parish to escape their workplaces, not to assume the same tasks. Many times, they grudgingly take on the tasks, while looking for another parish to move to (and do).

Independent of parishioners' skills, frequently people come to their church to grow, and to experience new challenges and opportunities. They look to their parish to pursue their true passions, which they often cannot do in their day-to-day activities outside the parish setting. If they are not given the chance to engage these passions, they tend to move on to a parish where they can.

Parishioners also tend to have wonderful ideas for how parish life might improve, and are only waiting for someone to ask them. Little things may happen during services or at parish social events that upset parishioners, but there is no process for feedback.

How can we be more careful stewards of our people, the parish's most critical resource? An annual parish survey may open the parish leadership team to a wealth of untapped skills, gifts, energies, and creative ideas for improvements.

Several parishes have attempted surveys, with disappointing results. Here are some reasons why:

- Surveys were designed to confirm what the leadership team wanted to see. Questions led the parishioner to "correct" conclusions; this approach was obvious to parishioners, and the surveys became recycling material.

- Surveys were designed with boxes to tick (Yes/No; scales, such as 1 to 5). Parishioners ticked the boxes and handed in the surveys, and the leadership team learned very little.
- Surveys were too complex. Parishioners either could not understand the questions or did not have time to decipher them (again, into the recycling box).
- Parishioners were asked to pick up survey forms as they left the church building, and complete and return them. Results were predictable—5% response rates.
- Following the survey, months went by with no feedback. This resulted in feelings of "Why did I bother?" and "They obviously aren't going to change anything, anyway." Some families left.

A successful parish survey requires both a clear focus and strategy. Before the survey is even designed, the parish leadership or survey team needs to determine

- the purposes of the survey;
- how the survey will obtain a 95% to 100% response rate from the families on the parish list;
- how the information will be used once gathered; and
- how and when follow-ups will be done, and by whom.

Next, the leadership or survey team needs to consider key objectives for carrying out the parish survey. At a minimum, the parish survey should

- build an inventory of the **skills and gifts** that parishioners are willing to share with the parish;
- build an inventory of the **passions** that parishioners are willing to develop within parish teams and programs; and
- solicit **feedback** from the parish membership as to what the parish does well and should keep on doing, what it does well but could consider ending and why, and what it does not do well or at all, and suggestions for improvements.

To ensure a maximum response rate, several parishes have successfully combined the survey process with a pot-luck lunch, observing popular Anglican wisdom: "Feed them and they will come." The survey team would hand out the surveys and pens, then lead the parishioners through the questions, allowing a few minutes for each response before moving on to the next question. For best results, this process should take no more than 40 to 60 minutes.

The survey team might want to "test drive" a draft survey with a small group of volunteers. Advisory boards have been used for this, again successfully. Not only was the timing confirmed, but the board members also suggested ways to clarify the questions and make them easier to understand.

While pot-lucks are fun, they tend to bring out only a portion of the parish's families, usually between 25% to 40% of the families on the parish list. For those parishioners who do not attend the pot-luck and survey event, the survey team will need to contact each family and complete the survey either by phone or through a visit. Visiting is ideal where the respondent is a family rather than an individual. At any rate, the survey team must be prepared to carry out these interviews, and to transcribe responses for each parish family that does not attend the pot-luck. The team will probably have to recruit volunteer callers. To calculate how many volunteer hours are needed for this task, add up the number of visits and phone interviews required to contact the pot-luck "no-shows," then multiply that number by the time estimated to complete the survey. Ideally the interviews should be completed within three to four weeks, with a maximum of six to eight calls per volunteer.

Another important step in designing the survey is to determine (1) how the information will be summarized so that a **parish member inventory** can be built, ideally on the parish computer, and (2) how the feedback responses can be summarized. For example, the inventory should be designed so that parish team leaders can ask the parish's volunteer coordinator questions like, "Who has a passion for outreach? I need three people to help launch the parish outreach program" ... "Are there any electricians in the parish? We have a light fixture that needs replacing" ... "Which of our parish programs rated the poorest and should be discontinued? We need to free up volunteers for the new programs" ... and so on.

To facilitate easy answers to these sorts of questions, the survey team might consider using a spreadsheet program, such as Microsoft Excel or Lotus 123 or, if it's possible to recruit someone in the parish who has database skills, Microsoft Access or Lotus Approach. When using a spreadsheet program, names of parishioners could be entered in the first column, with various skills/passions entered across the spreadsheet. A simple selection command will highlight the names of parishioners whose skills/passions are sought. With a database program, the skills could be codified, and a query would likewise result in a list of parishioners with the required skills/passions. This inventory of skills and passions will be a major asset to the parish's program teams as they move forward. Updating the inventory after each annual or bi-annual parish survey will keep it current, with minimal work in-between. The inventory could be maintained by the volunteer coordinator, using their personal computer.

The survey team needs to build the framework for the inventory before the pot-luck and survey event. That way, as responses are collected, they can be keyed into the inventory, and the results of the survey can be reported back to the parish, probably within three to four weeks. Quick feedback reinforces the idea that the member's contribution to the survey is highly valued, and that their input will be acted upon. Reporting back could be done in the announcements portion of a service, or during a coffee hour following the service. Copies of the survey summary should be available for parishioners to take home.

A summary of a parish survey should include

1. the response rate and a sincere thank-you to the congregation for their interest and participation;

2. a feedback summary that
   — highlights those parish programs that are highest ranked (and congratulating the associated program teams for a job well done);
   — indicates those parish programs that need improvement (along with sample suggestions). The survey team should have an idea from the associated program teams when they will begin work on the changes, and (perhaps) when they might be finished;
   — proposes new programs. The survey team needs to have an idea of next steps in these cases—at least, the name of a parishioner who has agreed to research the suggestion further and report back to the parish within four to six weeks;
   — indicates those parish programs that probably should be discontinued and why.

The survey team should have responses to these suggestions from the corresponding program teams—their concurrence, if the program team agrees, or feedback as to why they do not agree and what might be done to improve the program, to have it worthy of continuance.

3. a skills and passions summary that states
> — the number of parishioners in each skills and passions category; and
>
> — the intention of program teams to follow up with parishioners with corresponding skills and passions to discuss next steps, within four to six weeks.

Following the survey summary presentation, the survey team will need to make sure that parishioners are contacted by the program teams within the committed time-frame.

Once the survey process has been completed, the team can disband until the next annual or bi-annual parish survey. In the interim, the inventory could be managed by the parish's volunteer coordinator, to support the resource needs of the parish's program teams.

Here is a sample parish survey, adapted from several parish surveys that have been carried out in the last few years. The questions are a composite of those that resulted in the most valued feedback. The sample may be found on the enclosed CD in Microsoft Word format (see survey.doc).

Annual Parish Survey

Thank you for your interest in helping to improve the parish's programs by sharing your suggestions. We will follow up with you when we have completed gathering the survey information, in case you have any additional thoughts or ideas you would like to share.

_____   _____
Name   Telephone(s)

                                          _____
                                          E-mail address

Section 1: How are we doing?

For each of the parish's programs and projects last year, please let us know how you feel about them. Are they good in their current form? Could improvements be made—if so, what? Should some of them be discontinued—if so, why? Are there some things the parish should be doing but isn't?

1. *Worship Services* (hymns used, sermons, service format, duration):

2. *Outreach* (PWRDF, Anglican Appeal, food bank, drop-in):

3. *Sunday School* (curriculum, setting, duration):

4. *Bible Study/Adult Education* (topics, format, location, duration, time of day, frequency):

5. *Fund-Raising* (type of events, frequency, venues, turnouts, financial results, work involved, awareness):

6. *Fellowship Events* (type of events, frequency, venues, turnouts, awareness, results):

7. *Meditation* (frequency, location, turnouts, awareness):

8. *Pastoral Care/Visitation* (awareness, coverage, frequency, results):

9. *Building Maintenance* (general condition, follow-up on outstanding issues):

10. *Youth Program* (content, outings, duration, settings):

11. *New Programs* (for each one you suggest, why do you think these would be good for our parish?):

Section 2: How about you?

A lot is going on in the parish, with demands exceeding our resources. We count on each parishioner to lend a helping hand, from time to time. To make sure we best use the gifts you wish to share with the parish, please take the time to indicate which **skills** you have that you could bring to the parish, to help us out; those **passions** that you would like to explore with like-minded parishioners; and the **amount of time** you might be able to contribute each month.

1. The *skills* that I am willing to share with my parish (e.g., trades, team leading, events planning and execution, office support, pastoral care, teaching, bookkeeping):

2. The *number of hours per month* that I would be willing to provide to my parish, along with my skills:

3. My *passions* that I would like to explore and grow with others in my parish:

4. The *number of hours per month* that I would be willing to invest in growing with my passions:

Section 3: Other thoughts

Are there other comments/feedback you would like to provide to your parish?

Remember to keep these tips in mind when designing a parish survey:

1. Avoid Yes/No answer formats, or soliciting responses based on scales, for example, 1 to 5. You want parishioners to say in their own words what they would like to see in their parish.

2. Limit the survey to only the number of questions that can be completed in 40 to 60 minutes. Because of this restriction, limit the survey to only those questions the leadership team needs critical feedback about. Use a group of team members to "test drive" the survey before you approach the entire parish membership. Keep the questions simple.

3. Have the feedback section precede the skills/passions section. It is far easier for a survey respondent to critique parish programs than to self-assess their own passions. The feedback section will lead them into the process in an easy way, and warm them up for the second section.

The Parish Growth Plan

While many congregations may hope that newcomers will drive by and take an interest in their parish, this is not an effective way to grow the congregation. For those seeking social involvement, there are too many interests competing for discretionary time: organized sports for kids, service clubs, and entertainment venues. For those seeking a parish church, there are many different denominations, as well as other Anglican parishes a short drive away. We are no longer the only parish church within walking distance or a horse-and-buggy-ride's distance. We no longer "corner the market."

In today's world, we need to "market" our parish to ensure that it grows. We need to be proactive and seek out new families to join our parish. We need to learn from the techniques used successfully in the secular world, to "market" our "services" and package these approaches in a way that fits our faith and parish mission statement.

What are the elements of a secular marketing plan? How might they help us to achieve our congregational growth objectives? A well-developed product or services marketing plan would include the following aspects (see growth.doc in Microsoft Word format on the enclosed CD).

Parish Growth/Marketing Plan

For

Parish Name

1. Product Definition

In the secular world, the definition of the product or service to be marketed includes the functions and features that make the product or service unique. The "value statements" for consumers, or the principles and ideals that guide their thoughts and actions, are also described.

In the context of parish congregation development, this could give the congregation development team an opportunity to reflect on why a family might want to join their parish, and what aspects make the parish unique. Here are some ideas:

- Consider the parish's mission statement. What aspects of the parish might attract Christians seeking like-minded people and exciting, challenging programs in which they can grow?

- What "value statements" could be attributed to your parish's "offerings"? How might newcomers benefit by coming to your parish?
- Physically, what features make the parish a pleasing place to visit and spend time in?
- Which parish programs stand out? Which ones have appeal to parents, children, teens, seniors, singles?
- What distinguishes these programs from those of other denominations and other Anglican parishes closeby? What are the parish's **differentiation points**?

Once the congregation development team knows what "product features" they wish to "sell," they can develop the parish "image" (which should be obvious in all parish advertising materials).

2. Target Market

In the secular world, the term "target market" refers to the potential consumers of the product or service, and the ways or means of reaching them and holding their attention. The expected "win rate," based on conservative and realistic estimates (usually derived from past marketing programs for similar products or services), is also part of this definition.

In the context of your parish, this would include the number of families in your community that could become members of your congregation. Your diocesan office will have statistics from StatsCan of the number of registered Anglicans in your community. First, divide this number by 1.5 to get a good idea of the number of Anglican families in your community (1.5 being the average between single-person families and couples). Next, subtract the number of families on your parish list. From the balance, subtract a percentage (40% to 50%) who have registered their affiliation based on their baptism, but have no intention of returning to church. Last, divide the balance by the number of Anglican churches in and near your community (within 10 to 30 kms), as they represent your "competition" and so will likely tap into the same potential group.

For example: say, Statistics Canada indicates that there are 5,000 registered Anglicans in your community. Your parish has 100 families on its parish list and there are three other Anglican churches within 30 kms of town. Here is the math: the StatsCan number represents 3,330 families, of which 2,230 are not members of your parish. Of these, 1,115 are potential churchgoers. Of that number, you will need to compete with the other three churches for one-quarter of the potential parishioners (280). This represents your "target market."

For these 280 families, how might you determine your expected "win rate"? Consider these ways: first, will the parish be able to reach all of these families through a parish brochure, phone call, or visit? To do that, every family in your community would have to be contacted. So, of the community's population, how many families could your congregation development team contact each year? If you are planning on a brochure drop, for instance, your answer might reflect the number of copies you plan to produce and/or the number of parish volunteers available. For example, if your community has 5,000 homes and your team can contact 500 per year, that means you may reach only 10% of your target market each year (28 in our example). Such information makes a good starting point from which to calculate this year's win rate.

Over and above those newcomers you might contact in a proactive way, some families simply drop in: they may have moved into your community, they may have lost interest in another church, they may have been driving by, or scouting out churches for baptisms or weddings. If your parish has not had a proactive marketing/growth program in place in past years, add the historical or known number of new families you have been attracting over the past five years to your win rate.

Next, the congregation development team needs to consider any inhibitors to reaching potential targets, and how these might be overcome. The team also might ask, How do we measure success? How do we maintain the momentum or freshness of our parish's message, year by year?

3. The Competition

In the secular world, the competition are those entities or organizations that will contact the same target market. Success depends on assessing strengths and weaknesses in terms of their product/service features relative to yours, and knowing how to counter those strengths and take advantage of any weaknesses.

In the context of your parish, your competitors include not only other Anglican parishes, but also other Christian denominations within 30 kms of your community, as many families are not affiliated with a specific denomination.

The congregation development team should consider, What makes our Anglican parish more attractive than parishes of other denominations? If your team does not know, they might consider attending services at the other churches, to see. These visits may result in creative ideas that benefit your parish.

Concerning the other Anglican parishes in your area, your team might ask, What do they do that we do not? What do they do better? While Anglican parishes are not really in competition with each other, we might work together better, to provide alternatives to potential parishioners "shopping" the churches in the community. For example, one (older) Anglican parish in the community might emphasize traditional worship forms and programs, while another (newer) parish might emphasize contemporary forms and programs.

4. Advertising Plan

Once the congregation development team knows the parish's unique strengths and differentiation points, its target market, and the strengths and weaknesses of the "competition," they can then design effective parish advertising materials.

The first step is to determine which delivery channels to use. Here are the most popular:

Parish Web Site (see also page 67). In today's world, many families "shop" their community churches through the Internet. While a parish web site will usually inform parishioners of current and upcoming events, it should also serve as an advertising tool. The parish program features that are likely to appeal to newcomers, for instance, could be highlighted. The information should reflect the differentiation points of your parish versus those of other churches in the community, and include value statements that potential parishioners might quickly identify with. The parish web site needs to be dynamic and up to date. If potential parishioners return to the site more than once and see the same content, they may regard the parish as static, and pass on by.

Pamphlets (see also page 68) should be highly visual, and emphasize the parish's programs and key value statements to draw people's interest. Featuring the Sunday school and youth programs, for example, will attract parents; the parish outreach program and its results will appeal to community-minded people; the worship and Bible study programs will appeal to those who wish to grow in their faith.

How many pamphlets might your parish need to print? A good rule of thumb is to print only the number of pamphlets that the team can distribute in one year. Even though volume discounts for printing may apply and seem appealing, parish programs change and the differentiation points and value statements will need updating. Also, circulating new pamphlets with a new look each year reinforces the impression that the parish is dynamic.

If the team plans to drop the pamphlets door to door, the distribution strategy should be well thought out. If the team intends to distribute only to a portion of the homes in the community, the team needs to map out where the current year's supply will go. Some factors to consider are proximity to the church and to competitors, zoning, and density.

Timing is also important. Certainly a brochure drop just before Christmas or Easter will have more impact than one delivered mid-summer when many people are on holiday away from home.

Posters must emphasize the parish's differentiation points, visually and in the written content. To help accomplish this, the congregation development team might study posters from the secular world: what design attributes are eye-catching or enliven the message? Size the posters for the physical space where they will be displayed: they should fit neatly on a bulletin board or window in local stores, libraries, community halls. Don't let the posters remain up more than a year—replace them with a fresh look and new content so that your parish will appear vibrant.

Signage. The congregation development team should be responsible for design of the parish's signage and should take great care ensuring that all signs accurately reflect the parish's image. It's no wonder people remark, "Too bad that the church has closed," when they pass a parish church and see a peeling sign with service times posted in faded black and white paint, and the current incumbent's name and phone number poorly repainted over the previous incumbent's.

The team should check whether any signs need to be repainted, or possibly replaced if they are seriously detracting from the parish's image. The team might consider the ways business signs, for example, capture the attention of passersby. Bright colours attract, as do different shapes (not the usual rectangles). Perhaps there is a professional sign maker in the parish membership? If not, build the sign(s) at a team working party, and have a sign painter professionally finish the job. The team might ask for estimates from two or three painters, then pick the best.

To be effective, parish signs should feature the parish's slogan, web address, phone number, and service times.

All signage should be visible day or night—having the parish's sign in darkness suggests the church is "closed for business." Lighting for each sign (with daylight sensors, of course) should be installed. Again, the team could check the parishioner inventory for electricians. At the very least, the team could have a conduit-trenching/wire-stringing party, and leave the hookup to a professional electrician.

The congregation development team should include the parish sexton and assets management team in these plans since parish property is involved. They may have some good ideas where the signs should be placed, and help get them installed.

If budget permits, consider posting a duplicate of the new parish property sign on each main road into town. Have the sign painter create all the signs at one time, as it is much cheaper than returning a second or third time for additional sign work.

Also, in many communities there are welcome signs that include small versions of various service clubs signs. Your parish's name should be there, if possible.

Banners. For special events, consider rental tote boards and vinyl banners. Banners say in a big way that the parish is active and hosts exciting events. While the event itself will of course be worth advertising, a series of banners has a cumulative effect on passersby: "Wow, these folks sure are busy. They're into everything." Make sure the banners come down as soon as the event is over, so that the parish maintains an up-to-date image.

Newspapers. Consider a monthly advertisement for your parish in the local paper. Change the message each time it appears—don't let it get stale.

While the parish notice is important, there is a far more effective (and free) way to leverage your local press: as often as possible, contact the paper to cover a "newsworthy" parish event, preferably including photographs at least twice a year. Most local papers are starving for local good news stories, and what may seem a minor event to the parish may be a really good news story for the community. Possibilities include Sunday school and youth group outings, outreach projects such as car washes and walk-a-thons, donations or visitations to the local hospital, and installation of an organ or a new curate.

5. Partnerships (see also page 69)

In the secular world, an organization will link up, or partner, with other groups to increase the chances of successful growth.

In the context of the parish, the congregation development team could consider partnerships with service organizations in the community. If the parish is donating or renting space to organizations (e.g., Scouts, Guides, AA, ESL groups, daycare), the team should consider ways of "marketing" the parish to the associated families of members. At the very least, parish brochures could be distributed to the organizations' members; at best, members and their families might be invited for a tour of the church or a brief address about the programs of the parish and their value points.

The team could contact each service group in the community to explore possible means of joint sponsorship or involvement in their service initiatives. For instance, a parish might participate in a service club's fund-raising event where it complements the parish's outreach program. Through joint sponsorship, the parish might partner with service club(s), and perhaps become the church of choice for those members who are "church shopping."

The congregation development team should also contact other Anglican parishes in or near the community, to find ways of pulling together to achieve results not possible separately. Joint outreach programs in the community, for example, might be excellent projects. Joint fund-raising programs would likewise be more effective if adjacent parishes joined forces to share the work.

Another way for the team to market the parish is to ensure participation in community events, such as the Christmas parade, summer street festivals, and fall fairs. For these events, it is important for the parish to participate in a meaningful way, not simply be a presence. Rather than walking the Christmas parade route with a parish float, for example, the parish could distribute small toys and pamphlets along the route. Or, with a minimal amount of work and cost, the parish could invite the community to have hot chocolate in the parish hall after the parade—everyone attending the parade would then perceive the parish to be co-hosting the parade.

6. Financial Forecast

In the secular world, a financial forecast would include, for the course of an advertising campaign, the increased income expected and the non-financial benefits. Offsetting this would be the costs of the campaign.

In the context of the parish's growth campaign, the congregation development team must provide the parish treasurer and wardens with projected advertising costs for the year, so that sufficient funds will be set aside in the annual budget.

Since an advertising campaign will draw new families, the team should estimate the increased annual givings they will represent (multiply the number of new families expected by the average annual family givings for the parish).

When budgeting, the advertising costs should not be more than 20% of the expected increase in givings.

7. Management System

In the secular world, the management system outlines how the impact of the marketing campaign will be measured, monitored, and reported, and how to amend the campaign if results do not occur as planned.

In the context of the parish's growth plan, the estimated number of new families per month should be compared with the actual number of new families attending. The parish's greeters are best suited to report this information to the congregation development team each Sunday to enable close monitoring of the campaign.

The total givings of the new families will also need to be reported and compared with the team's estimate. To do this, the parish's envelope secretary should subtotal the givings from the new families and provide the total to the congregation development team each month. The team will need to compare this with the actual costs of the growth campaign, to determine the net result to the parish.

As with all plans, results may not match initial expectations. The congregation development team must consider how and when to change the growth plan if results are out of line. They will have to determine how quickly they might shift their approach, and how to handle any additional costs.

The team must also decide when the campaign will end, and what constitutes completion. With a growth program such as this, parishes may want the process to be continuous. In these cases, how will the team take a "checkpoint," to celebrate their successes, refresh their teams with new members (and let current members move on to other parish programs), and build plans for subsequent campaigns?

Parishioner Retention

Let's say the congregation development team has done a great job of bringing newcomers into the parish, having executed a well-designed growth/advertising campaign. But there is little point in a parish team working hard to attract newcomers if they do not stay, or if others are leaving. We must cherish the families in our parishes and ensure that they are well cared for, if we are to be good stewards of the parish's most valuable asset.

Newcomers' Events

A key task for the congregation development team is to keep track of newcomers to the parish, and to hold a "newcomers' event" every three months or so. The phone numbers of newcomers since the last event should be recorded, so that the team may invite them to this special event. To help make it a success, it's a good idea for the team to invite as many "old-timers" as newcomers, and have them "buddy" with the newcomers during the event.

The purpose of the event is to formally welcome newcomers to the parish, and to provide some education about the parish's programs. Buddies for the newcomers could also give them contact information for any parish programs that interest them. If the newcomers are new to the area, the buddies might provide other helpful information, such as what community services are available. It is important for old-timers and any program leaders present to appreciate that they are hosting a welcoming and information-sharing event, and so care should be taken not to pressure the newcomers into volunteering for parish programs and possibly scaring them off.

No more than one month after the event, each buddy should contact their partner newcomer. They should ensure that there are no lingering questions about what the parish has to offer, that program contacts are known, and that any queries are answered.

From the event, enough old-timers will be familiar with the new families, to help make them feel more welcome at church and to help the parish greeters monitor their attendance at subsequent services.

Parishioner Attrition

In considering how to keep the parish's families as active members, the congregation development team needs to explore the factors that resulted in families leaving the parish, then put in place corrective measures. The team members themselves can likely think of what factors might have made them leave. Also, families who have left should be contacted, to determine the causes.

The congregation development team can mitigate membership attrition in several ways. Here are some suggestions, along with typical reasons why families leave:

1. *Moving away from the community*
Obviously the parish team cannot do much about this. However, they could contact the rector of the Anglican parish to which the family is moving and

let them know the family is coming and their new address. They could also offer to send the skills/passions record for the family, so that the new parish will know the family's interests.

Since many families who move away wish to stay connected with their old parish, the congregation development team should find out if they would like to stay on the parish list for newsletters, etc. If so, they would be contacted during the parish survey process, as a way of keeping in touch. Some may wish to attend programs that their new parish does not provide, contribute to future capital campaigns, or simply return for some services.

In the congregation development plan, the team needs to factor in the reality of parish family attrition. It is appropriate to include a 10% loss each year due to moves or deaths. With this unavoidable attrition rate, the congregation development team will need to ensure a 10% growth rate in newcomers each year, just to stay even. So, if the plan is to grow in numbers, the team will need to target 15% to 20% growth in membership per year. While this may seem like a large number, it really is not.

For example, consider a parish that has a membership of 100 families. A target growth rate of 15% per year means that 15 new families must join the parish. Of this number, 5 to 10 will be new families that have moved into your community. They will come to the parish regardless of the team's efforts (the flipside of people moving out). The team then must proactively bring in another 5 to 10 new families per year—or one family every one to two months. This is certainly doable, even for a small congregation development team.

2. A feeling that other parishioners do not care if the family comes or goes

It is all too easy to lose track of parish families between visits. The congregation development team should review the parish list each month. Do any families seem to be drifting away? Which families have not attended recent parish events? This is an early warning signal that the family may leave in the near future, and one that should be heeded. It is much easier to bring families back into active membership before they decide to move to another church, than after. In these cases, the team might contact the family to ask how they are doing. Is there anything that they feel is missing from their experience in the parish? Might things be done differently? The act of calling or showing that the family has been missed is often enough to help them return.

In other cases, it may be found that a relatively small matter has caused the family to feel unwanted—this happens more often than one might think. Frequently these families can be welcomed back, through some caring discussion. Talking the issue out will help the family determine that it is not worth their leaving the parish, and they will return.

Sometimes the family agrees to work with a parish team to change or add a parish program that, in its structure or by its absence, had been causing the family to consider leaving.

3. A family crisis

During a crisis, some families find themselves unable to cope with attending Sunday services and having social contact with their fellow parishioners. They may be overwrought or embarrassed by the crisis. Unfortunately these absences may become permanent unless the parish follows up. This is precisely the time when the parish family can help the most. When families are contacted by the congregation development team and painful circumstances emerge, it is usually best to refer the situation to the parish's rector. A family visit may be very helpful, and may help the family recover sufficiently to return.

4. A scheduling conflict

Often children's organized activities (hockey, soccer, music lessons, etc.) will happen during the family service times. When the congregation development team member contacts a family and finds this to be the case, the team could suggest attending an earlier or later service, or a mid-week service. If enough families are caught in scheduling conflicts, the team could consider switching the family service time, or alternating it, to ensure that these families can attend at least once or twice a month.

The caller might also find that the activity causing the scheduling conflict is temporary. It becomes critical to call the family when the activity is finished, so that they will know the parish has missed them and is looking forward to their return. Often, after a scheduling conflict ends, the family has become so used to missing the Sunday service that they do not think to make the first move to return.

Whatever the reasons that people drift away from the parish, the congregation development team must monitor Sunday attendance by the faces they see, and follow up when families are away for extended periods. How can this best be done?

Many parishes have adopted a buddy system: members of the congregation development team pick a set of families whom they know, and monitor their attendance. A 10:1 ratio has worked well in several parishes. In a parish with weekly attendance of say, 100 people (or really, 40 to 60 families), the congregation development team would need only four to six members to act as buddies for the parish.

Apart from monitoring attendance, the buddy system has been highly effective in discovering family crisis, and enabling the parish to respond. Many families will choose isolation when bad things happen, and so the parish may be unaware of their difficulties. Through buddy phone calls, such situations tend to be minimized.

Fellowship Events

In addition to attendance monitoring, the congregation development team should be responsible for arranging fellowship events throughout the year. These events, intended to celebrate the parish family and share some of its good news stories, are morale boosters in tough times; in good times they reinforce reasons for being members of the parish.

Fellowship events focus on the social aspects of the parish family and should not involve fund-raising. If the congregation development team has a budget for fellowship events, food could be brought in as part of the celebration. Otherwise, the team should plan for pot-lucks. Note: it is important that at least half the fellowship events be funded through the parish's annual budget. If parishioners have only pot-lucks as their fellowship events, food becomes a substitute for bringing money, and the purpose may be lost. The events need not be expensive—a pizza lunch or dinner can be as much fun as an elaborate affair.

A fellowship event provides an excellent opportunity to celebrate key volunteers in the parish, perhaps with small but thoughtful gifts. The event also gives the parish's program teams a chance to highlight some of their achievements over the past few months. The outreach development team, for instance, might speak about the difference the parish is making in the lives of less fortunate people in the community, citing specific examples. The youth group could talk about a recent outing, and how the parish helped them get there. And so on. Program speakers should avoid attempting to recruit team members. Fellowship events are thanking, not asking, venues. (We do enough asking as it is.)

Four to six fellowship events each year is ideal. Timing is important, to ensure maximum attendance. Thanksgiving Sunday might be opportune, to welcome the parish back from their summer break and to give thanks for the parish family, its gifts, its caring, and its growth. A celebration in early December might give parishioners a pre-Christmas "breather" before they move into full swing. A post-Easter spring event might be an occasion to celebrate the return of the perennials in the parish gardens. The last day of Sunday school before summer break might be an ideal time to say thank-you to teachers and to celebrate the children's achievements, perhaps through a display of their work.

While fellowship events do need to be included in the parish calendar, to remind us that we are more than money-raisers, they should not compete with fund-raisers. Several parishes alternate fellowship and fund-raising events monthly from September to June. This seems to work well, and balances the events' schedule between the two venues.

Parish Greeters

Another way to help keep parishioners attending services, and to feel cared for, is to have parish greeters at Sunday services. Greeters are not sidespersons—the roles are quite different. Sidespersons are focused on the logistics of the service: seating; handing out bulletins, prayer books, and hymnals; collection; readings; communion. They do not have time to chat with families as they enter the church.

Parish greeters, on the other hand, are free to initiate conversations with parishioners as they enter and leave the church. Greeters should focus on current members who have been absent, and welcome them back. In this way, parishioners know they have been missed and feel valued as a result. Greeters also look for new faces, and ask if families are new to the parish. If so, they provide introductory information, such as the locations for washrooms, Sunday school, and the youth group, and provide coffee hour invitations. Greeters record the newcomers' names and phone numbers for later follow-up by the congregation development team. At coffee hour, the greeters spend time with newcomers, to describe parish programs and answer questions, ask about their interests, and whether they would like a follow-up phone call.

Depending on how many people usually attend Sunday services, two or more greeters may be appropriate. It is important to have a back-up greeter—often one greeter will be engaged in conversation with a newcomer while another person who should be greeted goes right by.

When recruiting greeters, the congregation development team should look for people who know a fair number of the parishioners and who like to socialize. This skill/passion should be included in the parish survey. A position description for a parish greeter follows, for adaptation to your parish. An electronic version in Microsoft Word format is available on the enclosed CD (see greeter.doc).

Role

The parish greeter is an important member of the congregation development team, and represents the parish as parishioners enter the church for Sunday services and leave. By welcoming established members of the parish to services each week, the greeter reinforces the fact that members of the parish family are valued, and is instrumental in keeping them coming back. For newcomers, the greeter is often the first face they associate with the parish. First impressions are important to retain newcomers, so the greeter's warmth and sincere interest in them are key to growing the parish's congregation.

Responsibilities

The parish greeter is like a host who welcomes guests into his or her home. As such,

- the greeter will wear a parish name tag, to give people arriving a head start on meeting them;
- the greeter will welcome each family as they enter the church with a smile and a handshake, as appropriate;
- for established members of the parish who have been away from the church for a time, the greeter will take the opportunity to ask where they have been. This lets the parishioners know they have been missed, and reinforces their feeling important to the parish. The interest shown in their well-being is also helpful in retaining them as members;
- for newcomers, the greeter will ask their names and, if possible, record their phone number as they enter. Newcomers should be told where the washrooms are, the locations of the Sunday school and youth group if they have children, and be invited to coffee hour as appropriate. If they cannot come to coffee hour, the greeter will give them a newcomers' welcome kit, and mention that they will be called within a week after the service. If they can attend coffee hour, the greeter will link up with them then;
- for parishioners needing special care (e.g., those who use wheelchairs, walkers), the greeter will recruit an established member of the parish to help the parishioner to their seat or location. If there is no one available to help out, the greeter will attend to the person needing help;
- during coffee hour, the greeter will make contact with newcomers and

help them to get coffee, then take the opportunity to describe the parish and its programs. The greeter will give newcomers the parish's welcome kit and ensure that the rector meets them. The greeter will also take the opportunity to ask newcomers about their interests and record these, as possible. Before the greeter moves on to other people during coffee hour, he or she will let the newcomers know that someone will be in touch to further discuss their needs and the expectations of the parish; and

- as well as welcoming attendees, the greeter will return to the church doors to say goodbye, using supportive phrases such as, "See you next week" or "Hope to see you again."

Duration

Greeters ideally should commit to a three- to six-month term. Note that several teams of greeters will need to be recruited, so that greeters may plan time off. Theirs is not a weekly commitment to the position, and individual schedules may be negotiated with the team leader when the year's master plan is drawn up.

Skills Required

- A friendly, caring disposition;
- a good talker and listener;
- a good memory (to help identify familiar and new faces and names); and
- a fairly good idea of the parish's services and programs.

Absentee Parishioners

Let's assume the congregation development team is successful at encouraging parishioners to regularly attend services. What about the families on the parish list that no one remembers seeing? It is not uncommon for 20% to 40% of families on parish lists to attend services only occasionally, such as at Christmas or Easter. Also, many parishes conduct baptisms and weddings each year for families that soon after seem to disappear. In terms of growing the weekly congregation, this group of absentees may be the easiest to tap, as they have been to a service at least once, and chose to do so for a particular reason.

The team might divide up the absentee list, so that each member will phone a certain number of families to discuss recent events in the parish, noting their presence has been missed. This may seem like a big job, but if the team looks carefully at the parish list, and checks with the rector and greeters as to recent attendance, they will probably find that the chronic absentees are not that numerous. In a parish with 100 families on the parish list, for example, the team may find 20 to 30 absentees. If three or four members on the congregation development team volunteer to make the calls, that represents 5 to 10 calls each. These may be spread out over a two- to three-month period (three calls per month, or one per week).

Before making the phone calls, the congregation development team should draft a script or approach to be followed, and "test drive" it with other team members to make sure it will achieve the objectives of the calling program. A suggested calling script follows. An electronic version may be found on the enclosed CD, in Microsoft Word format (see script.doc).

Absentee Parishioner Calling Script

1. Confirm the family's name.

2. Introduce yourself as a member of the parish, and say that you are calling to keep in touch with the family. Ask how they are doing.

3. Indicate that they are still considered to be members of the parish. If the family indicates that this is no longer the case, ask why not. Have they moved to another church? Do they not wish to return? Record their reason(s). This information will be good feedback for the team, for future program planning. Note that the family name should be deleted from the parish list.

4. If the family feels they are no longer members of the parish, and their reasons seem weak, take the opportunity to probe a bit—the family in fact may want to come back, especially if encouraged.

5. If the family wishes to remain on the parish list, record this. Ask when they might return. If there is hesitation, ask if there are scheduling conflicts that prevent them from attending services. If so, note this, and suggest other alternatives, such as attending an earlier or mid-week service. Record when they intend to attend the next service. (The caller should follow up with them two to three weeks after that date, to see if they attended and how they felt about the service.)

6. Ask if they would like the rector to visit them. Ask if they would like a copy of the latest parish newsletter mailed to them.

7. Mention upcoming parish events, and ask if any interest them.

8. Refer to the parish web site, and some of the past and future events described there.

9. Thank them for their time, and say that you hope to see them again soon. End the call.

10. Record your impressions of the conversation. Might another call be fruitful? Do you sense it might be helpful for the rector to visit? These notes should be passed to the congregation development team leader, to plan for follow-up calls within six months.

Enabling Passions

So, the congregation development team has a growth process in place, they ensure that members keep coming, and follow up on missing members. Is attendance all there is to congregation development? Of course not—parishioners belong to a parish, and as long as they can receive value from and give value to their parish, they will keep supporting it. Otherwise, they will disappear. When this happens, there is little a proactive congregation development team can do to bring them back.

Congregation development, at its core, is about building a parish environment that is exciting and stimulating, and fosters caring for each parishioner. It must also provide some means of enabling the passions of its parishioners to flourish.

Simply making an inventory of parishioners' skills and then linking parishioners with volunteer assignments on various parish program teams will not keep their interest. Skills assignments are ways of enabling the parishioner to give back to the parish, but if this is all the parish offers, volunteers will probably lose interest, or burn out, and disappear.

To build a congregation that is growing in faith and understanding, as well as in numbers, the congregation development team needs to create a way, within the parish context, for parishioners' passions to be satisfied. The parish programs need to reflect the passions of its parishioners. In summarizing the parish survey, the congregation development team will learn more precisely what parishioners need and want from parish programs. If parish programs do not match parishioners' passions, and there is no demand for those programs, they should be discontinued, and new programs built.

The congregation development team should meet individually with the program leaders to discuss the results of the parish survey, before presenting a summary to the parish. An unpopular program may be a bit off-focus, and with some work, could be brought back into demand. Others will need to be abandoned. In these cases, care should be taken to avoid suggesting that the program has no value or no future. A demand for the program may return, and so the team should ensure that program resources are retained. Programs that are discontinued in this process, however, often result in a feeling of relief on the part of the program leader: the poor level of interest has probably been self-evident, and the program leader may have been looking for a way out. The program leaders might see an opportunity to renew themselves—perhaps they can start up a new program development team, and get into some new, more exciting topics.

Program creation and amendment is not an overnight process: putting a worthwhile program together takes work. Look to the parishioners who identified their passions with the new program: they may want to learn by building the program for others. Look, too, for prepackaged programs to fill these gaps—there is no point in reinventing the wheel. Contact the program resources team at your diocesan office. If they do not have the requested program resources themselves, they probably know of a parish or diocese that does, or where resources might be purchased. Program leaders may also be available through the diocesan office, other parishes, or commercially.

This book will not cover the huge topic of program development. Many publications already cover the subject in detail. That said, it is vital for the congregation development team to appreciate that, to grow its congregation, parishioners themselves must grow intellectually, or they will lose interest. Parish programs must engage the passions of its congregation—adults, youth, and children—and be exciting and challenging for those participating.

The team must understand, too, that the needs and passions of its parishioners naturally change. This is why the parish survey needs to re-ask the question, What is your passion? every year, and adjust the parish's programs accordingly.

The Congregation Development Team

In this chapter you have read about the congregation development team and its great works. Who specifically make up the team?

The team begins with a leader, a member of the parish who cares deeply for the well-being of fellow parishioners. Every parish has natural leaders capable of filling this role: they tend to organize the parish's social events, speak at parish events, greet parishioners each week, follow up when parishioners are ill. You know them already.

The role of team leader may well suit one of the deputy wardens, if he or she has the interest. Certainly by leading the congregation development team for a year or so, the deputy warden will gain significant insights into the parish's membership, which would help prepare them for the role of warden, should they choose.

Recruiting a leader for the congregation development team may not be easy, as the scope of the position may seem daunting. However, if the approach to potential team leaders is positive and supportive, such as, "You've been doing the job for years already. All we need to do is spread the workload to other like-minded volunteers and formalize what we have done in the past. We could even improve on things," the team leader will emerge. To help in the recruiting process, the following position description may be helpful. An electronic version in Microsoft Word format may be found on the enclosed CD (see congdevlead.doc).

Position Description: Congregation Development Team Leader

Role

The team leader provides guidance to the congregation development team. The leader directs the team in executing the congregation development program for the parish, including parish marketing, design and execution of fellowship events, the greeting process, newcomers' events, and the annual parish survey. Through the work of the team, the team leader monitors the growth of the parish congregation, and takes appropriate action through the team, as required.

Responsibilities

The team leader

- works with the parish's volunteer coordinator to recruit the members of the congregation development team;

- schedules and chairs the congregation development team's monthly meeting;
- arranges for a facilitated team planning workshop each year, to develop or amend the congregation development plan for the parish;
- monitors and approves expenses for the team, according to the team's approved budget;
- allocates the work of the team to various members, based on their desires and abilities. The team leader monitors the work of team members to ensure that it follows the team's plan, and so that team members do not suffer burnout, or have so many priorities that they are at risk; the team leader may then reassign work to another team member;
- maintains a high level of morale within the team, by celebrating the team's successes and by working with team members having difficulty; and
- provides updates to the wardens and advisory board on a monthly basis about the team's achievements and its upcoming plans, and brings forward any issues the team may need their assistance with.

Duration

The team leader may be appointed by the wardens or elected by vestry. The leader will normally agree to lead the team for no fewer than 12 months, so that the annual congregation development planning and execution cycle can be completed within their term. The team leader may elect to remain as team leader for an additional 12 months. Ideally the team leader will remain with the team for an additional one or two months following the end of their appointment, to assist their replacement in the transition period.

Skills Required

- Some leadership skills (team members, as self-motivated volunteers with similar passions for the betterment of the congregation, will require minimal management);
- planning skills (to lead the team in preparing the congregation development plan);
- delegation skills (to assign work to team members);
- analytical skills (to lead the team in assessing the effects of the congregation development program, adjusting the plan as required);

- patience (to accept that results may be slow in coming to the parish); and
- persistence (to continue the program when results appear less than hoped for).

Note: most of the content of this position description for a program team leader can be easily adapted to the position of the other program team leaders in the parish.

The size and composition of the congregation development team will vary with the size of the parish and the planned workload. In small parishes the team will likely be effective with a leader, two or three team members, and the greeters. Once they have drawn up a congregation development plan together, they might share the workload in various ways. In the examples below, key responsibilities are noted in parentheses.

Team leader (team reporting): Develops the marketing plan; summarizes the parish survey results; reports team's progress to the wardens and advisory board.

Member 2 (survey): Designs the parish survey; records survey results; follows up with parish program leaders to have the programs better match parishioners' passions.

Member 3 (events): Oversees fellowship and newcomers' events; handles absentee parishioners calls.

Member 4 (marketing): Responsible for marketing materials, partnerships, liaising with newspapers, and coordinating greeters.

For large parishes, a greater workload (more parishioners to survey and call, more programs to be developed and amended, more extensive advertising programs and partnerships) will require a larger team: a leader, four to six team members, and the greeters. The workload might be distributed as follows:

Team leader (team reporting and monitoring): Prepares survey results report; prepares reports to advisory board; monitors team; initiates community partnerships.

Members 2 and 3 (marketing): Develop the marketing plan; oversee parish-community events; responsible for marketing materials, liaising with newspapers, and maintaining the parish web site.

Members 4 and 5 (survey): Design the parish survey and record results; oversee the parish survey and pot-luck event; interview pot-luck "no-shows," with additional volunteer callers as needed; identify program gaps and ensure that parish programs match parishioners' passions.
Members 6 and 7 (retention): Oversee fellowship and newcomers' events; handle absentee parishioners calls; coordinate greeters.

Both in small and large parishes, the congregation development team should try to meet monthly, to review their progress and to plan for the next one or two months. The team should work closely with the parish's volunteer coordinator (to build/amend the parishioner inventory), the fund-raising team (to separate fellowship events from fund-raising ones), and the program teams (to identify gaps and make improvements).

The Congregation Development Plan

Regardless of the size of the congregation development team and their many tasks, the team should take the time to plan their congregation development work for the upcoming year. This ensures that the program receives careful thought—what needs to be done this year; what can wait until next year. It also helps ensure that tasks will be done in the proper order, and will be given sufficient time and volunteer resources to do them well. The best time to have this planning session is in November or early December, since the congregation development program for the current year is finishing up, and the starting point for next year will be fairly well known. This also allows time to estimate the funds the team will need in the year ahead and pass the estimates on to the parish treasurer, before the parish budget is finalized (usually in late December or early January).

The following congregation development plan could be used as a starting point if the team has never prepared such a plan. To use this template, read the italicized notes in each section, then replace these notes with the content of your plan. An electronic version may be found in Microsoft Word format on the enclosed CD (see congdevplan.doc).

For

Parish Name

Table of Contents

Program Team/Scope

The Team. *List the names of members of the program team, their phone numbers, and street and e-mail addresses; their role(s) within the program team (e.g., their special interests, talents, passions); and their time available to support the team's work (hours per month).*

Include the organizational structure of the team, if it might prove helpful to readers of the plan.

Program Scope *for the year. List the team's scope boundaries. These may include financial limitations, workload restrictions, timing constraints (e.g., certain program events must occur at specific times or dates), and the parish's expectations of the team for the year being planned.*

For the congregation development team, consider the following scope attributes:

- *the number of volunteers likely to be available to do the work of the team during the planning year, and the hours per week/month they have available to do the work;*
- *for the growth/marketing sub-team, the realistic number of new parishioners that will be added to the parish list in the planning year, given the demographics of the surrounding communities;*

- for the growth/marketing sub-team, the amount of funds likely to be available for advertising in the planning year;
- for the retention/fellowship/visitation sub-team, the number of parishioners who will need visitations during the planning year, and the realistic number of visitations (telephone or in person) that can be carried out each month, given the resources available;
- for the retention/fellowship/visitation sub-team, the realistic number of fellowship events that can be accommodated during the planning year, and the number of attendees expected.

Program Objectives for 20__

The objectives for the congregation development team for the planning year include the team's and the parish's expectations for the year. The objectives should be specific and measurable. Use statements that will help move the parish from where it is today, to where the team hopes it will be by year-end. Include how the changes will be measured at year-end (i.e., How did we do?).

Example of an inadequate congregation development objective: "Increase advertising next year."

Example of a strong congregation development objective: "Through an aggressive advertising campaign, make the parish the most visible church in our community, by measuring public awareness through surveys twice during the planning year (before and after)."

For each objective, note those that are interdependent, and how. Also note if the objective needs to be accomplished at a particular time for proper measurement to start.

When the list of objectives is drawn up, inspect the objectives carefully: are they realistic for that year? Can all the objectives be accomplished, given the resources available to the team and the parish's ability to absorb the proposed changes? Do any of the objectives depend on the success of another program team? If so, are they in sync with yours?

It is better to drop objectives at the outset, and have the team meet a reduced set, than to overextend the team and have them fail. Remember, there is always next year. Still, the team needs to set objectives that "stretch" them—this is how teams grow and learn.

Here are some sample congregation development objectives for the team's consideration:

1. To increase the number of regular attendees at the 9:00 A.M. service by xxx and the 11:00 A.M. service by xxx. This will be monitored through the sidespeople's counts, and reviewed each month by the team. The number of attendees should grow on average by xxx per month (9:00 A.M. service) and xxx per month (11:00 A.M. service).

2. To increase the number of attendees at fellowship events by xxx by year-end. The number should increase by xxx for each subsequent event. Attendance will be measured by the team for each event held.

3. To carry out xxx visitations per month. This number will be recorded by the team.

Initiatives

List the program initiatives for the year that will address the objectives. For each, include

- **what** the initiative is, which objectives it will address, and a description of the development work required to complete it;
- **who** will develop the initiative;
- **when** the development work must be completed, related to when the initiative is to be provided to the parish; and
- **how** and **when** the program team will measure the initiative's success.

Note any initiative prerequisites or assumptions, and any interdependencies of other program teams' initiatives.

Schedule

Two schedules are needed in the congregation development plan:

1. A **schedule of published congregation development events** (fellowship events, celebrations, presentations, etc.), which should be reflected in the parish's bulletins, newsletters, and web site, so that parishioners can plan their attendance accordingly.

2. An **initiatives development schedule** that includes
- the resources and development time required for each event (e.g., fellowship event or visitations);
- target milestones (e.g., advertisement placements or parishioner inventory); and
- who will be developing the material.

This schedule will be used by the congregation development team to ensure adequate preparation for the published congregation development events and planned milestones.

When the congregation development team meets each month, they can use the development schedule to determine whether there are any problems with the planned development work and then take corrective action, if required (e.g., enlisting more people to help prepare, moving event dates, etc.).

Financials/Resources

Financials

With respect to the planned congregation development initiatives, the team needs to summarize the costs of the program for the year ahead (resource materials, advertising costs, event costs, visitor travel if applicable, etc.) and indicate when the expenses are expected to be incurred. This way, the treasurer will be able to include these costs in the parish's budget for the upcoming year, under the congregation development expense line. When approved by vestry, this budget line-item can be used by the congregation development team, as needed.

In addition, the estimated additional annual parish income (from the increased number of parishioners) should be summarized, and the information passed to the treasurer for inclusion in the upcoming year's budget.

If the team discovers significant variances between the actual costs and those planned in the parish budget (plus or minus), the team should advise the treasurer. A negative variance might be covered by a contingency budget line, or the treasurer may have to raise the matter with the wardens for resolution.

Resources

The team should summarize the monthly volunteer resources and skills required (beyond those of the team) to support the congregation development plan. The volunteer coordinator (see chapter 5) will use this information to recruit the appropriate volunteers.

When all parish program teams circulate their completed plans at the start of the year, the volunteer coordinator may advise the congregation development team that the required resources will not be available in the numbers or at the time planned. In these cases, the congregation development team will need to revise the plan.

Program Management Process

The congregation development plan needs to lay out how the team's progress will be monitored throughout the year. Some best practices for the team's consideration follow:

1. Team Meetings

The team should meet monthly (same time each month) to review planned activities, past and future. The team meeting should be chaired by the team leader. Minutes are not necessary, but the team leader will need to keep track of commitments made during the meeting, for follow-up purposes. The team should bring copies of their development schedule and events calendar with them to each meeting.

Team meetings should be issue-focused (e.g., issues with the development schedule/events calendar), not focused on brainstorming solutions. The meetings may then be conducted within one to one and a-half hours.

Here is a suggested meeting agenda:

- How has the team been doing since the last meeting? Achievements should be celebrated. Problems should be learned from and used to modify subsequent events as appropriate, or used when preparing next year's plan.
- What's next? Who is working on what, according to the development schedule? How is it going? Will we be ready for the event(s)? If not, what needs to be done? Are there any cost variances?
- Are there any proposals for changes to the plan? Any new events needed but not included? If so, how might they be resourced? Are there any events that should be cancelled?

2. Program Reporting

The team leader (or designate) should report the team's program status to the wardens and advisory board each month, following the team's own monthly meeting if possible. The team leader may wish to schedule the team's monthly meeting to be a week or so ahead of the advisory board's meeting, so that the board receives up-to-date information.

Team reports may be quite brief (e.g., one-half to one page in length). The program update for the wardens and the board should include: program events since the last update and results; upcoming development work and issues; issues for the wardens' or board's action, if any.

The program report might be tabled only for the advisory board's information. Also, it is not necessary for the team leader to attend the board's meeting, unless there are issues for the wardens' or board's action.

In addition to the advisory board's monthly report, the team leader should prepare an annual program report for vestry that describes the work of the program team in the year ending, lessons learned, and plans for the upcoming year. The team leader should attend, in case there are questions from the vestry on the program.

3. Parish Surveys

Before the team meets to develop their plan for the upcoming year, the team should ask the parish what they thought of this year's fellowship and visitation programs. (What was good? Not so good? What was missing?)

The team should use the same guidelines in the parish survey section of this chapter when preparing a survey of the team's work (e.g., avoidance of tick boxes, use of pot-lucks, etc.).

The team should use the feedback to plan next year's program.

By using a template such as the one above, the congregation development team can run the planning session as a "fill-in-the-blanks" type of meeting, which will make the process considerably easier. If the team is creating a program plan for the first time, they may need two or three sessions, up to three hours each. If the team is meeting to update the plan with next year's initiatives, they may need only two 2-hour sessions.

If the team decides to use the sample template, the most effective approach is to have the entire team contribute to completing the scope, objectives, and management process sections. (These may not change very much in subsequent years after the first plan has been built.) One member of the team might use flip charts or an overhead projector to record the team's information.

Once these crucial sections have been completed, the team could divide up the initiatives for next year, working in pairs to define them in more detail and decide what resources (funds and volunteer hours) will be required and what the schedule (timeline) will be for each. The team would then reconvene to review each other's initiative descriptions, add comments, and agree to the detail.

Later the team leader should review the new or revised congregation development plan with the wardens and advisory board for their input and concurrence. The plan should also be presented at vestry, as an information handout, to build excitement in the parish for the year's program.

While small parishes may feel this amount of planning is unnecessary for the congregation development work they need to do in a year, they may find that—by sitting down and thinking through what needs to be done, when, and by whom—their scarce resources will be used more efficiently than if they moved forward without a plan.

For large parishes, the planning process gives the congregation development team an excellent way to get to know each other, and explore how they work together, what their passions are, and which tasks they would prefer to work on during the year. The team twosomes formed during the planning sessions may remain for the year.

And if the congregation development plan is distributed to the parish, you will probably be pleasantly surprised when the time comes to execute the work. You will find volunteers waiting for you. The volunteer coordinator, the program leaders, and members of the fund-raising team will know how and when to connect with your team. You may find volunteers waiting for you. You may find the volunteers pre-scheduled to help with calls and event preparation. Think of the plan as your team's own marketing vehicle—building excitement and anticipation in the parish for your team's work.

Application to Your Parish

It might be helpful for the congregation development team to keep in mind that not all of the work that needs to be done can be done in any given year. To move forward, the team might select the key shortcomings of the parish, and work on them in year 1. In year 2, the team might proceed with tackling the second-most pressing issues, and so on. As long as the parish is increasing in numbers, and the parish surveys show that the members are happy with the progress being made, the team is doing a good job, and should celebrate their successes.

Here is a suggested priority list:

1. *Congregation Development Plan* (see also page 59)
The congregation development team should first create a plan. Otherwise it will be difficult to proceed in a coordinated manner, and no doubt waste precious volunteer time, with people going in different directions and reworking poorly executed efforts. Even if the team comprises only two people, as may happen in a small rural parish, it is important to decide what needs to be done, in what order, and when. A three-page plan is still better than no plan.

The plan should be circulated to the congregation so that everyone knows what's ahead and why, and can be prepared for events, surveys, and phone calls. The parish's volunteer coordinator will know when to recruit extra people to help with events or make calls. The treasurer will know when the team requires funds in the upcoming year, and will build them into the parish budget.

2. Parish Survey and Parishioners' Skills/Passions Inventory (see also page 31)

The next step for the congregation development team is to carry out a parish survey and, using the results, to build an inventory of parishioners' skills/passions. Without this inventory, the team won't get very far executing their plan. Also, by not having a skills and passions inventory, other program leaders in the parish cannot effectively tap into the parish list to obtain volunteers for their initiatives.

3. Fellowship Events

While gaining new parishioners will be important to the success of the congregation development plan, caring for current members should be the team's third priority. Fellowship events provide an excellent way to show care to parishioners, and the team should plan four to six such events annually.

When it comes to planning creative venues, a good way to generate ideas is to check out the experience of other parishes. The congregation development team could call local churches and find out what they have done for fellowship events. They might also surf the web sites of other parishes in the diocese—often stories will be posted about their latest events and how they put them together. The team could also ask members of the advisory board for ideas.

4. Signage (see also page 42)

If the team does nothing else in year 1 for parish advertising, checking the parish signage is paramount. Are the signs attractive and in good condition? Do any signs need to be repainted? Replaced? A weathered, black-and-white board does not attract positive attention. Selecting colours for the parish's signage that match the posters and brochures adds impact. A sign placed at each main road entrance into your community is ideal. All signs should feature the parish's mission statement (at least the slogan), web address, phone number, and service times.

5. Parish Web Site (see also page 41)

If the parish already has a web site, the team's next priority might be to add the parish's marketing content to it. Ensure that the site gives the location of the church, perhaps with a link to MapQuest. Exciting aspects of parish life should be featured on the home page. Highlight the programs, especially those in high demand in the parish and any that offer unique features within the community. Services that the parish provides to the community should also be highlighted, along with a parish contact list. Change the content on the web site often, to show the evolving, dynamic nature of your parish.

If your parish does not have a web site, raise the matter with the advisory board: creating a web site may be too big a project for the congregation development team, as the site will span all aspects of parish life. However, if no one else volunteers and the team feels a web site is necessary to move forward, proceed. Most computer software stores offer web-building kits that are reasonably priced. Check your parishioner inventory, too—many parishes have at least one computer-oriented person in their midst who might be recruited to design and build the site.

A word of advice: make sure the web site is designed so that parish volunteers can maintain it. It should be easy to add information, such as the weekly service bulletin, sermons, contact list updates, and the parish calendar, which keeps the site relevant for parishioners. The design should be developed with the team's input and mirror the care shown for the parish signage: attractive colours, inclusion of the parish's slogan, mission statement, etc. Lots of pictures (which change each month) will add a human touch.

6. *Pamphlets* (see also page 41)
The next priority for the team might be to create and distribute parish pamphlets. You could start simple (cheap), with photocopied and folded brochures. In terms of both design and content, keep in mind the parish image and any unique or exciting program features. Distribution of the pamphlets might be handled by the sidespersons, who could easily give copies to newcomers. A pamphlet drop to a portion of the community might also be considered in the team's first year.

In year 2, the team could upgrade the brochures, perhaps printing on higher-quality paper and including photographs, and extend the drop to more homes and local businesses that have community information racks.

7. *Greeters* (see also page 50)
The team's next priority might be to recruit parish greeters (these are in addition to the sidespersons), who would also help distribute pamphlets to

newcomers at Sunday services. As a start, try to have at least one greeter at each service. Depending on how the greeters and the congregation development team structure the schedule, four volunteers may be sufficient (one for each service, or pairs taking turns, alternating Sundays, months, etc.), although six is better since you should have two greeters at a well-attended service.

The greeters should wear name tags, be prepared to record the names and telephone numbers of newcomers, and to distribute parish pamphlets and newcomer welcome kits.

8. *Partnerships* (see also page 43)
With the basics covered, the team could now expand their congregation development program by exploring opportunities to partner with other nearby Anglican parishes, other churches, and service clubs as a way of attracting attention to the parish and adding new parishioners.

Consider first partnering with other Anglican parishes in or near the community. Parishioners who may be looking for a church with programs not offered at one parish might be picked up by the other.

Next, the team might approach other churches about running joint programs, such as outreach or meditation. This would strengthen the parish's sense of community, and enable more effective programs for all concerned.

Partnerships with service clubs (typically for community outreach programs and community celebrations) would likewise allow for more effective parish programs. Also, working alongside service club members on joint projects may be a way of inviting new families into the parish.

9. *Passion-Based Programs* (see also page 54)
Using the inventory of parishioners' passions, and the feedback from the parish survey on which programs are more or less in demand, the team could work with the leaders of various programs (outreach, Bible study, pastoral care, etc.) to build new programs, improve existing ones, and discontinue those not in demand.

In small parishes, the congregation development team may have to take the lead in developing and executing programs. Their own team objectives, however, are important and should not be pushed aside. Take advantage of the considerable program resources available from most diocesan offices, as well as trained facilitators.

In large parishes, program development and execution may be a logical stepping stone for congregation development team members who have served their terms and want to do something new.

10. *Newcomers' Events* (see also page 46)
The congregation development team might next consider formalizing the process for newcomers' events, usually held about every three months. (The frequency of these events will be driven by the number and rate of newcomers joining the parish.)

11. *Absentee Parishioner Calls* (see also page 52)
The congregation development team, having made sure that current parishioners and newcomers are cared for, might now proactively contact families on the parish list who have not been regular attendees. In a parish with 200 families on the parish list, for example, about 50 to 80 families might be in this category. The team may need help with the calling program—recruiting the greeters would be a good idea since their skills and experience match the task.

The process could be spread out over several months, to reduce the number of volunteers needed. In the above example, if the team scheduled three months to carry out the calling program, with a maximum of four calls per volunteer per month (one per week), they would need six or seven volunteers to complete the process (20 to 30 calls per month divided by four).

12. *Upscale Advertising*
With the basic parish advertising/marketing materials and processes in place, the team might lastly consider moving the advertising campaign into more widespread venues. The financial costs and volunteer resources needed may be prohibitive, however, and upscale advertising may be possible only for some medium- and large-sized parishes. If budget permits, the congregation development team might arrange to print posters for posting in local businesses, libraries, and recreation centres. Banners, newspaper slots, and rental display boards could be used to promote upcoming parish events (see also page 43).

Often local radio and cable TV stations offer free slots for community service groups—these should be researched by the team and utilized whenever upcoming parish events might appeal to the community at large (e.g., bazaars, fun fairs, walk-a-thons). Don't use this valuable venue to announce church service times and so forth—remember, you are showcasing the dynamism of your parish in a community context. At the parish events, the team should be prepared to welcome all participants and have parish brochures ready to distribute to potential newcomers.

Chapter 5

Volunteer Management

While volunteer management is part of congregation development, the topic merits special attention because it is critically important to the parish's life and success, and ... because we often do such a poor job of volunteer care (management). The volunteers of a parish define its culture and the priorities of its ParishWorks, its ability to serve its parishioners and its community. Given all these considerations, why ***don't*** parishes focus more on volunteer care? Because

- we expect parishioners to come forward, as part of their commitment to the parish—they are not ***asked*** to help out;
- we expect parishioners to pitch in, no matter what the task—even though the volunteers may dislike the tasks involved;
- we expect volunteers to know what to do, without their having position descriptions, coaching, or support;
- we expect volunteers to want to do their tasks indefinitely; and
- because we ***expect*** volunteers to do whatever needs doing, we do not think to thank them.

Much needs to be done to build a parish volunteer base, both in terms of numbers and expertise. How can we do it?

To begin, parish leaders might brush up on how to recruit and motivate volunteers. Many publications deal with these skills and considerations—the parish library should have two or three such books on hand for parish leaders to read and absorb. If the parish library does not have these resources, your diocesan office likely does.

Parish leaders should also consider the following aspects of volunteer management, which tend to be unique to parish situations, and are often those which we do most poorly:

Volunteers versus Employees

Many parish leaders are familiar with techniques used to motivate and "manage" paid employees in their workplaces. Unfortunately, they try to use these same techniques in building and managing parish teams of volunteers—and fail. Why?

First, volunteers are not paid to do the work of the parish. So, this tried and true leverage over employee performance and commitment doesn't apply. Now what? Several techniques that staff managers use to motivate paid staff *do* apply to volunteers—they simply need different emphasis.

1. *Leading by Example*

Never ask a volunteer to do what you as a team leader would not do or (better yet) have not done yourself. Take the initiative, and recruit others to help get the project off the ground. For example, carry out a key preliminary task, such as assessing the community's outreach need, before recruiting the rest of the parish outreach team to do the work. Or, carry out the work on a small scale (for instance, calling a sample of the parish families in a stewardship campaign) before recruiting the rest of the team. This shows the volunteers that the task is doable, that you are ready to help them learn, and most importantly, that while you are the team leader, *you are neither more nor less important to the team than they are.*

2. *Appealing to Passions*

Many parishes have found that, whenever volunteers have been asked to do tasks without regard for what they would like to do, the parish's volunteer base shrinks (the 20% doing 80% of the work problem). Assuming the parish has completed its member survey (see chapter 4), volunteers should be recruited only when the initiative matches their passions. Where there is no passion match, volunteers may be recruited with respect to their skills only, if the initiative is a parish necessity. If there is a parish initiative with no skills or passions match, the parish leadership might consider dropping it.

3. *Coaching*

In the workplace, paid employees are often assigned to carry out tasks as "tests" of their skill to adapt to new challenges, and then are graded on the outcome. This is no way to treat volunteers. On the contrary, volunteers want to be part of a parish initiative that is fun, successful, and spiritually rewarding. For this to happen, parish leaders need to spend more time coaching their teams than they might in the business world. Praise volunteers for sticking to a task and for bringing energy and new ideas to the team. Show them frequently how they have personally made a positive contribution to the parish and/or community as the initiative moves forward—don't wait until the team finishes the job.

Parish team leaders will find that keeping a volunteer team motivated will involve far more time than for employee teams, and they will need to plan accordingly. In fact, many volunteer leaders won't have time to do much of the actual work. So, if they are going to lead by example, they will need to do it before the team starts carrying out the work in earnest.

4. *Celebrating*

In the business setting, employees are formally acknowledged through their annual performance appraisal process. Waiting a year to thank volunteers, though, will not be at all helpful, and in fact may be regarded as too little, too late. In a parish setting, a volunteer team needs to be formally thanked by the congregation at large ***immediately*** following a major milestone, and at the completion of their work. The team leader should do this, as well as inviting a spokesperson from the group benefiting from the initiative (either a parishioner or a member of the community) to thank each member of the team. Team members need to know the difference they have made in the lives of those affected.

Team leaders might consider giving keepsakes or certificates of achievement to each team member, perhaps presented by the rector. These need not be expensive. Rather, volunteer thank-yous are most appreciated when they are personal and reflect the nature of the team and its initiative. For example, team members who set up a food bank might each receive a can of beans with a bow and sincere message of thanks.

Volunteer Recruiting

Often parish leaders approach experienced volunteers, or parishioners whom they know well, when building a parish team. While this approach may work in business, parish leaders at this critical stage of volunteer team building need to ask, Is this a task this person *wants* to do? Without having an inventory of potential volunteers' passions, one cannot really answer the question.

Let's assume the inventory is available and that parishioners' passions are included. Parish leaders should then go through the list to pick potential team members. Passions frequently will not exactly match the initiative. However, the parishioner's description of their passions may not be exact either, so if there is a "close enough" match, the parishioner should be asked to be part of the team.

Parish leaders may find that, in sifting through the inventory, a number of parishioners have not included their passions in the list. Also, leaders may come across several parishioners who attend services infrequently. Or they may notice parishioners who have tended to shy away from parish initiatives in the past. It never hurts to ask these people to help a team. The very act of reaching out to them may be a way of further engaging them in parish life. Often leaders find that people are simply waiting to be asked. If the parishioner passes on the team's initiative, the leader might ask if they would consider helping other teams, and describe some of the programs underway. Team leaders can always help other team leaders, even in the process of volunteer recruiting.

Volunteer Burnout

In business, staff managers tend to assign work to those with the most time available, or to those who seem to be the most energetic or experienced, using bonuses or promotions as incentives. Unfortunately, many parish leaders use the same approach with their volunteer teams, with poor results. While the team's task may be accomplished by these keen volunteers, frequently it is done at a very high cost to the parish: volunteer burnout. When this happens, the team not only loses a valuable resource, the parish often loses a family—and no parish initiative is worth this.

Unlike staff workers and other organizational volunteers, parishioners who volunteer to work for their parish do so from a moral and spiritual basis. As such, the commitments they make are often sacrificial. Parish leaders need to understand *why* volunteers have joined their teams, so that their best intentions are not taken advantage of. Many people cannot say No to their parish when asked to help—they feel they "owe" unlimited commitment to the work of their church as a part of their faith, regardless of their abilities and available time. Many make a commitment based on their current life situation and, when their situation changes, cannot bring themselves to adjust their role in the team, because this would represent a "failure" on their part.

Regardless of the reasons, parish leaders need to be sensitive to their team members, and to step in when any sign of burnout begins to show—a normally energetic person looking tired or unhappy; somebody who tries to "do it all"; a conscientious volunteer rushing through the work of the team; a gregarious member turned uncommunicative. Even though team leaders need to focus on getting the work done, they cannot do this at the expense of *any* of their volunteers. They need to take their team members aside, and ask them how they are doing. Are they still excited by the work? Do they still have time to do what they thought they could do?

In addition to guarding against burnout, parish leaders need to be proactive with all of their team members, and "check in" from time to time. Some burnout candidates do not show any of the typical signs, and leaders are surprised when they abruptly resign from their teams and even leave the parish. Parish leaders cannot let this happen if at all possible.

Often, burnout may start when a parish volunteer has been doing the same task for too long. Most volunteers look for variety in their work. Parish leaders need to make sure that longer parish initiatives have interim milestones or times when team members may shift gears, even move on to the work of another team.

Also, succession plans should exist for each key leadership position (e.g., the wardens, the treasurer, the secretary, the Sunday school superintendent). Think what might happen if one of these volunteers suddenly resigned. How long would it take to find a replacement? Who could train that person and how long would it take? During the period of change, what would happen to the parish's programs and administrative processes?

Each key position should have an "understudy," a person who learns the ropes in preparation for that time when the person in the key position retires. For the wardens, a deputy warden for each is advisable. Unfortunately, while many parishes manage to recruit deputy wardens, they are not given meaningful responsibilities. As a result, they are not prepared to take over when the time comes. To counter this, the wardens could consider having one deputy warden act as the parish sexton, so that they become knowledgeable about the upkeep of the parish's buildings and grounds. The other deputy warden might fill the role of treasurer, so that he or she gains a good understanding of the parish's financials. Regardless, without significant responsibilities, the deputy wardens will not feel they have anything of value to give to the parish, and may decline to serve as wardens when needed.

Other understudy possibilities include the parish's envelope secretary learning the work of either the parish secretary or treasurer. The Sunday school superintendent could be preparing a skilled and enthusiastic teacher to assume a leadership role.

The point is, if you have understudies in place, the volunteers holding parish positions will not feel pressured into continuing past the time they want to move on. Handing over the reins to someone who has been training for the position will make for a smooth transition—and it's an excellent way to avoid volunteer burnout.

The Parish Volunteer Coordinator

The previous chapter described the parish survey, and how to build an inventory of parishioner passions and skills. This is the first step in managing the volunteer base effectively. Once created, the inventory will be most effective when managed by a parish volunteer coordinator. This person would be responsible for keeping the inventory up to date, as passions and skills change, and as volunteer interests and time availability change.

The volunteer coordinator is the person parish leaders contact when they need additional help with a parish initiative. For example, the outreach development team might want to carry out a special outreach event, and need additional people to help set up. Or the parish may have decided to create a new parish marketing team, and parishioners with like passions and skills are needed to staff the team. The volunteer coordinator would go through the inventory, and match skills and passions of parishioners to the initiative at hand. The parishioners' names and telephone numbers would then be given to the initiative leader, for follow-up.

In addition to matching skills and passions to parish initiatives, the volunteer coordinator keeps track of who is doing what. In this way, the coordinator monitors the workloads of parish volunteers to determine if anyone has too large a workload or is subject to burnout. In these cases, the coordinator might follow up with the volunteer to see if they need to back off one or two of their commitments.

The coordinator will also use the "who does what" list to monitor the distribution of parish workload among its volunteers. If the parish is moving toward the "20% do 80% of the work" situation, the coordinator will follow up with underutilized volunteers to better spread the work. For key positions in the parish (wardens, treasurer, secretary/bookkeeper, etc.), the coordinator will look for potential succession candidates, as incumbents reach the end of their terms or wish to give up their roles.

As the parish's leader in volunteer management, the volunteer coordinator could also coach parish team leaders in volunteer management skills, so that they can build parish teams that are highly effective and motivated.

To help the parish leadership understand work distribution and potential issues with the parish's volunteer base, the volunteer coordinator could prepare a **monthly volunteers' report** for the wardens and advisory board. The report would include the percentage of active volunteers compared to the parish's total parishioners, in a framework of several months, to determine if progress is being made in the recruiting and workload distribution process. The report could also list who is assigned to what, to indicate likely burnout candidates and possible underutilized volunteers. Non-volunteers who might be called by the congregation development team, as part of their visitation program, should be included as well.

Last but not least, the volunteer coordinator will remind parish leaders to properly thank volunteers for their work, especially through volunteer appreciation events or services, held annually or more often.

By including a volunteer coordinator within the parish leadership team, the congregation will see the importance of its volunteers and the value the parish leadership places in them. A formal volunteer coordinator position, filled by a person who understands the significance of actively managing the parish's volunteer resources, will ensure that the parish will not fall into volunteer neglect patterns. A position description for volunteer coordinator follows. An electronic version in Microsoft Word format may be found on the enclosed CD (see volcoord.doc).

Position Description: Volunteer Coordinator

Role

The volunteer coordinator serves as the parish's focal point for determining volunteer availability and appropriate assignments. The coordinator assists parish team leaders in finding volunteers, recruiting according to the volunteers' passions, skills, and availability. The coordinator manages the parish's volunteer base by monitoring those volunteers who may be overworked or underutilized. The coordinator ensures that all volunteers are properly thanked for their contributions to the parish.

Responsibilities

The volunteer coordinator keeps track of the parish's volunteers. As such, the coordinator

- finds appropriate volunteers for parish projects, for team leaders' follow-up;
- monitors volunteers' workloads to determine if any may be overworked, and approaches them for possible reallocation of assignments;
- monitors the volunteer inventory to determine if any volunteers are underutilized, and follows up with them as required;
- updates the parishioner inventory, as volunteers' passions and skills change;
- coaches team leaders on best practices for utilizing and motivating team members;
- ensures that volunteers are properly thanked for their contributions to the parish; and
- reports volunteer utilization statistics to the wardens and advisory board each month, and compares those statistics against previous months; includes a list of underutilized parishioners, for follow-up by the congregation development team.

Duration

Appointed by the wardens or elected by vestry, the volunteer coordinator fills a term of one year, and may renew the term each year following.

Skills Required

- Awareness of the parish's initiatives and familiarity with the team leaders;
- ability to match volunteers to parish initiatives, using the passions and skills within the parishioner inventory;
- ability to coach parish leaders in volunteer management skills. Knowledge may be built through supervisory roles in business, leadership roles in volunteer organizations, courses taken in volunteer management, experience leading parish initiatives in the past, etc.;
- a caring personality, concerned with the potential of volunteer burnout in parish volunteers, and willing to take corrective action to avoid it; and
- ability to prepare the monthly volunteers' utilization report, and to determine historical trends behind it.

Application to Your Parish

For all sizes of parishes, coaching and thanking volunteers, along with celebrating the parish's accomplishments, are essential. Be sure to make both a part of your parish's processes and events planning.

Also, no matter how small a parish may be, there will always be several members who have shied away from volunteering in the past, and would come forward, if asked in the right way and for the right reasons. All parishes, large and small, need to increase their percentage of volunteering members. Even when you reach 100%, volunteers will need to be monitored so that they do not over-commit or drift away from their assignments.

For small parishes, volunteer burnout will be more of an issue than for larger ones. With fewer people to share the workload, the parish leadership team will tend to rely on core members to plan and run parish events, do calling programs, etc. Often the same people are called upon to do again what they did last year, and the year before that, and so on, regardless of whether they still enjoy it. So, for small parishes, the leadership team definitely needs to be aware of who has done what, and how often. Parish tasks might be moved around, to give volunteers at least variety, if not a complete break. One of the two wardens could act as the parish volunteer coordinator, and keep track of workloads and changes in volunteers' situations and preferences without a lot of overhead. In any case, someone needs to keep track.

For larger parishes, spreading the workload to those in the parish who have not yet come forward will require one or two people to proactively ask potential volunteers indicated by the parish survey results. A volunteer coordinator will be more of a necessity, to keep track of who is doing what, who works well with whom, who enjoys doing what, etc. Larger parishes may have 50+ volunteers, whose interests and personal circumstances will be continually changing. Someone in the parish needs to track these changes, and be able to offer other venues as opportunities arise. This will likely represent a significant time commitment, and the parish leadership team should consider appointing someone other than the wardens to carry it out.

Chapter 6

Communications Management

While many parishes seem to do the right things, rifts frequently occur among members that result in parishes losing key leaders, often to other denominations. Why does this happen?

Most causes point to poor communications within the parish. How could this be possible? Members worship together each week, share the same beliefs and values, and socialize during coffee hour. How can they not always get along?

The nature of our faith and our spiritual journey is one of forming new ideas and challenging old assumptions, through a belief system that is highly emotional by its very nature, and moralistic in its foundations. With this understanding, it is a miracle we even speak to each other. So, given the nature of a parish family in this context, and the risks imposed every day to its well-being and cohesiveness, parish leaders need to pay significant attention to parish communications. What can be done so that members keep in touch, are aware of parish news, and feel valued?

First, parish leaders should review the parish's communications plan (yes, there needs to be one) to determine its effectiveness. Here is a checklist, to see how your parish sizes up:

1. *The Parish and Its Mission Statement* (see chapter 3). Does the parish have a mission statement? Is it well understood by all members? Do parish leaders review the mission statement with the parish each year, to ensure that newcomers are aware of it, and that it continues to reflect the parish's values and objectives? Do all parish teams work toward the objectives in the mission statement? ___YES ___NO

2. *Parish Leadership Team* (see chapter 2). Does the leadership team touch base with each other every two weeks or so, not only to keep up to date on the affairs of the parish, but also on a personal basis, to ensure that they value each other and gain from each other's gifts? Can they fill in for each other if necessary and be consistent in their approaches to managing the parish's affairs? ___YES ___NO

3. *Parish Team Leaders* (congregation development, Sunday school, outreach development, etc.). Do team leaders keep in touch with each other (formally, each month, say, through the advisory board) to ensure that their work complements other teams' work? Are they aware of other teams' events, and do they work with their teams to support them? Do they review their team's direction each year, using the parish's mission statement, to ensure that they are on the right track? Do they review the work of their teams with the advisory board each month, and the congregation two to four times a year, to ensure that they are aware of the team's progress, and that teams receive valuable feedback on the progress they are making? ___YES ___NO

4. *Advisory Board.* Is the board kept up to date on key parish decisions and future issues? Does the board function as a team of advisors to the rector and wardens, or are they expected to "rubber stamp" decisions already made? Is the board doing the work of the parish teams instead of serving as a board of advisors (which is what they signed up for)? Does the board receive discussion materials four to seven days before their meetings, so that they can come to meetings prepared to discuss the issues raised?
___YES ___NO

5. *Congregation.* Do they know what services, readings, and worship themes are coming up, so that they can participate in a more meaningful way? Do parents know the Sunday school curriculum in advance, so that they can understand what subjects their children will be covering and when? Does the congregation know what the parish teams are doing? Do they know about upcoming events and parish project milestones?
___YES ___NO

6. *Newcomers.* Are they met by a greeter at the door on Sundays? Do they know where the washrooms are? Do they know where the Sunday school is? Do they receive a parish welcome kit? Are they invited to coffee hour? Does someone call them the following week to ask how they felt about the parish and if they will be returning? Is there a newcomers' event every few months to introduce them to the parish leaders and programs available?
___YES ___NO

7. *Community.* Is the community aware of the parish and its contributions? Does the parish participate in community events (Santa Claus parades, fun fairs, home weeks, etc.)? Does the parish have a web site with up-to-date information, including upcoming events? Does the parish have inviting

signage that gives the impression of vitality and excitement? Does the parish get reported in the local newspaper for its community projects and the differences these make?   ___YES   ___NO

For each of the above audiences, a communications plan needs to be prepared every year, and a team assigned to carry it out.

The Parish Leadership Team

The rector and wardens, as key leaders of the parish, must ensure that all members of the parish and its community know what has recently happened in the parish, what is about to happen next week, and what will be happening later in the year. And, the leadership team needs to remind the parish and community why these actions happen—how they are day-by-day examples of the parish living out its mission statement. If the leadership team leads by this example, the other parish leaders will follow and add their good news stories to those of the leadership team. Parish team leaders will understand that accurate and frequent communication nurtures an active and vibrant parish.

All three members of the leadership team should take turns sharing the good news stories in Sunday bulletins, on current events posters, on the parish web site, in the parish newsletters, in short talks at Sunday services, and in the newcomers' materials. A leadership team update or story should appear (at least) every second Sunday in the parish bulletin. Every time one of these stories appears in the bulletin, the web site should be updated, so that parishioners who missed the service and shut-ins can also be informed. By taking turns, the three parish leaders can spread the work of preparing these parish updates.

As well, each warden should speak to the congregation at least twice a year during a Sunday service. By alternating, the wardens might give a five- to ten-minute talk once every two or three months. Not only will this help in keeping parish members up to date, it will also help them get to know their wardens and understand what they do behind the scenes, to keep the parish growing.

While many wardens feel that parishioners do not particularly care what they do, parish surveys consistently prove the opposite. Parishioners want to know what their wardens are doing, and they want to thank them for their good works. The wardens' talks can highlight parish good news stories or be an opportunity for the wardens to share some of their feelings about why they volunteered to serve in their role, the differences being a warden has made in their lives, and some of the dreams they might have for the parish's future. The wardens are there to inspire other members of the parish—not just to review the parish's finances with the treasurer. The wardens' talks encourage potential parish leaders to come forward and to be a part of what's happening—some may even volunteer to be the next warden.

Chapter 2 contains many other tips for the parish leadership team. The most important task for each leadership team member, however, is to communicate with parishioners.

The Advisory Board

While chapter 2 offers lots of tips for engaging members of the advisory board, communication is key. If members of the board are to effectively advise the parish leadership team, they need to have discussion materials to review at least one week before each meeting. Each board member should know, going into the meeting, which topics are simply "FYI" items and which will require their feedback during the meeting. The leadership team needs to prepare and distribute a pre-meeting package with this information, along with an agenda and a suggested time allotment for each topic.

Issues for decision should be highlighted and refer to the appropriate preparatory reading materials. The wardens might include some decision options that they have been considering, but should ensure that the board members understand these options are not closed—the wardens, after all, are looking for other ideas from board members. Above all, the wardens need to convey to the board members that their ideas and opinions are highly valued and will be carefully considered, to keep the parish growing as it should.

In all board meeting agendas, the wardens should include 10 minutes for other business: issues, thoughts, any concerns the board members wish to raise. The board members are also part of the behind-the-scenes parish communication pipeline, and so may be aware of parish issues that elude the wardens—often because they are wardens. In many parishes, negative issues might fester simply because none of the parish leadership team is aware of them. The parishioners involved develop a feeling that the wardens and rector do not care about their issue; a simple issue can become a substantial crisis. Open communication and active responses to issues arising will keep the parish family moving in the same direction, building on one another's gifts.

The leadership team needs to ensure, once an issue is raised in a board meeting, that someone is assigned (during the meeting) to address the issue, and that a date is set when the issue will be reported back to the board (hopefully resolved).

The board could consider adopting a **parish issues list**, which would have four columns—a description of the issue/opportunity, who is assigned to look into the issue, the date when its status will next be reviewed with the board, and the target date when the matter should be closed. This list could be reviewed at each board meeting (for those issues due), which would help resolve issues and provide a sense of progress being made from one meeting to the next. Addressing issues cannot be assigned soley to the wardens and rector; rather, issues should be an opportunity to engage board members as parish problem-solvers, which would enrich the board members' role.

Lastly, the parish leadership team should make the minutes of each board meeting available to all parish members. Extra copies might be on hand for pick-up after Sunday services; the minutes might be posted on the parish web site. Without openly communicating the affairs of the board, non-board members will feel left out, which can be a source of mistrust and misunderstandings.

The Congregation

All affairs of the parish leadership team, the advisory board, the parish teams, and the diocese should be shared as soon as possible with parish members. There should be no intentional delay in distributing updates, and the parish leadership team needs to ensure that not only parish members attending services receive updates, but also the parish's absentee members and shut-ins. The parish web site will help in providing updates, but many shut-ins and absentees do not have computer access, and so arrangements should be made for them to receive updates through the visitation team.

While many of the day-to-day decisions of the parish can be handled by the wardens and rector, issues that may have significant impacts on the parish should be tabled at the advisory board. The wardens and parish team leaders (outreach development, congregation development, etc.) should all consider submitting their issues to the parish membership as a whole. These issues need not necessarily require a vestry meeting. Rather, a representative speaker could address the congregation, briefly table the issue, and ask for feedback over the following week or so. Even if some parishioners do not provide feedback, they will appreciate being considered for their ideas and opinions. By soliciting two-way communication in this way, a parish family will grow in a positive way, with fewer opportunities for misunderstanding and resentment. Again, the parish leadership team needs to include non-attendees in soliciting feedback through the parish web site or through visitation handouts and discussion.

The annual parish survey will also help parishioners who are less pro-active in expressing their views. Frequently, a face-to-face, non-threatening interview with a fellow parishioner over coffee will draw out ideas that the parish leaders have never considered. ***Often the best ideas are those that have not been asked for.*** (Read it again.)

The parish leadership team might also consider "lunch-and-learn" events, where a particular parish team is spotlighted during coffee hour, per-haps with table-top displays. An outreach development team could highlight the national outreach initiatives (e.g., the Primate's World Relief and Develop-ment Fund, Anglican Appeal) as well as the team's local initiatives (food banks, halfway houses, etc.) and use the opportunity to show parishioners how they work together to make a difference in the parish's community and beyond. A congregation development team could highlight the diversity of the parish family by showcasing families from other countries and their histories. Some family members might describe the forms of worship in their home countries, and talk about their links to Anglicans in Canada and in the parish. This would help give parishioners a stronger sense of parish family and an appreciation of who they are. An assets management team could highlight the history of the parish, the church building, and how the parish lands were obtained. A photo display could show restorations and renovations, along with some (no doubt) amusing stories. This would help newer parishioners feel part of the parish's history, as they continue in their predecessors' footsteps.

The congregation is the lifeblood of the parish. It has boundless energy and a wealth of ideas—use every member to make your parish what it wants to be and needs to become.

The Vestry Meeting

Far too many vestry meetings are seen as a waste of time—and in many cases, they are. This is largely because parish leadership teams tend not to put enough thought and preparation into them.

Vestry meetings ought to be times of celebration—a time to look back over the last 12 months, and review what the parish has done for its members and its community. Parish leaders might consider creating a party atmo-sphere—there is no reason why balloons and streamers can't be used. A photo display from every parish team would give attendees a visual retrospective on the parish's accomplishments that year. Sharing a festive cake might be fun, as might a game or raffle at the mid-point of the meeting, or a time to thank each parish volunteer with a memento. Consider interweaving a service through the meeting's subjects.

Let parishioners know ahead of time that the vestry meeting will be a fun and interesting event—if they are going to have cake and a chance to win something, the turnout will likely double.

Vestry reports should be made available to the parishioners at least two weeks before the meeting, along with an agenda. All parish members should be advised, through the vestry package, that no time will be available during the meeting for reading the reports. Also, members should be advised that, if they do not understand some of the content, it is up to them to contact the report submitter for clarification *before* vestry—there won't be time at the meeting to go through the reports line by line. As with a well-run advisory board meeting, parishioners need to know what is being circulated as an "FYI item" versus an item that requires feedback and voting. Vestry can then be issue-focused, with minimal chance of getting off track.

The parish leadership team should review each parish report in the vestry meeting package before it is distributed. If there are ambiguities or open items in any of the reports, the wardens should follow up with the submitters and have the reports amended. If any reports require a specific vestry vote, this needs to be highly visible in the report and included in the vestry agenda, along with sufficient time for discussion.

When opening vestry, the rector needs to emphasize that the discussion period for each report is strictly for content feedback and new ideas from vestry.

Probably the most "boring" part of a vestry meeting is the presentation of the closing financial report and next year's budget. Here are some more tips to make the financial presentation as painless as possible:

1. Always use a "narrative" financial statement and budget. Each line-item should be described in a glossary, with examples, and explain why the parish's books keep the item separated. For the year-end financial report, each line-item that varied significantly from last year's budget needs explanation, and an explanation of how the difference was covered. For the upcoming budget, each line-item that varies significantly from the past year's actuals needs to be explained—why it is different, and how the funds will be spent/obtained.

2. By distributing the narrative financial report two weeks before vestry, and asking parishioners to review it *before* the meeting, the treasurer and wardens will not need to go through the financial reports line by line.

Make sure that the reports include the treasurer's phone number and a statement to the effect that problems in understanding any detail of the report should be raised with the treasurer *before* vestry. During the vestry meeting, there won't be time to walk through each line for clarity.

3. When presenting the closing financials, the treasurer will note that the books have been audited, and that the report is in balance with the bank. At that point, the parish should be asked to approve the statement, noting that their approval for this is the adoption of what has already occurred and what has already been audited. With this understanding, discussion should be minimal.

4. When presenting next year's budget, the wardens should explain the overall approach—for instance, a cost-of-living increase has been added to each line-item, or the heating budget has been increased because of predicted increases in fuel oil. The wardens should *not* review every line-item, since everyone will already have had a chance to read and understand the financial reports.

Instead, the wardens should focus on the key line-items for next year—for instance, "Because the congregation development team is going to do a major membership drive next year, we believe that our donations will increase by x%, based on similar drives done by other parishes in this region." Or, "Because we need to replace the roof on the church, the maintenance amount has been increased by $x, based on the best of three quotes from contractors." While these notes will have been included in the narrative budget, the wardens still need to highlight the unexpected changes for the upcoming year. If the wardens have done the appropriate "homework" on these estimates, there should be a minimum of discussion.

Again, if the parish leadership team have been effective communicators throughout the year, none of these budget items will surprise parishioners. In the examples above, the congregation development team leader should have presented the membership drive plan during a Sunday service, long before vestry. Likewise, the parish sexton should have presented the contractor's estimates to the congregation well beforehand.

The Community

How many parishes do you know of that do a great job of supporting their communities with terrific outreach projects, service club sponsorships, and other community-building initiatives, and yet no one else seems to know? Far too many, probably.

It is the responsibility of the parish leadership team, through their parish team leaders, to communicate the good news stories that show how the parish makes a difference in the community. Not only is this good stewardship of the parish's efforts, it builds pride in the parish family and sparks additional initiatives. It also shows the community that the parish is a vital part of their day-to-day quality of life, and deserves to be valued and supported. The community is a source of new members, partnerships with other churches and service clubs (for community projects too large for the parish to take on by itself), and a springboard for wider recognition within the community's region, and potentially even larger programs.

While chapter 4 discusses the growth/marketing plan for the parish and its community, regular parish communication with its community goes beyond the marketing aspects. The parish supports local businesses by buying locally; parishioners volunteer for various non-parish community projects and are members of services clubs as well. The parish is an asset of the community, drawing new families and helping new development.

The parish leadership team needs to ensure that the parish remains highly visible in the community through local newspaper articles, local cable TV announcements, posters, banners, etc. The parish should make a point of being in every community parade/event (Christmas parades, homecoming weeks, corn roasts, etc.), as well as publicizing its outreach and other community enrichment projects.

Maintaining a visible community profile is such an important part of the leadership team's responsibilities that serious consideration should be given to appointing a **publicity coordinator** for the parish. This person could be the focal point for all parish good news stories. While the stories might be written by any of the parish's teams, the publicity coordinator would have editorial license to ensure that the stories will have the intended impact and that they best reflect the parish's image and mission statement.

The publicity coordinator would ensure that the parish has at least one story for the local media each month. In cases where two stories occur in the same month, one might be held back for a subsequent coverage. For community events in which the parish participates, the coordinator would ensure that the parish's story is included in the local newspaper. The coordinator would also track which issues are most important in the community, and match parish involvement to those issues. For example, the parish's efforts to provide housing for families in crisis might be linked to a story in the paper about a local single mom being evicted from her home. Often parish teams do not think to publicize their projects. The publicity coordinator would follow up with them to ensure that their good news stories are written.

The parish leadership team could also look for opportunities to co-sponsor and co-author good news stories with other churches and service clubs in the community. By pulling together, the parish and its partners might achieve what neither could do on their own—this is community building at its best.

Parish stories need not be limited only to the parish's good news. Parish involvement in diocesan programs or national church programs also interest the local community. By supporting the Primate's World Relief and Development Fund, for instance, the parish shares in many of the good news stories in Canada's Arctic and abroad. These stories need to match a local concern. For example, when the tsunami ravaged south Asia in 2004, many small community newspapers covered this world event. Showing how the local parish, through their support of the Primate's World Relief and Development Fund, helped to make a difference in the countries affected would have been newsworthy to those community newspapers.

At any rate, the parish needs to make a noise to be heard. It has many good news stories to share, and should do so, every month.

Application to Your Parish

Regardless of the parish's size, the leadership team needs to stay in touch, week by week. By discussing parish issues sufficiently, they will be able to form a joint approach and, if necessary, act consistently in each other's absence.

In small parishes, the advisory board and vestry meetings tend to be quite informal—these meetings resemble social get-togethers with some business to discuss. This is often a successful way to manage parish business, but it is still a good idea to distribute discussion materials in advance of the meetings. Attendees then won't have to spend time reading the materials during the meeting, and losing time they need to socialize. Also, the business agenda will receive the attention it deserves.

For large parishes, advisory board and vestry meetings usually involve more attendees and more diverse opinions and ideas. This is why it is important to take as much of the guesswork out of the meetings as possible—otherwise the duration of the meetings may be extended well beyond what was planned, and not all agenda items may be covered.

In small parishes, parish leaders might claim that everyone knows everyone and that parish news gets around—there is no need for formal communications. Well, yes and no. Have you ever played the game of whispering a message from one person to the next, then comparing the final whispered message to the original? The end result is often quite different. So, while the intimacy of a small parish is a treasure, the parish leadership team would be wise not to assume that everyone will hear all of the news in the same way all of the time. Often this does not happen, and misunderstandings pop up. ***Don't let informality substitute for clarity.***

Also, in small parishes leaders might feel that their community is well aware of the good works the parish does, and so publicity isn't necessary. Maybe yes; maybe no. Before casting aside the need for publicity, it might be a good idea to test the theory: take a walk up the main street and drop into a few businesses. Ask the owners a few questions, such as, Do you know how many needy families our parish fed last year? Do you know how many families are members of the parish? Do you know how much our parish contributed to the town's fun fair last year? If there are any information gaps, the leadership team needs to consider a low-key publicity program.

For large parishes, especially those with two or more congregations, the need for congregation communications will be obvious. For parishes with multiple services, the leadership team must find ways of pulling these groups together, so that everybody's understanding of parish events and good news stories is consistent.

Large parishes in large communities will need to publicize their good works more often than small parishes. Many other churches and service clubs will be blowing their horns, and your parish will be competing for attention. The larger the community, the noisier you will have to be.

Chapter 7

Worship Program Development

The suggestions this book offers to help build parish teams also apply to many aspects of building a worship program that engages the congregation and lay volunteers—team building, program planning, authority distribution, creating variety, and making improvements.

While the rector is the parish's spiritual leader, he or she cannot do everything alone. In fact, if the parish left all matters pertaining to worship to the incumbent, this would represent a failure by the parish to help lead in its faith.

How can we help the rector and become richer in our faith as a result?

The Rector as Worship Leader

Not infrequently, wardens have expressed the opinion, "We pay the rector to be our worship leader, so it is up to them to do the job," and then leave it up to the rector to do it all.

True, we pay our rectors, and true, they are the worship leaders in our parishes. Worship, however, like all aspects of parish work, is not a one-person job. While our rectors are well trained and have numerous gifts to share, they are also human: they don't have all the answers, either.

It is up to the parish leadership team to ensure that worship within the parish is experienced as participatory, with all members being seen as equals who have unique gifts to share. One of the rector's success measurements might be the number of laity involved in the worship team, and the depth of their involvement.

How do we demystify forms of worship so that lay people feel comfortable being part of the worship team? Certainly the rector can be instrumental, explaining in sermons the history of the worship components and why things are done the way they are. Worship elements might change from time to time to show what Anglicans in other countries do. The rector could describe his or her training, and explain the ordination process and the role of the rector in the parish. In other worship services, the role of the laity might be described.

The wardens and parish team leaders might lead talks during the Sunday service from time to time, which would encourage others to come forward to share their faith ideas and stories. The rector could assign a service to one of the parish teams to conduct from start to finish, assisting with communion. The rector could invite "guest rectors" to the parish to lead services. It is key for the rector to lead the congregation by example, and to include the laity in worship planning and participation.

The wardens might assist the rector in this aspect of parish growth, by helping to demystify worship and recruit volunteers. As lay people, wardens also demonstrate how members may participate fully in all aspects of parish life, including worship.

The Laity as Worship Team Leaders

To encourage lay involvement, the rector should create a worship development team to help plan and execute the parish's worship program each year. The team should include the servers; the coordinators for the sidespersons and the readers; the Sunday school teachers; the leaders for the choir, youth group, pastoral care, and Bible study; and others who might wish to participate.

The worship development team should meet monthly to plan in detail the services for the next month. The team would need to know the theme of each service, so that the hymns, sermon, children's lessons, and Bible study lessons could contribute to that particular theme and be consistent across all age groups. Each lay leader would plan their part, in discussion with the worship development team, gaining valuable input as to their program content and tips for keeping it vibrant.

For example, if the first week's theme was outreach, the rector's sermon might refer to kindness extended to some groups in the community that he or she had witnessed. The prayers of the people might offer thanks and blessings for local outreach programs, and prayers for those with less among us. The Sunday school lesson might be built on the Good Samaritan story. The youth group could discuss any kindness shown them, and their personal responses. The hymns could be selected for outreach themes, to help form the overall effect of the service. The pastoral care team could drop off copies of the sermon to the parish's shut-ins.

By involving all parish team leaders in developing a worship theme, the lay members of the parish not only grow in faith, but the overall worship experience is enriched through the ideas and good works of many. When members of the youth group and Sunday school later join their parents for communion, all have a common message and experience to share. Members of the Bible study group will have the Sunday service to reinforce what they discussed that week. Members of the congregation will see (through the obvious keen involvement of lay members of the worship development team) that worship components are not a mystery, and that others (including themselves) can participate. Members of the worship development team can discuss the worship content with others in the parish, to see if they would like to join the team or participate in one or two worship events during the year.

Members of the worship development team might also help out more easily when illness strikes—a server, for instance, could step in to lead a Sunday school session if the regular teacher was absent, and be well aware of the theme content that was discussed in the team's planning session. Members of the team could also swap roles (with sufficient training) if they wish to try a new approach to worship development. For example, a Sunday school teacher may want a break from his or her semester with the children, but still wish to serve in some way, perhaps as Bible study leader or as a reader. Swapping roles allows for back-up resources, flexibility, and growth, and helps the team develop greater resources to create ideas and approaches to worship.

The Worship Program: Mapping Out the Year

While it's important for the worship development team to plan themes for the coming month, the team should also consider meeting every fall to map out an overall worship program for the year ahead. This helps the team maintain a context in which each month's worship themes can be developed.

One approach that has worked well for parishes is to have the team meet in a planning session and plot next year's calendar on flip chart pages. Major festival times, such as Advent, Christmas, Easter, Lent, are noted. During these periods, worship planning naturally focuses on appropriate themes. The team then marks in other occasions that may have themes, such as Thanksgiving and All Saints' Day.

The team should then check with all parish team leaders to see if and when other worship themes need to be included in the calendar. For example, the outreach development team might be planning to launch their outreach campaign in March of the coming year, and might need two or three consecutive weeks to get the campaign underway. The outreach development team may want the sermons and service hymns, as well as Sunday school and youth group lessons, to be focused on outreach. Or, the financial management team may be planning to launch a stewardship drive in September, and would benefit from a stewardship worship theme. Or, the congregation development team may want to complete a parishioners' survey, perhaps using a "share your gifts" worship theme.

As a last step to completing the worship theme calendar, the worship development team might assign program team leaders to take charge of, or "own," a particular theme. For example, if children's worship is an upcoming theme, and children will lead a service, the Sunday school leader might own that worship theme. Or, if there is an outreach theme, the outreach team leader could own it.

Each theme owner, however, would not plan the details alone—the entire worship development team would participate, each bringing their expertise to all themes. For instance, an outreach development team leader may know nothing about Sunday school lesson planning, but still could suggest content for an outreach worship theme to the Sunday school teachers, who would incorporate theme messages into the lesson, craft, game, etc.

Once the program themes have been decided for the upcoming year, the worship development team should make sure the calendar is posted on the parish web site. Also, they might put up a notice in the parish hall that outlines the next two months' worship events and themes, so that people know what's coming and can plan accordingly.

For the worship development team, knowing the worship program themes in advance means they can properly prepare content. While many themes can be planned for during the monthly team meetings, some details may require more lead time (e.g., booking special speakers, or preparation of posters and brochures). In these cases, the team needs to decide how far in advance resources should be developed and include them in the appropriate planning sessions, using the worship calendar to trigger component planning work as the year unfolds.

Alternate Forms

Another way for the worship development team to add variety and depth to the parish's worship program might be to introduce other forms of Anglican worship in one or two Sunday services every three months or so. Our Anglican tradition takes many forms in many countries throughout the world—it is a shame we do not get to experience them in many cases.

If interested, the worship development team might ask members of the congregation for their countries of birth. If there are two or three from one particular country, for instance, and they remember the Anglican form of service used there, the team could invite them to help lead a service with parts in that form. They might begin with an explanation of how the service is structured, and why, and share some memories of attending services before they came to Canada.

Such a service would offer the congregation a better appreciation of the diversity and breadth of the Anglican communion, to realize how close we actually are in our world, and perhaps to better understand our own Canadian form of worship and its roots.

Another way to add variety to the Sunday service is to have the Sunday school lead a service. The hymns could all be children's hymns, the readings taken from a children's Bible, the sermon geared to children (or given by the children—a play, or some such). This would highlight the children's worship program to the congregation, and give both groups a better sense of togetherness in worship.

The worship development team could invite the youth group to do the same, on a different Sunday. The youth group could include more contemporary music, and prepare a sermon through a play or dialogue.

The choir, as part of the worship development team, might use different instruments to accompany the congregation, or introduce contemporary music, rounds, etc., to inject variety into the worship.

For at least one Sunday per year, the team could also arrange a "rector swap" with a nearby Anglican parish.

Regardless of the worship forms introduced, the worship development team should plan three or four Sundays in the year with different worship form components (a go-slow approach). In the second year, once the congregation has responded favourably to experiencing these changes, one different worship form each month might be planned, but not more, as the parish needs to retain its standard service for a majority of Sundays through the year.

Application to Your Parish

The first step in building an exciting parish worship program (regardless of parish size) is to form a worship development team, if one does not already exist. Some parishes may think they have a "worship team" because they have lay servers, readers, a choir, a Sunday school program, and sidespeople.

But take stock—do the lay people involved in the services actually have a hand in selecting the content of services? Do they proactively plan services well in advance, considering worship themes for two or three Sundays in a row, to build on each other? Do they integrate the adult service with those of the Sunday school, Bible study group, and youth group? Do they experiment with alternate forms? If not, the parish does not really have a worship development team. They may instead have a group of people following the rector's direction, week after week.

Empowering the laity in worship planning does not come easily in all parishes. Sometimes an incumbent may feel threatened by lay people trying to take on a rector's "responsibilities." (In these cases, your diocesan office can often help facilitate a win-win solution.) Sometimes, too, seeing is believing, and so the rector and two or three of the worship leaders might attend a Sunday service at a parish that has happily survived the "transition," to see the benefits of worship development as a program of continuous evolution.

In some parishes, the long-established families may feel that changes to the Sunday service are undesirable, no matter how small or beneficial the change. They would rather repeat the service week after week, with no surprises. Certainly having the Sunday school and youth groups lead a service (a major change) would illustrate that our faith is alive and evolves from one generation to the next, with room for all. Again, the diocesan office could be contacted if the worship development team finds itself facing resistance bringing even small changes to the weekly service.

The team of course must recognize the validity of everyone's concerns, including those who want change and those who wish to maintain familiar, and loved, worship traditions. The resistant members could be invited to lead a service from the past (Morning Prayer, perhaps) in remembrance of their childhood church services. *By bridging the generations and celebrating all worship forms used throughout the years, the congregation can grow in understanding how their faith can grow in them.*

Once the parish has established a worship development team, what might be the team's next course of action? Well, for both small and large parishes, planning worship themes in advance of the upcoming year would be a good first step. For small parishes, this may be even more necessary, as attendance tends to be fragmented, and so several consecutive Sundays may be required to get the theme message across. Developing the materials for worship themes may be a daunting task for small parishes. Consult with your diocesan office—they will have plenty of resource materials for common worship themes such as outreach, fellowship, stewardship, and healing. Small parishes also might invite guest speakers to give the homily for one or more theme services, if members of the congregation lack the expertise to carry out the full worship theme on their own.

For large parishes, the worship development team might assign each worship theme to one or two team members to develop. While the whole team would pitch in, the ownership of the theme would rest with those assigned. In this way, ideas might be sparked by all team members, and then three to four theme development teams might build content concurrently. Large parishes should also take advantage of any theme materials available through their diocesan office, rather than redeveloping content that has already been "test-driven."

Once the worship development team has gained the confidence of the rector and congregation (and this may take a while), alternate worship forms might be considered. Probably the least threatening change is to select a contemporary hymn for one or two services. Also, having a few members of the congregation share a part of their birth country's Anglican service with the congregation, along with personal stories of how it affected their faith journey and their transition to the Anglican service in Canada, tends to be felt as non-threatening.

Regardless of how alternate worship forms are introduced to the congregation, the worship development team needs to emphasize that these brief glimpses of alternate worship forms are just that—glimpses. The parish will not switch from its *Book of Alternative Services* or *Book of Common Prayer*-based services. But through appreciating the Anglican traditions of other countries, we grow in our own faith, and respect others as they grow in theirs.

Chapter 8

Outreach Program Development

Everyone these days seems to be bombarded with appeals for donations to hundreds of causes, many to help the helpless, and by such worthy organizations as United Way, Rotary International, and CARE. As for our church, national causes such as the Primate's World and Relief Development Fund and Anglican Appeal exist alongside diocesan-level causes such as houses for the homeless and drop-in centres, as well as parish-level causes that include parish nurses, pastoral care programs, and not-for-profit day cares. In all of this noise for donations, and a sea of worthy causes, how can a parish member properly respond?

Donors are often not clear about the differences among charitable causes and about the details of their programs. They tend to gravitate to the most publicized cause (e.g., United Way) or the most convenient response (e.g., payroll deductions). Donors have a vague sense of helping others less fortunate, while personally receiving some tax relief.

Our parishioners are not all that different in the way they see the various causes that confront them. However, they *are* different from secular donors—they are giving through their faith and trying to follow the example of Christ. Habitat for Humanity has coined a key difference for us: they give others "a hand up, not a handout." While United Way, food banks, CARE, and others respond to famine, war, and natural disasters by donating food and water and temporary shelter to victims, these donations tend to be "handouts." They serve an immediate need, but they do not address the root cause. As such, the victims continue to need donations, and the need is self-perpetuating. By contrast, the Habitat program provides permanent housing for people in need, rather than just temporary shelter. They no longer need donations—in fact, they become Habitat volunteers for the next family in line.

This is how our Anglican outreach programs differ from secular charities—the Primate's World Relief and Development Fund focuses on root causes, and funds projects to dig wells in areas of chronic scarcity; or teaches people ways of growing low-intensity crops in areas with poor soil; or pressures repressive governments to move to more humane treatment of their refugees and minority groups. But above all, our Anglican outreach programs support the spirits of those in need, giving them much needed *hope in their futures, so that they can help themselves* when conditions allow. While the quick fixes of secular charities get much of the press, our church's ongoing, self-help programs do not, as their impact tends to be much more gradual, and brings on change that others do not readily see.

In this context, the parish leadership team needs to help members of the parish make well-informed choices that support others in ways that our faith teaches. Every parish should consider creating an outreach development team that focuses on educating parishioners about the differences between secular charities and Anglican outreach. Once informed, parishioners can then make choices that more directly match their commitment to their faith.

The Parish Outreach Team

All parishes have some form of outreach program in place. On a local level, most parishes have fund-raisers for charities in the community, contribute to the local food bank, or may be involved in community housing projects. Many parishioners give to the Primate's World Relief and Development Fund, Anglican Appeal, or other national or international outreach causes. So why change?

Well, for the reasons cited above: if you asked members of your parish why they donate to United Way and not to the Primate's World Relief and Development Fund, they probably could not give a coherent answer. If you asked them the difference between the Primate's Fund and Anglican Appeal, or a local cause, they likely won't know—but will be donating anyway, because "it's what we should do."

Wouldn't the acts of kindness by your parish's donors be far more enriching if parishioners better understood the context for their gifts? Wouldn't they learn more about themselves and their faith journey if they fully understood how their gifts make a difference in the lives of people they have not even met? Wouldn't they want to know how to direct their gifts to causes that they as Anglicans understand and value? Of course.

What is needed then, is a parish team responsible for

- educating the parish about outreach, as an expression of our Anglican faith, about opportunities in the parish, community, diocese, nation, and abroad to make the kinds of differences that parishioners want to see in our world;
- helping parishioners make sense of the many outreach causes, and formulating an integrated outreach program that best matches the outreach goals of the parish;

- conducting the parish's annual outreach campaign (ranging from a pass-the-hat approach to a proactive calling program); and
- thanking parish donors, through individual letters, recipient speakers, and parish celebrations.

What should a parish outreach development team look like?

To start, every team needs a leader. Who would you recruit for this role? You already have a potential leader in your parish. Who cares the most for the parish's shut-ins? Who collects the food for the parish or community food bank? Who puts up the Primate's World Relief and Development Fund posters in the church hall? Who worries about refugees and international justice issues? That person is your leader.

The outreach development team leader need not be an expert on donation campaigns, know how to get the parish fired up for a new outreach project, or be able to track outreach donations. Rather, a parish outreach leader will have the natural care and compassion for those in need in the parish family, the community, and around the world. They will lead the outreach development team and other members of the parish by their example. The leader can use the skills of team members to look after the logistics of outreach projects and campaigns.

How big does an outreach development team need to be? In small parishes, two or three people should suffice. In this size of team, the lead might focus on the parish's outreach theme, education, and arranging program and thank-you speakers, while the other team member(s) would handle program logistics—phone calls, tracking donations, forwarding donations, etc.

For large parishes, an outreach development team of four or five people may be more appropriate. Apart from the team leader (who keeps everyone on track concerning the outreach development plan), one member might focus on national and international outreach causes, including parish education, speakers, and campaign integration. Another member might focus on diocesan or partner-parish outreach projects, including education, donation allocation, campaigning, and speakers. Other members might focus on the parish's own outreach projects for their community.

The Needs Hierarchy

Before the outreach development team starts to plan its annual program, it may be helpful if they understand a key piece of information about the hierarchy of human needs. The model below describes this hierarchy, and it might be useful for the team to consider what "needs level(s)" their parish can address.

Three levels of human need are shown below: survival, protection, and independence. Depending on how fortunate we are, we may be in the middle of the hierarchy, or at the top.

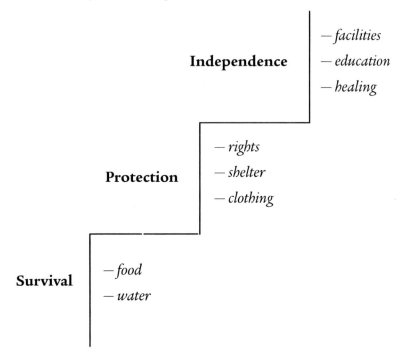

At the first level, human survival depends on water, without which we cannot live more than a few days. Food is the next imperative. Secular charities focus mainly on meeting human needs at this first level. Hurricane relief efforts, for example, first ensure a source of drinkable water, then food staples, airlifting these to the affected areas. In some Canadian parishes, outreach programs also focus on the survival needs of street people and runaways.

At the second level, the need for protection is met by clothing the body, once the person has received water and food. In colder conditions this is especially important. The next need is for shelter, even of a temporary nature, such as tents and lean-tos. The establishment of human rights is the final need at this level. Without this protection, the food, water, and clothing may be stolen, and the people beaten. This exposure could return those in need back to square one. While some secular charities also ship clothing and tents to disaster areas, most stop short of ensuring human rights. Unfortunately, there have been many instances of donation theft, with the result that victims regress back to their initial level of survival. The establishment of human rights, to protect and nurture human life, is central to the work of the Primate's World Relief and Development Fund and Anglican Appeal, among our other Anglican outreach programs.

At the third level, human needs move from dependency on outreach donations to independence, or a state of self-sufficiency. This first requires physical and emotional healing. People cannot move beyond dependence without their physical and mental health intact. Emotional healing is one of our church's primary focal points for outreach (a focus that secular charities do not share). As the Rev. Jayasiri Peiris, General Secretary of the National Christian Council of Churches of Sri Lanka (one of the Primate's World Relief and Development Fund partners), said during the tsunami recovery effort in 2005:

> We might be doing a lot of good things, but now is the time to make sure that we do not miss the goal. And make sure that we don't make people more dependent on donors than they were before the tsunami in Sri Lanka. We're starting to move out of this first crisis phase and into reconstruction, trauma counselling, and livelihood generation, of working with people at a community level to help them solve their own problems and rebuild their lives. We are also called to provide pastoral care to the people. *Otherwise we will (re) build all this infrastructure without building up the people.*

The next step toward self-sufficiency is education: for a person to move beyond dependence on others for food and shelter, new skills may need to be learned to enable independence. In agrarian communities, the educational focus might be on crop planning and livestock care. In urban communities, it might be on trades and business skills.

The final step in establishing independence is through community infrastructure projects—e.g., drilling new wells, sewage treatment facilities, community centres.

Self-sufficiency is seldom addressed by secular charities, since these initiatives require a lengthier time-commitment by volunteers in the communities affected. They also require more significant funding than short-term food drops. As well, these initiatives need to be community led; the charity does not get a lot of visibility from them.

This third level of independence is the most important in Anglican outreach initiatives. Through our local volunteers and clergy, and through worship and fellowship, hope and confidence are restored to those in need. Many of the Primate's World Relief and Development Fund and Anglican Appeal projects retrain refugees and rebuild community infrastructures.

At local levels, our dioceses and parishes provide drop-in centres to foster hope and retraining, and eventually self-sufficiency. In Canada's north, our clergy help native communities build the necessary infrastructure to improve community health and individual self-worth.

When a parish outreach development team understands the needs hierarchy described above, it can best decide where, and how, their parish might participate in outreach initiatives.

For small parishes, or parishes with limited resources, continued support of national church and diocesan projects may be all that they can manage. Parish donors, though, tend to become frustrated, in that they are not able to help their local communities. Speakers from the parish's outreach team may address the congregation and explain how their gifts make a difference, but it remains difficult for parish donors to "see" the results. For this reason, even very small parishes should try to include a local outreach initiative in their outreach development plan. Food banks are the least demanding, in terms of resources required. Donors need to know the impact of their gifts, and so it is important to have a representative from the local initiative visit the parish and say "thank you" to the congregation for their kindness, and to show how their gifts have made a difference right here, in their community.

For mid- to large-sized parishes, the outreach development team should (as next year's objective) try to move the parish up the needs hierarchy. For example, if the parish is running a food bank, consider also a used clothing program. Or, if the parish hall is available through the week, perhaps the parish can create a drop-in centre (by partnering with the community's social services people and/or other local churches) to provide counselling to street people. With appropriate assistance from social services staff, volunteers could help street youth and adults with job placements and training, and resumé writing. The rector or curate could be available to provide moral support and crisis counselling.

When local outreach initiatives are included in parish outreach programs (along with diocesan and national church programs), *the outreach development team will need to integrate the various initiatives and causes in a parish-oriented outreach program that will make sense to its donors.* Having the Primate's World Relief and Development Fund "compete" for parish donations with a local food bank will not only confuse donors, it will result in parishioners turning away from their church's outreach programs to seek clarity through well-publicized secular charities.

So the outreach development team needs to decide what their parish is able to do with the resources available, decide what level of human needs they will focus on, and where they will focus the resources available—local, area (diocese), national, global. Only when these aspects of the parish's outreach program are known can the team prepare and execute an appropriate outreach development plan.

The Parish Outreach Development Plan

For an effective outreach program, the outreach development team should prepare a plan for the upcoming year, each fall. The following template has helped other parishes successfully build their plan. To use this template, read the italicized notes in each section, then replace these notes with the content of your plan. An electronic version in Microsoft Word format may be found on the enclosed CD (see outreach.doc).

Outreach Development Plan

For

Parish Name

Table of Contents

Program Team/Scope
Program Objectives for 20__
Initiatives
        Outreach Theme Development
        Outreach Target Inventory/Financials
        Outreach Program Launch/Calling Program
        Outreach Thank-Yous
Schedule
Financials/Resources
Program Management Process

Program Team/Scope

The Team. *List the members of the outreach development team, their phone numbers, street and e-mail addresses; their role(s) within the team (e.g., their special interests, talents, passions); and their time available to support the team's work. Include the organization of the team, if it might prove helpful to the readers of the plan.*

Program Scope *for the year. List the team's scope boundaries. These may include financial limitations; workload limitations, timing limitations (e.g., certain events must occur at specific times or dates), the parish's expectations of the team for the planning year. Consider the following scope attributes:*

- *the number of volunteers likely available to do the work of the team during the planning year, and the amount of time per week/month they have available to do the work;*
- *the financial capacity (total amount) of the parish for outreach donations. Consider a percentage (say, 7% to 10%) of the parish's annual gross operating income from parishioner donations as a reasonable outreach target; and*
- *the likely amount of funds available in next year's parish budget for promotional materials and outreach events.*

Program Objectives for 20__

According to the team's understanding of the resources available in the parish for outreach, and the parish's desired orientation (local versus global), the team should include their plan's objectives (on a flip chart page). Here are some ideas:

- *to decide on the need level(s) that will be the focus of the parish next year (remember the hierarchy);*
- *to determine the ratio of donations to international, national, area (diocese), and local (parish and community) causes and why;*
- *for the local portion of the outreach program, to define the most urgent needs of the community (the team may need to meet with the social services agencies, service clubs, and hospitals in the area, to fully understand these, if they do not know already) and how the parish's program will address them;*
- *to develop an integrated program for the different outreach initiatives;*
- *through a series of educational events, to clarify the difference between secular charities and our church's outreach goals, as exemplified by Christ;*
- *to increase parish involvement in outreach activities (by xxx volunteers) and givings (by $xxx); and*
- *to better integrate the outreach program with the worship program of the parish, so that parishioners understand how we live our faith through our actions in helping others.*

When the list of objectives is drawn up, inspect the objectives carefully. Are they realistic for the year? Can all the objectives be accomplished given the resources available to the team and the parish's ability to absorb the changes proposed? Do any of the objectives depend on the successes of another parish team? (If the stewardship team, for example, plans to have a stewardship drive in the fall of next year, probably the outreach campaign should be synchronized with it.)

It is better to drop objectives at the outset, and have the team meet a reduced set, than to overextend the team and have them fail. Remember, there is always the following year. However, the team should always have objectives before them that "stretch" them—this is how teams grow and learn.

Initiatives

List the program initiatives for the year that will address the objectives—for example: community needs survey, outreach education day, social services speaker and luncheon, outreach campaign. For each, include

- **what** the initiative is, which objectives it will address, and a description of the development work required to complete it (example: survey the parish to determine who gives to secular charities and who does not give to our church's outreach programs and why);
- **who** will be working on developing the initiative (which team members and number of hours for each; additional volunteers and number of hours for each);
- **when** the development work must be completed, related to when the initiative is to be provided to the parish; and
- **how** and **when** the program team will measure the initiative's success (e.g., parish feedback, donor feedback, outreach recipient feedback).

Note any initiative prerequisites or assumptions, and any interdependencies of other parish teams' initiatives.

Schedule

This plan document should include the year's **schedule of outreach development events**, to be added to the parish calendar for next year.

The outreach development team also needs to maintain an **initiatives development schedule** that includes the resources (e.g., an outreach worship event or beneficiary parish visits), and the development time required for each event, or target milestones (e.g., "outreach theme published to parish" or "donor calls start"), who will be developing the material, etc. This schedule will be used by the team to prepare for the published outreach events and planned milestones. When the team meets each month, they can use the development schedule to determine whether there are any problems with the planned development work and then take corrective action, if necessary (e.g., enlisting more people to help prepare, moving event dates, etc.).

Financials/Resources

Financials

With respect to the planned outreach development initiatives, the team needs to summarize the costs of the program for the year ahead (resource materials, advertising costs, event costs, visitor travel if applicable, etc.) and indicate when the expenses are expected to be incurred. This way, the parish treasurer will be able to include these costs in the parish's budget for the upcoming year, under the outreach development expense line. When approved by vestry, this budget line-item can be used by the outreach development team, as needed.

The team needs to note that donations received from the parish do not belong to the parish (i.e., the parish cannot use the funds for operating expenses). Records of these donations must be kept separate from the parish's operating funds, and be accounted for (donations "in" versus contributions "out"). Also, the team must consider ways to ensure that all donations raised in a given year are distributed in that same year (since this is the expectation of the donors).

Resources

The team should summarize the monthly volunteer resources and skills needed (beyond those of the team) to support the outreach development plan. The volunteer coordinator (see chapter 5) will use this information to recruit the appropriate volunteers.

When all parish program teams circulate their completed plans at the start of the year, the volunteer coordinator may advise the outreach development team that the required resources will not be available in the numbers or at the time planned. In these cases, the outreach development team will need to revise the plan.

Program Management Process

The outreach development plan needs to lay out how the team's progress will be monitored throughout the year. Some best practices for the team's consideration follow:

1. Team Meetings

The outreach development team should meet monthly (same time each month) to review past and future planned activities. The team meeting should be chaired by the team leader. Minutes are not necessary, but the team leader will need to keep track of commitments made during the meeting, for follow-up purposes. The team should bring copies of their development schedule and events calendar with them to each meeting.

Here is a suggested agenda:

- How has the team been doing since the last meeting? Positive feedback should be celebrated; negative feedback should be used to modify subsequent events as appropriate, or used when preparing next year's plan.
- What's next? Who is working on what, according to the development schedule? How is it going? Will we be ready for the event(s)? If not, what needs to be done? Are there any cost variances?
- Are there any proposals for changes to the plan? Any new events needed but not included? If so, how might they be resourced? Are there any events that should be cancelled?

2. Program Reporting

The team leader (or designate) should report the team's program status to the wardens and advisory board each month following the team's own monthly meeting if possible. The team leader may wish to schedule the team's monthly meeting to be a week or so ahead of the advisory board's meeting, so that the board receives up-to-date information.

Team reports may be quite brief (e.g., one-half to one page in length). The program update for the wardens and the board should include program events since the last update and results; upcoming development work and issues; and issues for the wardens' or board's action, if any.

The program report might be tabled only for the advisory board's information. Also, it is not necessary for the team leader to attend the board's meeting, unless there are issues for the wardens' or board's action.

In addition to the advisory board's monthly report, the team leader should prepare an annual program report for vestry that describes the work of the program team in the year ending, lessons learned, and plans for the upcoming year. The team leader should attend, in case there are questions from the vestry on the program.

3. Parish Surveys

Before the team meets to develop their plan for the upcoming year, the team should ask the parish what they thought of this year's outreach development program. (What was good? What was not so good? What was missing?)

Most parish surveys, if they involve forms to be filled out, are failures. Many people do not bother to complete the survey; others leave spaces blank. Those surveys that do result in good feedback are those that engage the respondents. In parish settings, surveys are best done in two ways:

- *pot-luck lunch-and-learn events (see chapter 4); and*
- *telephone surveys (team members, and additional volunteers if necessary, ask questions and record responses, coaching for feedback).*

A combination of both is ideal: a lunch-and-learn event that most parishioners will attend, and telephone surveys to catch those who did not attend.

The outreach development team should use the feedback to plan next year's program.

The most effective way to build the outreach development plan is to have team members review the above template on their own, and form their own ideas of what next year's outreach development program should look like. Then the team should meet in two to four 2-hour workshops. A facilitator or scribe (this need not be the team leader) could record everyone's ideas on a flip chart. Another member should include the information recorded into a plan document following each session. The plan could then be passed to the wardens and the advisory board for feedback, as well as to the congregation for theirs. This process ensures that the entire parish has input into the outreach development program—it also gives everyone a good idea of what to expect next year and what goals the outreach development team has set for all.

The Annual Outreach Campaign

Most outreach programs include a campaign, during which parishioners are asked for their support to help meet the needs of those who are the focus of the program. Both financial aid and/or volunteer time may be requested.

For parish teams planning outreach campaigns, here are some tips that have proven invaluable:

1. *Know Your Objectives.*

While outreach objectives will be clearly stated in the outreach development plan, often campaigns will have less obvious or "below the surface" objectives. For example: a parish may choose to use a calling program to solicit financial support because of a wish to directly engage with parishioners—to educate them about the importance of outreach in practising our faith. In this case, a very different kind of campaign from simply asking for donations is required. Or a parish may want to shift a large percentage of expected or "usual" outreach donations from national/international causes to local causes. Again, the campaign must be tailored to help long-time donors appreciate why local needs are now taking precedence. These less obvious objectives need to be fully understood by the campaign team before they start their campaign design.

2. *Know Your Timing.*

There is little point in running an outreach campaign when many retired parishioners are snowbirding in warmer climates, or when half the parish families are away at the summer cottage. Choose a time for the campaign when most parishioners will be able to participate, such as April to May, or September to November.

Know what other teams are doing, too. If the worship development team, for example, intends to develop a worship theme at Thanksgiving, a time when we celebrate and share the gifts we have received and remember those less fortunate, that would be an ideal time to launch the outreach campaign.

3. *Know Your Approach.*

Parish outreach campaigns range from informational to very proactive. Some parishes are highly successful in laying out the outreach case and collecting donations. Others need to shake the trees a bit, to obtain an appropriate response. Use whichever approach works best in your parish's culture. However, do not let historical precedent drive this decision. While some parishes have run very low-key outreach campaigns in the past, maybe a different approach would do a lot of good.

The point is, each year your team should want to stretch your parish a bit more for outreach support. If support has plateaued over the past two to three years, another approach is necessary. Also, if during your parish survey the team finds that the percentage of parishioners who participate in outreach is low (i.e., less than 60%), your team will need to shake some trees.

Regardless, the team needs to know at the outset what type of campaign they will be designing.

4. *Integrate Causes.*

The overall outreach program must make sense to donors, and the campaign should be designed so that each cause—local, area (diocese), national, international—complements one another. If the team's approach to supporting the Primate's World Relief and Development Fund, for instance, runs along the lines of, "Well, it's a good cause, too, if you are interested," the campaign will fail.

Rather, build your campaign to highlight the needs level (see page 102) that the parish is focusing on and why, and how the outreach program will address those needs at each level in the plan, from local to international. Some campaign veterans have likened their parish's donations to dropping a pebble in a pond: the ripples closest to the donation are local recipients, and those farther out are area recipients, and so on. "You can and do make a difference," they tell parishioners, "right here in our community and around the world."

It is helpful, in this context, to create a parish outreach slogan and banner under which print material for all causes might be included—for example, "St. George's Anglican Parish—Helping Here and Around the World." Instead of having posters and brochures all over the parish hall for local outreach projects, the Primate's World Relief and Development Fund, Anglican Appeal, and diocesan outreach campaigns, these might be grouped under the banner so that parish donors would better understand how they work together. Otherwise, parishioners might be completely at a loss and pass on this year's campaign.

5. *Educate.*

Make sure the outreach campaign fully describes the "targets" for the donations, as well as the allocation formula that will be applied, and the rationale. The campaign should clarify the difference between secular charities and the outreach programs of our church. Highlight examples of the church helping suffering people regain their spirit (as in the Sri Lankan example, page 103), not just enabling their physical survival. Remember the Habitat for Humanity slogan: "A hand up, not just a handout." Make sure the campaign includes examples from Jesus' teachings—*why we are called to help others help themselves, as we live our faith.*

6. *Make It Easy for Donors.*

The goals should be clear and simple; use examples—e.g., "To reach our target, we need our parish to average $500 per family this year. That works out to $10 a week, or what you spend on your daily morning coffee." Make the donation process easy—set up a pre-authorized giving facility; add a monthly outreach envelope to the parish's envelope sets.

7. Thank Donors.

Don't wait for the end of the campaign—thank donors throughout the campaign, every month, and talk about the results. This practice often encourages new donors and/or increases initial commitments—everyone likes to support a winning cause. These thank-yous are most effective when made during Sunday services, and particularly when representatives from the beneficiaries describe how the gifts that donors have made, to people they don't even know, have changed their lives for the better. Some outreach development teams also invite donors to local causes (e.g., shelters or food banks) to show them how their gifts are put into action. At the end of the campaign year, the outreach development team leader and rector should co-sign a formal letter of thanks to each donor, highlighting what their gifts did for the campaign's beneficiaries this year.

8. Repeat but Change Every Year.

The needs of those among us with less never go away ... so neither should we. Your parish should have an outreach appeal every year that will challenge the parish to surpass last year's givings. Membership for the outreach development team might change, but not the essential message. Each year, the outreach program should seem different, to continually inspire regular donors and attract new ones. The parish outreach slogan should be kept (for continuity) even when the projects or the emphasis changes (e.g., from local to area, or vice versa). Consider changing the program colours each year; change which speakers come to the parish; change the venue of the fund-raising events—anything to make this year's outreach program fresh.

Application to Your Parish

For small parishes with outreach teams of two or three volunteers and small to non-existent program budgets, both outreach donations and volunteer involvement will be limited. How do you maximize your small parish's capabilities for outreach? For local initiatives, the simplest way is to direct donations to a local food bank. This project is "hands on," relatively inexpensive for donors, and does not commit donors to specific amounts. Also, it should be easy to have a speaker from the food bank thank the parish during a Sunday service. Your donors could also be invited to visit the food bank, so see how their gifts are put to work.

For area (diocese) and national/international outreach appeals, small parishes might have the rector focus a Sunday sermon on outreach; the following Sunday a lay speaker could speak about the area and national/international causes. If not, a guest speaker (perhaps from the diocesan office) might be asked. If possible, the outreach Sundays should fall within the first three months of the year, so that potential donors will have the balance of the year to make donations. Use the Primate's World Relief and Development Fund and Anglican Appeal posters sent to each parish, to maintain awareness of others' needs beyond the parish. Consider setting a parish target for the year, and create a "thermometer type" of poster, to show the parish the level of their success month by month.

For large parishes, the outreach development team might have four to six members. Try to assign teams of two to each cause (local, area, national/international), with the whole team working together to ensure a consistent message. Two could work with local churches and service clubs, for instance, to determine any gaps in the community's safety net and to build a local outreach program in response (with or without local partners). Two might work with diocesan outreach staff to get additional information on area outreach projects and arrange guest speakers from the area projects. Two could work with the national church team to get additional information on the Primate's World and Relief Development Fund and Anglican Appeal good news stories and arrange guest speakers.

The team should work together to come up with a parish outreach slogan, and to create posters, brochures, and service bulletin updates. Consider special outreach Sundays with table-top displays for each outreach project. The parish's overall outreach slogan should be included in the display to reinforce the idea of an overall program. Set up outreach fund-raising events (golf tournaments, walkathons, car washes, etc.). Integrate all levels and groups of the parish—Sunday school, youth group, Bible study group, choir, advisory board—in the program. Give them fund-raising objectives too.

Track who are your donors; who are not. For those on the parish list who are not participating, consider recruiting a team of phone callers to ask these potential donors if they have thought about participating in their church's outreach program. Your diocesan office can provide resource materials and on-site guidance if and when you want to start a calling program.

Consider partnering with other Anglican churches in your area, other churches in your community, and with local service clubs, etc., to build critical mass in creating and supporting a local outreach program, such as a half-way house, parish nurse, or youth drop-in centre. ***What your parish may not be able to do alone may be possible when you work in partnership.***

Consider sponsoring a parish or refugee family overseas. Again, your diocesan office can help with this.

And, as always, remember—***thank you, thank you, thank you.***

Chapter 9

Parish Assets Management

Proper stewardship of the parish's buildings and property is an obvious priority for parish leadership teams, and the most visible to parishioners (and newcomers), especially when neglected. If the church looks shabby and rundown, how will members of the parish feel when they attend services each Sunday? It is hard to feel uplifted when you are surrounded by peeling paint, grimy carpeting, gouged pews, and tattered banners. Imagine how newcomers feel about your church when they enter it for the first time. Would they consider making your church theirs? Or leave to find another?

The same may be said for the parish's grounds. Does the property look inviting and cared for, or derelict, without pride of ownership? Are the gardens full of weeds? Is the grass cut? Are the signs freshly painted and lit at night? Are the walkways and parking lot shovelled in the winter?

What about the rectory? Would we live in it the way it is? Shouldn't we do our best to make it as comfortable as we can for our valued rectors? Don't they do their best for us?

How do we set about getting our own homes in order, as well as sustaining their appearance and soundness? Caring for parish buildings and property is not very different. We need to approach them as *our* assets, and apply good stewardship principles to these important ParishWorks.

Stewardship of Our Legacies

We need to remember how the parish got to where it is today. Look back into the parish archives: see what it took to establish the parish from nothing; the efforts of the first parishioners to eke out funds to build the first church with nothing but a vision to guide them; the memorials that helped adorn the buildings and inspire future parishioners. These heroic efforts were not done for them, but for us: that we could enjoy the fruits of their labours, and continue to build on them. As members of the parish, we are in positions of trust—to carry on the ParishWorks, and to care for the assets members before us have left behind. Once the parish membership understands this fundamental point, there should be no question of whether building and grounds maintenance is worth the effort or cost. From these early stories and this understanding, it should be easy for the parish leadership team to recruit a parish sexton and an assets management team to help (see pages 148-153 for position descriptions).

To raise awareness of parish legacies, use your parish's patron saint day—every year—to celebrate its history. The closest Sunday service could focus on this theme. Consider having the sexton or the wardens provide the address in place of the sermon. This might include a chronology of the parish history, including past rectors and key lay members; how the church was built from nothing; and how memorials were used. Coffee hour could be a celebration of the parish's inception, and include a birthday cake and historical picture display. The wardens could take the opportunity to formally thank the sexton and assets management team for their good works over the past year, highlighting some of their efforts. This annual reminder to members of the parish will reinforce the idea that we all share responsibility for preserving parish assets, as our predecessors expected of us. Also, it will help ensure ongoing donations to the parish's building maintenance and/or capital funds, and encourage volunteers to maintain parish grounds and buildings.

Assets Maintenance Versus Capital Works

While it is critical that the difference between parish assets maintenance and capital works be well understood by the wardens and all parish volunteers involved in parish assets management, many do not know the difference. Simply put, capital works add value to the parish's assets, while assets maintenance does not. Examples of assets maintenance include cleaning the church and parish hall, landscaping of church grounds, repairing light fixtures, resurfacing the parking lot, repointing brickwork, upgrading electrical services, installing locks, replacing plumbing fixtures, a furnace, or a fence, and so forth.

However, adding a meeting room to the parish hall or buying a new photocopier for the church office does add value to the parish, and so are described as capital works. Other examples include purchasing statuary or other decorations, furniture, a stove, or a computer; building an addition onto the church or parish hall, a new kitchen, or washroom.

Operating costs—such as assets maintenance—should never be mixed in with capital costs. Operating costs need to be budgeted for each year, and based on past and projected expenses. These costs should be funded out of the operating income from the parish's general donations throughout the year. In Canada, this income is included in the parish's diocesan assessment formula.

Capital works, on the other hand, tend to be discretionary for the most part, and should be funded out of the parish's capital fund, as approved by the wardens, advisory board, and/or vestry (depending on the size of the project). When the parish has sufficient funds in the capital fund or approval to borrow, the capital project may be carried out. Capital funds often come from designations by parishioners, memorials, and bequests, or from capital campaigns. Capital works income and expenses are usually exempt from diocesan assessments in Canada. (For more information, see page 137.)

Assets Maintenance

Every parish has gone through the process of budgeting costs for next year, to maintain parish buildings and grounds in good condition. After costs for the parish's ministry team, assets maintenance costs tend to be the most expensive for the parish. It is surprising then, that budgeting for and management of these expenses tends to be given little thought by many wardens and treasurers. In these cases, the process tends to be, What did we spend last year? Add x% for inflation, and that is our budget for next year. As a result, situations arise throughout the year for which there is no maintenance budget, and a financial crisis not infrequently hits the parish. Or assets maintenance costs continue to rise while the parish's operating income remains static or drops, putting the parish into a financial crisis.

Rather than being a victim of circumstances, parish leadership teams need to approach parish assets maintenance proactively, building contingency into parish budgets, looking for problems before they emerge, and managing the costs down.

Inspections

A good place to start being proactive is to arrange for an inspection of the parish buildings and grounds by an accredited inspector, if an inspection has not been done for five years or more. First, look to the parish list for members who might be qualified, or who may know an accredited inspector, and might get the parish a discount on the inspection fee or even carry out the inspection as a donation (for a tax receipt). Also, consider contacting your diocesan office to see if they know inspectors they might recommend. Make it clear to the inspector that all parish buildings are to be included (church, parish hall, rectory, etc.), as well as the grounds. Part of the process should include the parish securing their land survey and deed. The documents will probably be filed in the parish office, or copies may be available through the diocesan office. Reviewing the survey and deed will ensure awareness of the parish's legal entitlement to the property, and that there are no encumbrances.

As mentioned, the inspection should include the grounds. While there may not be any major issues with the parish's buildings, sometimes significant problems with property crop up—contaminated wells, shifting/collapsing land, failing septic tanks, by-law issues, etc.

Once the inspection is complete, make sure the parish retains a copy of the inspection report and supplies another to the diocesan office. From the report, the parish must prepare a remediation plan for any items needing repair. If it has been a while since the last inspection, the list of repairs may be more than the parish can afford in the current year. This is fine. The remediation plan should list those items that are most urgent for year 1, followed by those to be addressed in year 2, etc. The plan must also identify the approximate costs for each repair (the inspector could provide rough estimates), and how those expenses will be covered by the parish's annual operating income. If the urgent or "must-do" repairs in year 1 exceed what the parish's annual income allows for assets maintenance, the parish leadership may decide to hold a fund-raising event or carry out a campaign to cover the costs. Regardless, these details need to be included in the remediation plan, so that parish members and the diocesan team understand what the parish is up against.

Once the remediation plan is accepted by the leadership team and the members of the parish, the parish sexton and the assets management team must plan for and execute the necessary work to properly repair the parish assets.

Cleaning

Keeping the parish buildings neat and clean is an important ParishWork. Newcomers at a Sunday service who are considering whether to make the parish their own won't think much of the church if the floor is stained, the paint peeling, and the bathroom messy. They won't be back. As for current members of the parish, how will they be retained under the same conditions?

The first step to maintaining good order in church buildings is to create a cleaning checklist. For each building, list what needs to be cleaned, then indicate the frequency. For example, the church may need vacuuming every two weeks, but dusting and polishing only once a month. Or the church hall may need floor cleaning every week if used heavily, but dusting only every second month. The checklist should be used by the cleaning team to ensure that everything receives proper care. A sample cleaning checklist follows. An electronic version in Microsoft Word format may be found on the enclosed CD (see cleaninglist.doc).

Parish Cleaning Checklist

Light Cleaning (weekly)

1. Church

- clean chancel door windows ____ done
- "low" dusting (altar, statuary, lecterns) ____ done
- clean toilets and sinks ____ done
- restock bathroom towels and soap ____ done
- wash bathroom floors ____ done

2. Church Hall

- clean toilets and sinks ____ done
- restock bathroom towels and soap ____ done
- wash bathroom floors ____ done
- sterilize kitchen counters and sinks ____ done
- empty garbage cans/take out garbage ____ done

Heavy Cleaning (monthly, in addition to weekly)

1. Church

- vacuum and wash worship-area floors ____ done
- "high" dusting (organ, choir loft, lights) ____ done
- wax wood (lecterns, altar, statuary) ____ done
- wash all windows ____ done

2. Church Hall

- wash and wax floors ____ done
- launder towels ____ done
- wash all windows ____ done

The parish can keep its buildings in good order through a cleaning team of volunteers, or by subcontracting the cleaning to a professional firm if the funds are available. For small parishes, cleaning the church and church hall could be done by volunteer teams that take turns. For example, teams of two could commit to do the cleaning for one month of the year. Depending on usage, the weekly cleaning could be done by a team of two in one to two hours, with the monthly cleaning requiring one to two additional hours.

If the parish rents its space to other groups, ensure that the rental agreement includes a cleaning checklist. By having renters do their own clean-ups, the parish's volunteer cleaning team will have much less work to do.

Also, make sure that the work of the altar guild and the cleaning teams does not overlap—by adding a light dusting and a (perhaps) light vacuuming task to the altar guild's responsibilities, the cleaning team may not need to deal with the church building on a weekly basis (only the parish hall).

If the parish decides to subcontract the cleaning to a professional cleaner, here are some cautions:

1. Professional cleaners run their businesses on a tight margin, and often the quality of their work reflects this. In many parishes that use professional cleaners, the wardens spend a significant amount of time following up with the cleaners on failures to carry out the cleaning work. Sometimes the parish leadership spends as much time and effort chasing up professional cleaners as they would have had they done the work themselves. Members of the parish may become increasingly unhappy as they see parish income going to contractors who are not living up to their responsibilities.

2. The cleaners will not care about the parish's buildings as much as the members of the parish. Don't enter into a subcontract assuming that the work will be done with the same care as by a parish volunteer team.

3. Before selecting a cleaner, get two or three references, and check their track records.

4. Include a cleaning checklist form in the contract to ensure that both parties understand what is to be done and when. The parish sexton should use the checklist to inspect the work from time to time.

5. Include penalty clauses for minimal or non-performance in the contract. For example, define minimum performance criteria for the cleaner, and include actions that will be taken for noncompliance (e.g., the parish will

not pay the monthly charge if the cleaner's performance falls below a pre-defined level).

A large parish might consider using volunteer cleaning teams as well as a contractor. A parish volunteer team probably could manage the weekly (light) cleaning requirements, while the contractor could handle the heavier, monthly work. This is an excellent arrangment for many parishes—parish members retain a sense of ownership of the care of their church while the drudgery tasks are subcontracted. Because the contractor does the harder tasks only once a month, say, the sexton need inspect their work only once a month, resulting in fewer chances for performance failures. Also, contractor costs are kept to a minimum.

Recruiting a volunteer cleaning team usually isn't easy. The best way is to tie the cleaning requirement to good stewardship of the parish, and to accentuate the positive aspects of parishioners personally caring for the church buildings. The rector could include these themes in a Sunday sermon, as part of a recruiting drive for volunteers.

Groundskeeping

Well-kept grounds, along with clean buildings, are key for newcomers and member retention. Trimmed lawns and weeded flower beds, exterior lighting in good working order, attractive signs, and sidewalks, driveways, and parking lots cleared of snow all show pride in the parish and good Parish-Works. As with cleaning, groundskeeping can be done by a team of parish volunteers, contractors, or both.

In parishes with low-maintenance grounds (e.g., small lawns and gardens, short sidewalks and driveways, small parking lots), groundskeeping may be done fairly easily by parish volunteers. Ideally groundskeeping duties should be separate from those of the volunteer cleaning team. Inside cleaning versus outside weeding and grass cutting often attracts different volunteers. Also, the groundskeeping work cycles are less repetitive—fall clean-ups and spring plantings tend to need additional volunteers, over and above the month-by-month volunteer team. Usually checklists are not needed for groundskeeping—the needs are visible.

For volunteer teams, consider using teams of two on a monthly basis as described above. During the summer, grass cutting might take only one hour per week (assuming the parish owns a riding lawnmower), with another 15 to 20 minutes for weed pulling. Recruiting volunteers for this level of care should be easy. (Note: when planting gardens and trees in the parish's grounds, try to reduce future work—e.g., use edging around gardens to inhibit growth, line trees up in rows for easier grass cutting.)

During the winter, weekly clearing and salting of sidewalks should take one hour or so. Replacing exterior light bulbs could be done by the sexton, as needed. Parish signage could be maintained by the congregation development team (see page 42).

For parishes with large grounds or large parking lots, the grounds-keeping requirements could overwhelm a volunteer team, and subcontracting may be necessary. Use the same guidelines as above when selecting contractors:

- check references;
- include a checklist with frequencies; and
- include penalty clauses with minimal/non-performance criteria.

As with interior cleaning, groundskeeping could be done by a volunteer-contractor mix—a parish's lawns and gardens might easily be cared for by a volunteer team, for example, while clearing the parking lot of snow might be best left to a contractor. Or vice versa.

Do not consider adding groundskeeping to the responsibilities of your cleaning contractor. The skills and capabilities required for each are quite different, and you will likely get unsatisfactory results.

Maintenance Projects

While cleaning and groundskeeping are year-round requirements, other maintenance issues will crop up from time to time. These tend to be repairs, but minor (proactive) improvements also fall into this category of parish operational expenses.

While parish inspections will highlight key maintenance issues (and some capital items) that the parish must address, many other maintenance projects that an inspection doesn't cover will need to be added to the parish's "to-do" list, such as

- repainting/restaining;
- replastering;
- recarpeting/retiling;
- upgrading plumbing fixtures;
- refencing; and
- resealing windows and doors.

How can the parish manage all these "to-dos"? Well, the best way matches the way you manage the care of your own home—the "to-do" list is an excellent way to track what needs doing and when, as well as bringing forward additional items or jobs that are coming due. Maintenance jobs always seem more numerous and more expensive than most parishes can undertake or afford in any given year, and so should be prioritized and cost-estimated. The sexton, wardens, and treasurer can then properly budget for the work, year by year.

Maintenance priorities should reflect the following order:

Priority 1: ParishWorks needed to ensure the safety of parishioners and renters (e.g., repair of loose roofing materials and flooring; levelling of uneven walkways; covering exposed wiring; cleaning contaminated wells; pumping/replacing failing septic tanks).

Priority 2: ParishWorks needed to prevent more expensive work in the future (e.g., roof or window resealing; exterior wood staining or repainting).

Priority 3: ParishWorks needed to reduce the cost of maintenance in the future (e.g., improved roof insulation; window resealing; installation of storm doors, higher efficiency furnaces/hot water heaters, timed thermostats).

Priority 4: ParishWorks needed to maintain the image of the church and hall as valued assets (e.g., patching drywall; interior repainting; weeding gardens).

Priority 5: ParishWorks needed to improve parish facilities (e.g., new kitchen countertops, bathroom fixtures, coat racks, carpeting).

The tendency in most parishes is to reverse the order (so that parishioners see the new stove in the kitchen as a visible sign of their Sunday offerings). However, as good stewards of our buildings and property, the less visible but more important things really do need attention first.

In many cases, a maintenance item (such as a new roof for the church) may exceed the sexton's maintenance budget for the year. The funds may be found through a few fund-raising events, or perhaps a low-key appeal to those in the congregation who have expressed an interest in financially supporting the project. Many parishioners will buy materials for the parish, for the charitable tax benefit. As with all maintenance work, the sexton should first determine if volunteers can do the work, and if any parishioners have contacts in the associated trade, to see if materials can be obtained more cheaply.

If the need is too large for these subtle approaches, the sexton and assets management team may need to mount a special maintenance campaign to get the job done. Here are some guidelines to keep in mind:

1. *Campaign Focus.* Keep the need front and centre—use it in the campaign title: "Raise The Roof"; "Buy A Brick"; "Foundation Of Our Fathers"; etc. The campaign materials must clearly convey the urgency of the need, and the consequences if left unmet. The financial need must be well understood—the amount required is the bare-bones cost to get the job done.

2. *Campaign Timing.* Make sure the time of asking for additional financial support does not conflict with a parish stewardship campaign or outreach initiative. Or, if there is a conflict, work with the other team to ensure that both appeals are integrated, so that parishioners are not asked twice.

3. *Appeal to "Ownership."* Emphasize to parishioners that the church building, church hall, and rectory are theirs to care for. The rector might include a history of the parish in a sermon, along with teachings of good stewardship. Use displays during coffee hour to show parishioners who came before, and their valiant efforts in building the church/hall/rectory. Consider incentives—for example, if the maintenance project involves rebricking a wall, insert brass commemorative plates that highlight donors' names.

4. *Ask Everyone.* Every parish has a number of families on its membership list who are seldom seen. Don't assume they won't be interested in the campaign. Make sure they get the opportunity to participate, along with the "regulars." If this requires a team of phone callers, make the effort.

5. *Community Support.* Consider soliciting donations from local businesses. Local suppliers of materials for the project should be informed of the possibilities for receiving tax receipts for charitable donations. Remind businesses of the good works the parish has done for the community, creating a better place to live for all. Also, business donors might contribute to the project if their gifts were made known in the community, perhaps through the parish's good news stories in the local paper or thank-you plaques mounted in the work.

6. *Diocesan Support.* If the parish is facing a major project, such as restoration of the church building, check with diocesan staff. Often funds are available as grants or as low-interest loans for parishes facing such crises.

Maintenance Budgeting

The sexton and the assets management team should be given "ownership" of the parish budget lines associated with maintenance of the church buildings and grounds. Specifically,

- utilities (for each building);
- cleaning;
- groundskeeping (including snowploughing);
- repairs; and
- insurance.

This ownership includes letting the team focus on ways to reduce maintenance costs, while ensuring that the "to-dos" for the year are carried out as inexpensively as possible. Let's consider each expense category:

1. *Utilities*
For the parish's heating or air conditioning (AC) costs (gas, electric, or oil), first consider the contracts for utilities. Are there options for "locking in" unit prices for a length of time? While it may seem that the lock-in fee is higher than the current fee, locking in gives the parish price stability—a critical need for parishes trying to budget in many cases on a static income base.

Next, look at the usage patterns of the buildings. When are they empty? When they are empty, is the heat or AC turned off or lowered? Often, in parishes without thermostat timers, people using the parish buildings forget to turn down/off the heat or AC when they leave. Purchasing a timed thermostat will pay off. Make it an early priority if the parish does not have one. Also, decide how low to set the temperature in the winter when no one is using church buildings. Generally, temperatures set at 16 degrees C will ensure that plumbing doesn't freeze, and will keep the inside reasonably warm. If you are using a timed thermostat, remember to set it to resume normal heating temperatures an hour or so before people are due to arrive. It can also be set to begin dropping 20 minutes or so before they leave.

Air conditioning potentially will be the parish's largest utility expense. As with heating, determine when people will be present. Use AC only when the outside temperature is above 23 degrees C, and set the AC to maintain this temperature inside.

In many parishes, the secretary and rector are often the only people in the building during the week. Does it make sense to heat up or cool down the entire building for these two people? Consider space heaters for the secretary's and rector's offices, and fans or portable AC units in the summer. The AC could be turned off while the secretary and rector are kept comfortable, and in winter, the rest of the parish buildings could be set at 16 degrees C while they are nice and warm in their offices.

Also, consider timers for the hot water heater, for the same reason—in many parishes, hot water is needed only one or two days per week.

For maintenance projects, have the volunteer team check the parish buildings, paying special attention to

- the sealant around windows and doors—reseal as necessary;
- the insulation in the attic—if underrated, initiate a project to upgrade it;
- all windows—if they are not at least double-paned, aim to replace them (gradually, if necessary);
- the water heater—if it is aging, have a professional verify the heating element, and replace if necessary; and
- forced air vents in meeting rooms—if they are seldom used, block the vents temporarily.

2. Cleaning

As outlined above, parishes need to consider leveraging their renters and parish volunteers, to minimize the costs of professional cleaning services. If a renter uses the parish hall every Friday or Saturday, for instance, and then cleans it according to the checklist (which forms part of the rental agreement), the building might be ready for Sunday use—significantly reducing parish volunteer cleaning time and effort. A small volunteer team of six, using a rotation system of two volunteers at a time, could commit to two months a year (say, October and March), without becoming worn out.

For those occasional cleaning tasks that require professional help, shop around for the best service at the best price. Call other churches and service clubs in the community to see who they recommend. Once a cleaner is appointed, make sure someone from the assets management team is responsible for monitoring the work, to ensure that the parish gets value for the fees they are paying. Again, the task of monitoring could be rotated among the assets management team members.

For maintenance projects, consider changing high-maintenance features in parish buildings:

- carpeting in high-traffic areas—cover with easy-to-clean area carpeting or replace with washable vinyl flooring;
- paper towels in the parish's bathrooms—replace with air dryers if the electrical services permit;
- exterior wooden soffit, fascia, and window frames—recover with matching vinyl or aluminum;
- hard to reach light fixtures—use long-life bulbs;
- high-use area walls—repaint with medium-gloss washable paint; and
- painted steel or wooden fencing—replace with plastic or aluminum material.

3. Groundskeeping

Consider parish volunteers for carrying out the smaller groundskeeping chores—grass cutting and weeding might be handled by rotating teams, if the grassy areas are small; snow shovelling and salting might also be done by rotating teams; for fall clean-up and spring planting, plan as whole-team or all-parish events. If someone in the parish has (or knows someone who has) a tractor or truck with a snow-blower or plough, ask to use the equipment for driveway snow removal.

Only when all of these options have been explored should the sexton turn to contractors. Again, check with other churches, service clubs, and local businesses for recommendations; then arrange for two or three estimates before selecting the best.

4. Repairs

The sexton should examine the parish's "to-do" list for the upcoming year, and determine which jobs can be done by parish volunteers versus those needing contractors.

For those which can be done by volunteers, the sexton should consult, through the parish's volunteer coordinator, the parish's "skills and passions" inventory (see chapter 4) to see who might have an interest in which projects, and who might have the appropriate skills. Repair projects should always be handled by at least two people, to ensure a sense of fellowship and for safety reasons. The sexton should have a fair idea of how many volunteers will be needed for each project, and recruit accordingly. A key source of repair project volunteers should come from the assets management team.

Some projects may need a professional contractor to supervise the work of volunteers. In these cases, the sexton will need to keep the contractor's involvement limited to supervision, otherwise the labour-savings gained by using parish volunteers may be lost.

The sexton should not forget about the parish's youth group—there are many maintenance projects they might be keen to assist with. Often high schools in Canada have a community service component in their curriculum—parish projects may be a great way for the youth group members to earn these credits. Their friends, too, might wish to join in.

The sexton should see who in the parish might know where the materials for the repair project can be acquired, free of charge (as a donation to the church for a tax receipt) or at very low cost.

When contractors are required for repairs (complex plumbing, wiring, re-roofing, etc.), the sexton needs to keep in mind the above tips for subcontracting. Also, the sexton should try to negotiate fixed prices upfront. Many parishes have seen their budgets go up in smoke when "time and materials" contracts exceed the contractor's initial estimates. In fixed price contracts, however, the sexton must present precise requirements for the project. While contractors will bid on fixed-price contracts, some will try to get in the door with the lowest bid, then use any vagueness in the parish's requirements to claim that several aspects of the project are "changes" to what they bid on, and add a change fee. Before the sexton knows it, a large number of change fees may create a runaway budget. To avoid this, precise specifications at the start are critical. When in doubt, have a contracting professional not involved in the bidding process review the requirements document to make sure there are no gaping holes. Better yet, ask a contractor from the parish membership to review the document.

5. Insurance
The sexton should ensure that the parish has appropriate insurance for its assets, at the best possible price. Often it is possible for the diocese to negotiate a group-type policy at rates much better than the parish could negotiate alone. At the very least, your diocesan office will have guidelines for parish insurance, which the sexton should follow.

The sexton and the assets management team should be responsible for preparing the assets maintenance budget for the upcoming year, taking into consideration last year's costs, inflation rates, initiatives the team has undertaken, or will undertake next year, to reduce costs for the parish, and the costs of the upcoming "to-do" projects. The team should be able to show vestry that, year by year, they are carrying out a valuable stewardship program for the parish's buildings and grounds, and will continue to reduce costs wherever possible through innovative projects.

When the budget has been approved by vestry, it should be up to the sexton and the assets management team to monitor actual costs throughout the year, to ensure that they stay on track.

The sexton should assist the wardens and treasurer in preparing the monthly financial report for the advisory board, explaining any variances in the line-items for assets management, and indicating how these will be addressed. If the sexton wishes to tap the advisory board for ideas on how to resolve budget issues, the financial report distributed before the meeting should mention this, so that members have a chance to review the issue and form ideas. The sexton should attend the advisory board meeting in these situations, and lead the discussion, soliciting all helpful feedback. Some advisory board members may volunteer to help the assets management team with the problem.

Rentals

To supplement income, many parishes rent their space to community organizations. This, too, shows good stewardship of the parish's assets, since the facilities would otherwise be empty much of the time, when they might be used for others' benefit.

The parish leadership team needs to decide at the outset how to view such use of parish space—as an outreach program (i.e., offering the space at minimal or no cost to service-type community organizations), as supplemental income, or both. If both, the parish needs to be clear to avoid misinterpretation by the community that it is exercising a double standard.

Regardless, the parish should appoint one of its members to be the rentals coordinator. In parishes where rental space is scarce or where demand is limited, the parish sexton will often take on the responsibility for rentals, with good results. Because the sexton is the parish's focal point for the cleanliness of the buildings, and is facilities-focused, rentals coordination has been a natural fit. In parishes that have an active rentals program, many have found it best to appoint a volunteer as their rentals coordinator. In these cases, ideally the rentals coordinator will report to the parish sexton, and may be a member of the assets management team, for the reasons cited.

Rental Agreements

The parish should not let renters—organizations using the parish facilities, whether paying or not—use parish property or buildings without having a formal rental agreement in place beforehand. Here are four main reasons why :

1. *Liability*

Regardless of whether the organization pays to use the parish's facilities (grounds or buildings) or not, typically the parish is liable for any injuries sustained by the renter's members or guests while on parish property—unless an agreement specifies otherwise. Examples: a Cub Scout breaks a leg tripping on a loose cobble stone on the sidewalk outside the parish hall; an ESL student suffers a burn while using the stove in the kitchen—both could sue the parish for damages if the parish did not have a proper rental agreement in place with the renter. If you look at the parish's insurance policy, you will see that it covers only accidents involving members of the parish—not renters. This is standard practice. Unfortunately the injuries sustained by the Cub Scout and ESL student above would not be covered by the parish's insurance, and either could sue the parish for any amount, which (if granted) could bankrupt the parish.

A rental agreement therefore is essential, specifying that the renter is responsible for securing liability insurance for their people while on the parish's premises, and that the renter must provide the parish's rentals coordinator with a copy of the insurance, to prove that their coverage is adequate and paid up **before** they start using the parish's facilities.

In some cases, as a courtesy, parishes will arrange for the renter's insurance through the parish's insurance broker. However, it must be completely understood by both the parish and the renter that the insurance is the renter's—**not** the parish's.

2. *Damages*

If the renter's people break equipment or furnishings within the parish buildings or grounds, typically they would not be liable for damages—unless specified otherwise in an agreement between the two parties. Without this, renters could run amok, breaking priceless assets within the church and grounds, and not have to take responsibility. Most parish rental agreements include a security deposit paid to the parish, before the renter uses the facilities. The deposit covers initial damages and clean-ups that might be required, in the event the renter does not pay for them after they use the facilities.

3. *Clean-Up*

As with damages, renters could make a large mess inside the parish buildings, leaving the parish to clean up after them, without an agreement in place. A security deposit will ensure that, if the renter leaves a mess behind, cleaners can be hired to do the work, at no cost to the parish.

4. Payment

Without an agreement as to the amounts to be paid and when, the parish might find itself chasing after delinquent renters with no recourse.

Most dioceses can offer a form of rental agreement for parish use, which allows minor amendments to note specific rental spaces, locations, rates, etc. If the parish makes significant changes to this basic rental agreement, check back with your diocesan office to make sure the document is sound before using it.

If the parish decides to create its own rental agreement, a legal opinion of its enforceability should be obtained before using it. This could involve considerable expense for the parish, unless one of the parishioners happens to be a lawyer and agrees to do the review free of charge, or as a charitable donation to the parish for a tax receipt.

Here are some suggested amendments for parish-specific content in diocese-supplied rental agreements:

1. *Describe the rental space to be used* (free or not). Without knowing the specific space to be used, the renter could wander into other areas of the parish's buildings and cause problems. The best way to prevent this is to list and describe each space the parish is willing to rent. Using this checklist, the renter simply ticks off which areas they wish to use and notes the dates.

2. *Note the rental fee for each space.* This ensures that the fees are consistent for all renters. For renters whose fees will be waived, the amounts should be crossed out, and "$0.00" substituted. This makes clear the degree of outreach the parish is giving the organization.

3. *State the amount of the security deposit*, the timing of its payment to the parish (xx days before the renter's use of the facilities), and the conditions for its release back to the renter (i.e., an inspection by the parish of the facilities used, xx days after the renter's use, with an acceptable result).

4. *Include the parish's clean-up checklist for renters*, to ensure that both parties are clear on what is expected of the renter. The checklist for renters will be a subset of the parish cleaning checklist. A suggested checklist follows:

- dry bathroom sinks (with paper towels)   ___ done
- clean up bathroom floors (remove paper)   ___ done

- sterilize kitchen counters and sinks (if used) ___ done
- wash floor in kitchen (if used) ___ done
- wash, dry, and put away dishes and glasses (if used) ___ done
- mop and vacuum carpet for spills ___ done

During the post-rental inspection, the rental coordinator can use the checklist to make sure everything has been properly cleaned before closing out the rental agreement.

To ensure the accuracy of rental bookings and to prevent double-booking, the rentals coordinator will need to refer to the parish calendar that includes all parish events and facilities usage, as well as facilities booked by renters. In most parishes, the congregation development team or parish secretary are in the best position to maintain a parish calendar (see chapter 4). The rentals coordinator should refer to the calendar when renters call to book facilities, updating it whenever rentals are confirmed or changed.

To lessen the workload of the rentals coordinator, parish team leaders should consider placing their events on a calendar on the parish web site. The online calendar could also include a description of each space, along with photographs, and if applicable, rental rates. In this way, potential renters could decide whether the parish's facilities would meet their needs and budget, before calling the rentals coordinator. This would reduce casual inquiries.

Since rentals are part of assets management, any income from the rentals program should be seen as part of the team's contribution to the parish. Rental income might be used to fund facilities maintenance and improvement projects. If this were the case, the assets management team could also consider the attractiveness and utility of the parish's facilities to potential renters, and make improvements to draw in more renters, and more income, for the parish. The parish leadership team might decide to move responsibility for the rentals-income budget line to the assets management team. This way, the assets management team would have responsibility for both sides of the assets ledger—both expenses and income, and work to balance the two, as possible.

Cemeteries

Parish cemeteries must meet several recordkeeping, financial, and caretaking requirements by provincial governments, which may not be obvious to parish leadership teams. These vary from province to province, but your diocesan office will have the details.

Dioceses also have standards for cemetery management, described within their canons. Again, the details vary from diocese to diocese, and it's best to check the canons for the requirements of your parish.

Lastly, parishes have their own duties of care inherent in the management of their cemeteries. These include:

1. *Recordkeeping.* Every parish cemetery should have an up-to-date, accurate plot layout with designations.

2. *Purchases.* Every parish should know if their cemetery is active (plots available) or in custodial care (full). If active, the parish needs to know the price for plots and the documentation to be completed when sales are made. Some of the documentation requirements are part of the provincial Cemeteries Acts. Ensure that these are well understood by the parish leadership team.

3. *Financial Management.* In most cases, funds from the sale of new plots are held in trust for the cemetery's use, including the costs of internments, relevelling, grass cutting, fencing, and monument repair. Cemetery funds are not to be intermingled with the other financial records of the parish. Most parishes find it simplest to have the funds in a separate bank account, named as such. All funds "in" (new plot purchases) and "out " (repairs and maintenance) of the account need to be reported to vestry and audited each year, along with the other accounts of the parish. In most cases, the wardens will need to review the cemetery account only quarterly, unless there are numerous transactions. Normally the advisory board does not need to review the cemetery account.

4. *Caretaking.* The provincial Acts, the canons, and the parish's own standards will indicate the level of care required for the cemetery. Typically, however, the parish is required to keep the cemetery's fencing in good order, the monuments repaired and in their original positions, and the ground level and trimmed.

The best person in most parishes to assume responsibility for the parish cemetery is the sexton, especially when the cemetery is adjacent to the parish's other property. In these cases, the lawn cutting and levelling work carried out by the assets management team is simply extended to include the cemetery. Righting and repairing monuments are simply added to the assets management team's "to-do" parish maintenance list.

If the parish sexton and the assets management team have "ownership" of the other parish assets income and expense lines, adding oversight of the cemetery account to the team's duties will not be onerous. The sexton has overall responsibility of the parish's grounds, and so will initiate any work needed to maintain the cemetery grounds. In this context, the sexton may be best suited to arrange internments by a contractor, as they likely do other work for the sexton.

For plot purchases, most people will likely approach the rector, who can handle the process. Since the parish bookkeeper/secretary will no doubt handle the payment and the credit to the cemetery account, ideally he or she should maintain the plot layout (adding new designations). However, the secretary should advise the sexton of these changes. In parishes with large and active cemeteries, a separate board may be required to maintain the property and finances.

Rectories

In days past, providing housing to the parish rector made a lot of sense, since the cost of land and building materials was relatively cheap and volunteers could easily be found to build the rectory. Energy costs, too, were low, and rectory maintenance was a minor cost for the parish. This offset the costs of adding a housing allowance to the rector's costs, which tended to be the most expensive item for the parish. For their part, rectors were quite mobile, and purchasing a house each time they were assigned to a parish made little sense. Also, rectors tended to be paid much less than what they needed to purchase housing, and to furnish it. So rectories made sense all around.

In today's world, however, rectories may not be as sensible as they once were. Average rectory costs to a parish have mushroomed over the last 30 years, including municipal taxes, utilities, contractors' fees, and building materials. Additionally, rectors don't always view rectories as "perks" since they don't allow for a build-up of equity for the rector's retirement plan. With a housing allowance, however, the rector can pay a mortgage on his or her own property. Rectors also are not as mobile as they once were. Incumbencies of 10-plus years are not uncommon. Putting down roots is not so much of an issue for rectors these days. Even when home-owning rectors are reassigned to parishes 30 kilometers or so from their current parish, they have the option of commuting.

Clearly the parish leadership team should take a hard look at any decision to recommit to ongoing maintenance of the parish rectory for years to come. Add up the annual costs. Include utilities, municipal taxes, groundskeeping fees, contracted repairs, replacing appliances, etc. With that total, compare the rectory cost to the rector's living allowance for your area, as recommended by the diocese. You will no doubt find that maintaining the rectory is more expensive for the parish than simply paying the rector a living allowance. Add to this the fact that the rector will be able to purchase a home and begin to build up personal equity. This seems only fair.

As a homeowner in the community, the rector may experience a dimension of life that was missing before. Putting down roots changes one's view of their community. Consider, too, the parish equity tied up in the rectory—would the value of the house not be better used in parish outreach projects, or badly needed capital works?

Lastly, consider the drain on your volunteer base that rectory maintenance adds. While parishioners could be doing good works to serve the community, often they find themselves spending precious time repainting the rectory, cutting the grass, replacing the windows, etc.

If the parish leadership team does decide that the parish would be better off without a rectory, the wardens should contact the diocesan office to determine next steps. In most cases, the diocese will split the proceeds of a rectory sale with the parish; some portion may need to be held in trust for future uses. Check your canons—they should be specific concerning the sale of rectories.

Another idea to consider is whether the parish might use the rectory for a community outreach initiative—that is, if the parish can afford to pay the rector's living allowance without receiving any proceeds from selling the rectory. If so, perhaps the rectory could be used as a halfway house for families in crisis, or to offer temporary shelter to abused family members. In some parishes where the rectory is used for outreach purposes, the community's social services team has agreed to manage the property, and to place and supervise the clients of the facility. Often municipal and/or provincial social services have found the funding to help carry the upkeep of the house. However, parishes that have chosen to use their rectories in this way usually have kept a hand in the program, as part of their outreach mission.

If you are considering this option, get the diocese involved at the outset, and enlist support from all levels of government. Just think what could be done, with some imagination.

If, after analyzing the situation, the parish leadership decides to maintain the rectory, it would be best to assign its upkeep to the parish sexton and the assets management team. In these cases, the team simply adds the rectory to their list of responsibilities and manages it along with the other parish property, using the same maintenance priorities as described above. As with the care of all parish buildings and grounds, the assets management team should be given "ownership" of the budget lines for the rectory—utilities, municipal taxes, groundskeeping fees, repairs, etc. *Un*like the other parish buildings, however, the rectory probably will not have an income component from renters (assuming the rector is using it). The team, as part of its mandate, can look for ways to reduce the maintenance costs to the parish (e.g., through improved insulation, resealing windows, upgrading windows and doors, installation of energy-efficient appliances and furnace).

Capital Works

So far, this chapter has outlined the maintenance aspects of parish assets management, where funds are allocated from the parish's operating account. The other aspect of assets management relates to capital projects. These are parish initiatives that add asset value to the parish, such as an addition to the parish hall or building a new washroom.

Why is the difference between operating costs and capital acquisitions so important? One reason involves adherence to proper financial accounting—an organization's operating income and expenses should not be mixed with its capital income and expenses. Different tax laws apply, as well as different depreciation costs. Within the parish structure, the diocese also treats capital income and expenses differently from operating income and expenses. While operating income forms part of the parish's diocesan assessment, capital income does not. Check with your diocesan office if you are unclear on this—they will give you the assessment formula that describes what is "in" and what is not.

Also, often parish donors designate their financial gifts for capital works, and do not wish to have them "swallowed up" by operating expenses. Most memorials and bequests are specific (e.g., to be used to purchase new stained glass windows or a new organ). Since these donations have been given to the parish in trust for a specified use, the funds need to be segregated from the operating income for obvious reasons.

Many parishes have made the critical error of mixing operating and capital funds. As a result, bequests have gone missing in the operating account, parishes have paid higher diocesan assessments, and the parish's bookkeeping has resulted in disarray. It is critical that the parish leadership team understand the difference and ensure that the treasurer, bookkeeper, sexton, and anyone else involved in the parish's finances understand and maintain proper records.

The best way to guarantee that the parish's capital funds and transactions are not mixed in with its operating funds is to set up a separate capital fund bank account. The extra banking charges for the additional account are well worth the simplification and clarity in parish bookkeeping. If the parish is adamant on having only one bank account, then their internal bookkeeping records must ensure that the capital and operating records are kept completely separate. The bookkeeper will need to reconcile the parish's two internal ledgers—operating and capital—to one bank account statement, which will make reconciliation a more difficult task.

Who should be responsible for the parish's capital account? Many parishes have assigned ownership of the capital account to the parish sexton. Why? Because the funds are used for the assets of the parish (buildings and property), which is the responsibility of the sexton and the assets management team.

When ownership of the parish capital fund rests with the sexton and his or her team, they will be responsible for monitoring the funds available as they work with the list of capital projects for that year. This list would be prepared at the end of each year (as with the maintenance "to-dos") based on priorities set by the team, the wardens, the advisory board, and vestry.

Unlike maintenance priorities, capital works priorities are parish-specific. However, some considerations include:

1. *Designated Gifts.* A portion of the capital fund will likely be made up of funds that have been designated by the donor, as a bequest, an in-memorium, or some other purpose. The designations and balances need to be kept separate from the parish's open capital funds (where no designation has been included). The sexton and the assets management team need to consider the future use of these designated funds. While the donor had the best interests of the parish at heart, their designations may not be realistic. For example: a parish may receive a bequest "for a new church." If the parish does not intend to build a new church in the foreseeable future (or ever), the bequest may be held in trust forever, not benefiting the parish or anyone else. In these cases, the wardens should contact the donors or estate executors to explain the situation, and ask that the designation be changed to "open," or directed to support a parish initiative that has a better chance of being realized.

If the parish has a designated gift of significance that would benefit the parish and the sexton has not initiated a project to pursue the designation, the sexton and the assets management team should do so. Perhaps the designated amount will be sufficient to carry out the capital project. If not, the sexton could consider a capital campaign to "top up" the designation, to allow the project to go forward. Otherwise, the donor's gift will not be transformed into its intended purpose.

2. *Cost-Reduction Projects.* While most maintenance projects described previously will reduce costs, other capital-based projects will also help reduce the parish's operating expenses. For example—building a vestibule and a second set of doors for the church building or hall will reduce heating/cooling costs. Or upgrading to a more efficient computer or accounting system may reduce the number of hours worked by the paid parish secretary/bookkeeper.

3. *Appearance/Facility Upgrades.* To attract newcomers and better retain current members, capital improvements should be considered, such as property lighting, additional washrooms and meeting rooms, etc.

4. *Growth Projects.* Ironically, research shows that as a parish fills its pews to 80%-plus capacity, attendance begins to drop. Parishioners like to have some "personal space" when they worship, and if they feel the church is cramped, they will go elsewhere. The parish leadership team needs to know that if one service is at 70% or more capacity, it's time to add another service, rearrange the seating in the church, or begin planning an expansion of the worship space (a capital project). Similarly, if the church hall is inadequate for its current uses, a capital expansion should be planned.

Generally parish capital projects should follow the above order in terms of priority, although each parish will experience differences. The sexton and the assets management team are most likely to identify the need for a capital project, and whenever they do, they should prepare a capital project plan. The project plan should include:

1. *Description of Need.* Why is the project needed for the parish? What are the expected benefits (financial and non-financial), and how will these be measured? Describe the costs and how they will be tracked. Include detailed specifications of the work to be done.

2. *Proposals Received.* Arrange for at least two estimates from contractors for the work to be done. Ideally the sexton and the assets management team should try to obtain a fixed price estimate from the bidders. In these cases, specifications for the work must be very precise, as some contractors will low-bid fixed-price work to secure the contract and then use "change notices" wherever specifications seem vague or misleading to increase their bill.

For capital projects that rely on parish volunteers, get cost estimates from two or three suppliers of the required materials. Include, too, any fees for a supervising contractor—for some work, inspection by the municipality may be required, in which case a professional contractor should be hired to oversee volunteers' work. If the parish has a licensed contractor within its membership, the fees might be donated to the parish for a tax receipt.

3. *Recommended Solution*. The sexton and the assets management team should outline the pros and cons of each bid or materials supplier, and recommend the best solution for the parish, along with their rationale.

4. *Financials.* Depending on the recommended solution, the team will prepare a financial plan for the project. If funds for the project are available from the parish's capital fund, the team should show how the funds will be replenished in part or in whole over time, to ensure that future capital projects will be supported. If there are insufficient funds to cover the costs of the project, the team should outline how the balance may be obtained—e.g., through a transfer from the operating account, fund-raising event(s), a capital campaign, sponsorships, diocesan grants, capital loans, or several of these in combination. The financial plan must be realistic—parishioners should not be asked to approve a capital project that risks putting the parish in an unplanned deficit position from which it might not be able to recover, or that is based on unrealistic expectations of the parish's donors.

In cases where the capital project will result in increased income for the parish (e.g., increased membership donations, rentals income) or reduced costs (e.g., utilities, rental expenses), the estimates should be included on a 5- or 10-year spreadsheet. The project costs will be incurred in "year 0," with the increased income/reduced costs beginning when the project ends (in year 1, year 2, etc.). By the end of the time-period, the expected income/cost reductions should eliminate the project costs, unless the capital project is very large in scale (e.g., a new church), in which case a 15- or 25-year spreadsheet may be required.

Let's look at an example: a parish wants to increase the seating capacity of its church by 50%, say, by adding an addition to the building (a cost of $250,000). The parish leadership team estimate that by expanding the seating area and by improving the parish's advertising and newcomers programs, they could attract 20 new families each year over the next 5 years. Since the average givings of a parish family is $1,000 per year, this represents additional parish income of $20,000 per year, compounded. Also, by including a vestibule within the addition, the parish leadership team estimates that the heating and air conditioning costs for the church will be reduced by $300 per month. The corresponding financial spreadsheet follows:

Costs/Benefits (in 000s)	Year 0	Year 1	Year 2	Year 3	Year 4	Year 5
Project Costs	$250					
Increased Income		$20.0	$40.0	$60.0	$80.0	$100.0
Reduced Heating Costs		$ 3.6	$ 3.6	$ 3.6	$ 3.6	$ 3.6
Total	($250)	$23.6	$43.6	$63.6	$83.6	$103.6
Net (year over year)	($250)	($226.4)	($182.8)	($119.2)	($35.6)	$68

The above shows that the capital cost of the project would be recovered 4 years and 5 months after the project was completed. The project plan should also indicate how the capital fund will recover the initial cost of $250,000. For example, the team could propose that the increased income and cost savings be transferred from the operating account to the capital account, until the initial cost is recovered.

5. *Schedule.* The team lays out when the project should begin (allowing time to raise funds, appoint contractors, obtain building permits, etc.). The schedule should also include interim milestones (usually highlighted by interim contractor payments) and the projected completion date (including some contingency for slippage). As well, the schedule should include any ancillary tasks to be done by the parish, such as temporary parking and walkways, alternate accommodations for meeting rooms and offices, etc.

6. *Transition Plan.* With most capital projects, parish facilities are temporarily altered, and the parish leadership team must ensure that the parish continues to function as normally as possible while the changes are being made. Lack of planning for transition periods has resulted in Sunday services that are poorly planned, inadequate access to the church or parish hall, inadequate parking, etc.—all of which has caused many parishes to lose members. Most capital projects will require two facility changes (transfer to the temporary

set-up; transfer back to the new set-up) and sometimes more. This section of the plan needs to describe, ***in detail***, how normal operations will be accommodated, week by week.

7. *Management Plan.* Describe how the various project team members—e.g., contractor(s) and their employees, parish team leaders and their team members—will be coordinated to ensure synchronization of the various tasks required to achieve the scheduled milestones. Details should include how and when team members will meet to plan upcoming work, how and when the parish will receive progress reports, how and when payments will be made, how and when municipal inspections will be made, etc.

Once the capital project plan is completed to the team's satisfaction, it should be passed to the wardens and/or the advisory board for review. When they have approved the plan, the wardens should present it at vestry for approval. In most cases, the parish leadership team will try to schedule the review of a capital project plan at the parish's annual vestry meeting. In these cases, the sexton and the assets management team will need to have the plan to the wardens and advisory board in November, to ensure that it can be ready for vestry in January-February. During December the team can revise the plan according to feedback from the wardens and board members. The sexton and the assets management team should also consider reviewing the plan with the appropriate diocesan staff before vestry. They may have valuable tips for the team to include in their plan.

If a capital project plan cannot be delayed until the parish's annual vestry meeting, the wardens will need to call special vestry for parish presentation and approval.

When the parish is ready to go ahead with the project, the sexton and the assets management team will need to decide who the parish's project manager will be. For large capital projects (such as building a new church), parishes often hire their own consulting project manager. In these cases, the parish should ensure that the project manager is not affiliated with any of the contractors or suppliers, to avoid conflicts of interest. Also, ***in cases where the parish hires a project manager, parishes should not make the mistake of assuming that they need not "manage" the project themselves.*** While the hired project manager will focus on the construction work and the contractors, the parish must still manage certain parts of the project, such as transition planning, project updates, alternate facilities, etc.

Also, the parish needs to lead the project, even if they have hired a project manager to deal with the day-to-day issues. For these reasons, a **parish**

project manager is required. The parish project manager does *not* need to be an expert on the construction details of the project—that is why the parish has contracted a professional project manager. However, the parish project manager will need to ensure that the contractor and parishioners involved in the project are in sync with the plan, and are working toward the completion target and within the project budget.

The parish project manager should hold a **project kickoff meeting** with the contractor(s), hired project manager, wardens, sexton, treasurer, and other members of the parish on the project team, to review the plan and identify any issues before the project gets rolling. Once it is underway, the parish project manager should hold project status meetings every month (at a minimum) with the same group who attended the kickoff meeting, and whenever deemed necessary. (Note: interim meetings should be held with the parish project manager and the contracted project manager and/or contractors each week, to keep the project on track in between full project team meetings.)

Monthly meeting agendas might follow the format suggested below. In cases where the parish has hired a project manager, that person would lead the meeting. Otherwise, the parish project manager would lead.

1. *Review the schedule*, describing progress since the previous meeting, milestones met/upcoming, and the current forecast. The prime contractor should provide an up-to-date schedule to the hired project manager, the parish project manager, wardens, etc., showing planned events versus actual.

When interim milestone dates have slipped, both parish and hired project managers should ask the contractor how the time will be made up and if not, what will be the impact to the overall schedule. If necessary, the contractor should provide a revised schedule to the project team, highlighting any dependencies on parish team members. The parish project team needs to review any revised schedules with healthy pessimism—approaching it with an attitude of "convince me" will ensure that the entire team has properly thought it through and that it is realistic. (Few things are worse for a parish's morale than for its members to become victims of a runaway project, with no idea of the completion date.) The parish project team should also "quiz" the contractor whether this revision will be the last—what assurances can be seen that would make the new completion date 100% reliable.

2. *Review the budget*, describing costs since the previous meeting, payment milestones met/upcoming, and the current forecast. The contractor should provide up-to-date project costs to the parish project management team,

comparing it to the plan. For the work done to date, the costs should match the plan to date. Differences should be explained and the contractor asked when and how the costs will be (re)covered. Even in fixed price projects, the parish and hired project manager should keep track of costs—if costs are rising too quickly, the contractor may try to find ways of cutting out work, using cheaper materials or labour, or claiming additional fees through change requests. If the parish and hired project managers are not prepared for any of these events, the contractor could adversely affect the project budget.

In cases where the project is based on contractor costs passed to the parish ("time and materials" contracts), and the budget review reveals significant increases in the projected total cost, the parish project team must determine if they can afford to complete the project, given current projected costs. When carrying out this assessment, the parish team will need to keep in mind that this budget change may be only the first of several subsequent increases. If so, how will they respond in the future? For example: if the schedule shows that 20% of the work is done, but the contractor indicates that they are 40% over budget for that amount of work, what level of confidence should the project team place in the contractor's budget (re)forecast? Extremely low, with only 20% of the job done—subsequent increases are very likely.

On the other hand, if the project is nearing completion, on time and on budget until the contractor indicates a recent overexpenditure of 40%, the parish team can be reasonably sure that this will be the only increase. With early overexpenditures, the parish project team must look very closely at the project. Should the contractor be replaced? Should the parish cut back on some aspects of the project (and do them later)? It is critical that these decisions be reached as soon as overexpenditures are reported. If the parish needs time to reconsider the scope of the project, the contractor should be told to stop work temporarily. This happens quite often in construction projects—the parish risks losing the workcrew assigned, as well as some time when work is resumed, since the contractor has to put together a new crew. However, this is far preferable to watching a runaway project clean out the parish bank account. Again, try to negotiate fixed price contracts whenever possible.

3. *Issues.* The project team should be given the opportunity to raise any concerns. While it may seem that some issues won't affect the contractor and his/her crew, it is important that the contractor be present when any concern is discussed—some issues may impact the work underway, even though the parish project team might not think so.

Many capital projects are undertaken to retain current members and to accommodate new ones. In these cases, when the capital project ends, the parish project team should make the most of the occasion, to maximize the impact of the changes made. The bishop should be invited to consecrate the new facilities, the mayor encouraged to attend, local newspapers asked to cover the event, posters and pamphlets might be distributed, and a reception planned. The congregation development team (see chapter 4) could be enlisted to help plan and execute such a celebration. The event should draw as many community people—potential members—as possible. Displays of the parish's history should be on hand, to illustrate the parish's commitment to the community as it grows for the future. Any project investments within the community, such as materials and labour, should be highlighted to reflect the parish's value to the community as it reinvests in its future.

Capital Campaigns

When parish capital projects exceed the capital funds available and cannot be covered by the usual fund-raising events carried out for small parish initiatives, the sexton and the assets management team should consider a capital campaign. If the project will not require a major financial commitment from its parishioners (say, less than 10% of their annual givings for a year), the assets management team can probably run the campaign on their own. However, if the project will require a multi-year financial commitment from parishioners, it is time to call in the experts to help plan and carry out the campaign. Contact your diocesan office for guidance—staff will know which firms are most successful in this field, and will know of parishes who have held campaigns similar to yours, which the team can check out.

Even when a parish hires a fund-raising consultant or firm, it is critical for the parish's capital campaign team to retain ownership of the initiative. All too often, parishes "out source" their campaigns to firms who have little background with the parish, and the campaign comes across to parishioners as being artificial. The financial results in these cases are very disappointing. Professional fund-raisers should be in the background, taking care of the campaign's logistics. It is the parish leadership team that the parishioners will respond to, not some stranger brought in only for the duration of the campaign. In this context, the parish campaign team will need to lead the campaign—with or without a professional fund-raiser. While the professional will offer their own methodologies (which the parish team should follow), the parish team should also keep the following best practices in mind as they carry out the campaign (see also chapter 8, The Annual Outreach Campaign, and chapter 11, Stewardship Campaigns, for additional tips):

1. *Know Your Goal.* Know how much the campaign needs to raise, and over what period of time. For large sums, spread the donor payments over several years. Determine how the difference will be funded if the project will be completed before all the funds are collected. Ensure that the amount is realistic—compare the goal to the last three years of operating income received from parishioners, to calculate the average annual donations by family. Most capital campaigns can count on only 10% to 15% additional funds from their parishioners each year. Even by spreading the campaign over several years, the team still may not cover the entire costs of the project.

Let's consider an example: an addition to the church is estimated at $250,000, say. With respect to the records kept by the envelope secretary over the last three years, the average annual donations per parish family for general operating funds is $2,000. This means that the campaign may see $200 to $300 per family per year (on average). The parish has 150 active families, so the annual potential donations would be in the $30,000 to $45,000 range ($40,000 is a conservative estimate that should be used). If the campaign runs for five years (the maximum the parish can expect for these types of campaigns), it could raise $200,000 toward the project cost, leaving the parish to fund the remaining $50,000 through other means. To accomplish this, the campaign team could consider other sources of donations (e.g., local businesses, partnerships, diocesan grants) before opting for long-term financing from the parish's banker.

The campaign goal is the amount parishioners will need to contribute over the duration of the campaign. While other sources and financing options should be included in the campaign details, do not focus on these—you will only confuse your donors. The parish treasurer should be aware that, during capital campaigns, donations to the parish's general operating account will go down somewhat, even though the campaign team will make the point that capital donations should be in addition to what families regularly give. General operating donations still tend to go down by about 3% to 5%, and the treasurer should take this into account when preparing operating budgets during capital campaign years.

2. *Know Your Timing.* There is no point in the assets management team launching a capital campaign at the same time as a parish stewardship drive or an outreach appeal. Make sure you are not "competing" for the same donors. The parish leadership team should ensure a moratorium on other active campaigning in the parish during the capital program. Also, launching any campaign needs to be done when the maximum number of parishioners is

attending services. April to May and September to October are regarded as the best launch times.

3. *Make It Appealing.* Give your campaign a title that not only focuses on the goal, but also inspires parishioners to give. Ask your diocesan office for suggestions. Look at other parish web sites for ideas for campaign names. Include the parish's history in the campaign messages—try to impart a sense of our inherited legacy and responsibility to continue our ministry for those following us (e.g., "... from generation to generation ..."). Make the campaign highly personal, and emphasize the donors' ownership of their church.

4. *Leave No One Out.* You may think that only "active" parishioners will respond to the campaign, but infrequent attendees have been known to surprise campaign teams when asked to help. To reach these potential donors, try a telephone approach, after campaign materials have been mailed out. Also, know your key donors. In most parish campaigns, 5% of the members often account for 50% to 70% of the funds. Have the rector call on these families directly to ask for their best-effort support.

5. *Make It Easy for Donors.* Set up the donation process to be as simple as possible. For donors whose regular givings are through pre-authorized payments (PAP), make the capital campaign a PAP option. For envelope donors, add monthly capital campaign envelopes to their envelope sets.

6. *Thank Donors.* Track the pledges and actual donations to date, and regularly report these to the congregation. Thank donors who have committed, and remind those who have not that their support is also needed—it is not too late. A monthly update in the parish's service bulletin, and bi-monthly updates from the campaign team during service announcements, will help everyone stay current and the campaign remain visible.

7. *Repeat for Newcomers.* In many parish capital campaigns, the team tends to disband once the initial launch is over and the multi-year donation collection cycle kicks in. ***This is a serious error.*** Most parishes see member turnovers of 5% to 10% per year, as people move out of, or into, the community. This means that, ***during a 5-year capital campaign, the parish may see up to 50% of its members arrive as newcomers.*** These potential donors will have missed the campaign launch, and will not participate unless asked to. The campaign team needs to keep the "ask" process operating every year that the campaign

is active. As new families arrive in the parish, their names should be supplied to the campaign team for telephone follow-up (after the family has had a few months to settle into the parish).

No doubt, campaign team members will come and go during the campaign, especially if it is five years long. However, the parish leadership team needs to regard the campaign being as active in year 5 as it was in year 1.

The Parish Sexton

In many parishes, assets management is left to the wardens—or rather, no one else will take on the job. Often parishioners feel that taking care of the buildings is the wardens' "job." Of course it is, according to the canons. However, the wardens need to work at distributing this responsibility to other members of the parish, or they will get bogged down taking care of buildings and property, and end up neglecting other duties.

The most successful way to ensure that parish assets are well taken care of is to appoint a parish sexton. Who should this be? Look for someone in the parish who takes pride in the buildings and grounds, and who wants them to stay in good condition. The sexton should not be regarded as the parish "handyperson," as the position involves much more than fix-it jobs. The position description below might help in recruiting your sexton, as well as helping everyone understand the sexton's role and responsibilities. An electronic version in Microsoft Word format may be found on the enclosed CD (see sexton.doc).

Position Description: Parish Sexton

Role

The parish sexton is responsible for the care and upkeep of the parish's buildings and property, and reports to the wardens. The sexton is the parish's focal point for issues regarding building maintenance and property upkeep. An assets management team, led by the sexton, will assist the sexton in these duties. The sexton also supervises the work of the parish custodian, ensuring that cleaning is properly taken care of. In addition, the sexton arranges for building inspections by qualified engineering contractors.

The parish sexton and assets management team also track the costs of maintaining the parish buildings and property, and initiate ways to reduce costs through increased use of parish volunteers, improved energy efficiency initiatives, and contract negotiations.

The sexton and assets management team are also responsible for the parish's cemetery, ensuring that the cemetery records remain current and accurate. The sexton is the focal point for those wishing to purchase burial plots, and for contracting internments.

The sexton (assisted by the assets management team) is also the focal point for renting space within the parish's buildings. The sexton keeps track of vacancies and contracts rentals with outside renters.

For capital improvements, the sexton manages the parish's capital fund and recommends expenditures to the wardens based on the needs of the parish. The sexton may select contractors to carry out capital improvements, assisted by the assets management team.

In order to replenish the parish's capital fund, the sexton and assets management team may also create and carry out parish capital campaigns.

Responsibilities

The responsibilities of the sexton and assets management team include

- stewardship of the church buildings, including regular cleaning, periodic inspections for potential problems, and remedial work to repair damage; selection of contractors and monitoring of their work when contractors are hired to perform these tasks to ensure the work meets the needs of the parish;
- for routine repair jobs (e.g., painting interior walls, patching drywall, minor flooring repairs, minor electrical wiring, etc.), arranging work parties of parish volunteers, and purchase of the required materials;
- for complex repair jobs (e.g., exterior repairs, plumbing, major electrical, wall framing, etc.), contacting contractors for work estimates, appointing the approved contractor, and managing the contractors during project execution;
- stewardship of the church property, including regular lawn cutting, garden weeding, snow ploughing, driveway and parking lot repair, and lighting; selection of contractors and monitoring of their work to ensure the work meets the needs of the parish (in cases where the parish uses contractors to perform these duties);
- monitoring and reducing costs for the upkeep of parish buildings, through energy reduction initiatives, contracting reduced fees for maintenance services, and use of parish volunteers;

- maintenance of the cemetery records, arranging for the sale of new plots, and subcontracting internments; upkeep of the cemetery monuments and plots, including relevelling and repairs;
- maintenance of the parish's capital account, including the planning and execution of capital campaigns, small fund-raising initiatives, annual capital project budgeting for vestry approval, and capital bank account tracking, assisted by the parish bookkeeper; and
- supervision of the parish's rental program, including contracting with renters, income collection, and post-rental inspections.

Duration

The sexton is appointed by the wardens or vestry for a term of one year, renewable each year following. Members of the assets management team volunteer for a term of one year, renewable each year following.

Skills Required

- Strong sense of "ownership" of the parish's buildings and property, with a highly responsible outlook toward their upkeep;
- knowledge of the parish's buildings and property, and the costs of their upkeep;
- ability to negotiate, to balance parishioners' demands for improvements while working within the annual maintenance budget, to contract work to contractors, and to ensure that parish's rental fees are paid;
- knowledge of the contractors available for parish buildings and grounds maintenance, inspections, and capital improvement projects;
- knowledge of requirements for building inspections and the contractors available to perform inspections;
- reasonable knowledge of building improvement costs;
- knowledge of the parish's rentals standards, and the capacity to ensure these are followed by renters;
- knowledge of cemetery recordkeeping, and attention to detail to ensure records are properly maintained;
- knowledge of fund-raising techniques, and the ability to inspire parish members to contribute to the capital fund;
- leadership skills, to recruit volunteers, lead the assets management team, and to chair assets management team meetings;
- volunteer-management skills to inspire the assets management team to carry out their work throughout the year; and

- basic accounting knowledge, to track capital expenses to the annual budget and report variances to the wardens as required.

The Assets Management Team

Maintaining the church building, parish hall, rectory, grounds, and cemetery is too large a task for one parishioner, even in a small parish. This is why the sexton needs to form and lead a team of parishioners focused on stewardship of the parish assets. How large should the assets management team be? Consider the following roles and how responsibilities might be delegated:

Cleaning Coordinator. If the parish has elected to contract out cleaning of the church building and parish hall to a professional cleaner, the team need include only the owner of that business (or a representative). If the parish has a volunteer cleaning team, appoint a team member to be the leader and a member of the assets management team.

Rentals Coordinator. If the parish rents any of its space (either free or for a cost), outsiders will need a contact person. If the parish's space is limited or demand for space is low, the sexton can probably fill this role. (A word of caution: rentals coordination can be surprisingly time-consuming, even in parishes with low demand. Before trying to do this along with everything else, the sexton needs to understand what he or she is getting into.)

Cemetery Coordinator. In most parishes, cemetery recordkeeping is delegated to the parish secretary/bookkeeper, which works well. The secretary/bookkeeper need not attend the assets management team meetings, but should be included in the distribution list of any minutes. The secretary/bookkeeper should report the cemetery fund balance to the sexton each month (based on the bank statement) and any account transactions. The sexton, as the focal point for people wishing to purchase plots, must keep up to date on any changes made. In parishes with large cemeteries, however, a cemetery coordinator may be required, and possibly a board to assist.

Property Maintenance Coordinator. In parishes with little property and/or no parking lot, the sexton may carry responsibility for property maintenance, coordinating a small team of parish volunteers to cut grass, weed gardens, and shovel snow from sidewalks. In parishes that have a parking lot, cemetery, and large parcels of property, the sexton should try to delegate property maintenance to a team leader, who will coordinate a small team of volunteers and may oversee the work of contracted snow removal and lawn cutting services.

Building Maintenance Coordinator. In small parishes where buildings have been well maintained, the sexton may carry responsibility for building maintenance, coordinating a small team of parish volunteers to keep the church and parish hall clean and in good order. If the parish has an active rentals program, buildings with a backlog of repairs, or a contracted cleaner who needs close supervision, the sexton should consider appointing a team member to be building maintenance coordinator.

The maintenance coordinator would

- monitor the contracted cleaner, coordinate with the rentals co-ordinator to ensure post-rental clean-ups are done, and manage the "to-do" list for the maintenance team, arranging maintenance work-parties and obtaining any materials needed;
- schedule building inspections every five years or so, and provide the inspection report to the wardens and sexton;
- monitor the maintenance budget lines to ensure that the mainte-nance team's expenses stay within the approved budget;
- work with the parish's congregation development team (see chapter 4) to plan fund-raising events for maintenance projects whenever necessary; and
- if maintenance work requires a contractor, arrange for the contrac-tor to carry out the work.

Capital Works Coordinator. If the parish has no capital projects pending, this position can be carried out by the parish sexton. Even without active capital projects, the sexton will still need to monitor the capital funds of the parish to ensure that they are accounted for in the correct parish account. If the parish is about to launch a capital project or campaign, the sexton should not attempt to handle this—a project or campaign coordinator should be appointed from the assets management team.

In summary, the assets management team could operate with as few as two or three members (sexton and cleaner/cleaning coordinator), but will more likely require four (sexton, cleaner/cleaning coordinator, building mainte-nance coordinator, and property maintenance coordinator), and possibly six (addition of rentals coordinator and capital works coordinator). Note that the parish volunteers who make up the assets management team may need to assist the volunteer cleaner, property maintenance coordinator, building maintenance coordinator, and capital works coordinator, as the occasion demands.

The team should meet each month. The sexton should chair the meetings. Meetings may be brief and informal—minutes are probably not required. It is important for the sexton to know the general condition of the church buildings and property, so that he or she can advise the wardens and advisory board of improvements underway and upcoming. In turn, parishioners' concerns about completed work or new repair issues should be communicated to the sexton for the team's follow-up.

While capital projects tend to be more formal and self-contained (because of a contracted workforce), the assets management team must still be made aware of project progress, to ensure that all are in sync. For example: the cleaner/cleaning coordinator will have to know where the contractors will be working next, so that needless cleaning is not done.

The sexton needs to provide the assets management team with the year-to-date maintenance budget and actuals, so that all members know the parish's financial status and what funds are available for future work.

The Assets Management Plan

It would be helpful for the assets management team to create an annual assets management plan. This plan would not only guide the team throughout the year, but could be to used to inform the parish of the team's plans. Other team leaders (financial management, outreach development, etc.) would also appreciate having such information, to ensure that their team plans complement it.

The team would meet each year in the fall to plan the ParishWorks for next year. The team would prepare,

- from the outstanding repairs list, a "to-do" list for next year, including cost estimates for each item. The total cost of the "to-dos" for next year should be in line with the maintenance budget for next year;
- estimates for next year's cleaning costs, based on expected increases in supplies and labour rates—the cleaning plan for next year might include plans for shifting some or all of the work from paid cleaners to parish volunteers or renters, thereby reducing parish costs;
- estimates for rentals income for next year—this may include planned rate increases, increased usage, increased marketing costs for the

parish's rental space, and any shifts from free rentals to paying rentals, or vice versa;

- estimates for cemetery income (based on previous year's income) and upkeep cost;
- estimates for groundskeeping costs, including plans to shift from paid groundskeeping to parish volunteers, or vice versa; and
- if any capital projects or fund-raising projects are planned, the team should include the details in the assets management plan for next year. In most cases, capital projects will have their own project plans, so these should be included in next year's assets management plan as an appendix.

When the team has completed the plan to their satisfaction, the sexton should provide copies to the wardens, treasurer, and advisory board for their feedback and approval. The plan would then be included in the vestry package for vestry approval. The sexton should attend vestry to motion adoption of the plan, and to respond to any questions.

The following template has helped other parishes' assets management teams (e.g., building committees) to successfully build their plan. To use this template, read the italicized notes in each section, then replace these notes with the content of your plan. An electronic version in Microsoft Word format may be found on the enclosed CD (see assetsplan.doc).

Assets Management Plan

For

Parish Name

Table of Contents

Program Team/Scope
Program Objectives for 20__
Initiatives
> *Volunteer Management Project*
> *Rentals Improvements Project*
> *Costs Reduction Project*
> *Rectory Study: Retain or Sell*
> *Capital Campaign*

Schedule
Financials/Resources
Program Management Process

Program Team/Scope

The Team. *List the names of members of the assets management team, their phone numbers, and street and e-mail addresses; their role(s) within the program team (e.g., their special interests, talents, passions); and their time available to support the team's work (hours per month).*

Include the organization of the team, if it might prove helpful to readers of the plan.

Program Scope *for the year. List the team's scope boundaries. These may include financial limitations, workload limitations, timing limitations (e.g., certain program events must occur at specific times or dates), the parish's expectations of the team for the year being planned.*

For the assets management team, consider the following scope attributes:

- *the number of volunteers likely available to do the work of the team during the planning year, and the hours per week/month they have available to do the work. Estimate this separately for each of the team's volunteer focal points: cleaning, building repairs, groundskeeping, etc.;*
- *the expense budget lines available to the team for next's year's work. These should include each parish budget line for which the assets management team is responsible: church, hall, and rectory maintenance, rentals advertising, and capital costs;*
- *the income budget lines expected by the parish next year, for which the team is responsible. This should include each income budget line: cemetery income, rentals income, capital project(s) projected income (e.g., additional parishioners, increased rentals, etc.); and*
- *if the capital project is claiming additional income from increased parishioners, the projected number for next year should be included here.*

Program Objectives for 20__

The objectives of the assets management team for next year include the team's and the parish's expectations. The objectives should be specific and measurable. Use objective statements that will help move the parish from where it is today to where it will be by year-end. Include how the changes will be measured at year-end (i.e., How did we do?).

Example of a poor assets management objective: "Increase rentals next year."

Example of a strong assets management objective: "Increase rentals income by 20%, generating an additional $xxx income for the parish. This will be tracked each month by the assets management team, and proactive marketing activities carried out to ensure that the targets are met."

For each objective, note those that are interdependent, and how. Example: maybe to start a rentals marketing campaign, the assets management team must first complete a premises improvements project or revise the rentals agreement. Also note if the objective needs to be accomplished at a particular time for proper measurement to start. In the case of the rentals initiative, the premises improvements should be complete by year-end in order for the marketing effort to kick in and to ensure maximum income starting in January of the year being measured.

When the list of objectives is drawn up, inspect the objectives carefully: are they realistic for next year? Can all the objectives be accomplished, given the resources available on the team, the extra volunteers available in the parish, the parish's ability to absorb the changes proposed, and the parish budget lines available? Do any of the objectives depend on the successes of another program team? If so, are they in sync with yours? Example: if the team plans to switch groundskeeping from a contractor to a volunteer team of eight in the spring, and the team learns that the outreach development team is planning a major campaign that will require twelve volunteers for the visitations from April to June, one of the teams may have to reschedule or move the project to the following year.

It is better to drop objectives at the outset, and have the team meet a reduced set, than to overextend the team and have them fail. Remember, there is always next year. Still, the team needs to set objectives that "stretch" them—this is how teams grow and learn.

Here are some sample assets management objectives for the team's consideration:

1. *To reduce cleaning costs for the church and parish hall by 50% next year ($10,000), by using a volunteer team to do the weekly light cleaning.*

2. *To reduce utilities costs for the church and rectory by 30% next year ($30,000), by installing programmed thermostats, resealing all windows and doors, replacing the church doors with insulated doors, and installing space heaters in the rector's office.*

3. *To improve the retention rate of parishioners, by improving the appearance of the church entrance through replastering and repainting.*

4. To reduce the groundskeeping costs for the church and parish hall by 60% next year ($10,000), by using a volunteer team to do the weekly lawn cutting, weeding, and sidewalk snow removal, using a contractor only for parking lot snow removal.

Initiatives

List the program initiatives for the year that will address the objectives. For each, include

- **what** the initiative is, which objectives it will address, and a description of the development work required to complete it;
- **who** will develop the initiative, including the number of volunteers needed in addition to the assets management team members;
- **when** the development work must be completed, related to when the initiative is to be provided to the parish; and
- **how** and **when** the program team will measure the initiative's success. (e.g., how and when the team will recalculate the cleaning costs, groundskeeping costs, utilities costs, and so on, to confirm that the objectives were met).

Note any initiative prerequisites or assumptions, and any interdependencies of other program teams' initiatives.

Schedule

Two schedules are needed in the assets management plan:

1. A **schedule of upcoming assets management parish events** (fund-raisers, spring clean-ups, repair work parties, capital campaign launches, etc.), which should be reflected in the parish calendar, in the parish's service bulletins, newsletters, and web site, so that parishioners can plan their attendance accordingly.

2. An **initiatives development schedule** that includes the resources and development time required for each parish event (e.g., capital campaign launches) or target milestones (e.g., "rental agreements revised" or "cleaning team recruited," etc.). This schedule will be used by the assets management team to ensure adequate preparation for the published parish events and planned milestones.

 When the assets management team meets each month, they can use the development schedule to determine whether there are any problems with the planned development work and then take corrective action, if required (e.g., enlisting more people to help prepare, moving event dates, etc.).

Financials/Resources

Financials

With respect to the planned assets management initiatives, the team needs to summarize the costs of the program for the year ahead (advertising costs, event costs, contractor costs, materials costs, etc.) and indicate when the expenses are expected to be incurred. This way, the treasurer will be able to include these costs in the parish's budget for the upcoming year, under the appropriate expense lines. When approved by vestry, the budget line-items can be used by the assets management team, as needed.

In addition, the estimated additional annual parish income from the team's improvement initiatives (increased number of parishioners, rentals, contracting cost reductions, etc.) should be summarized, and the information passed to the treasurer for inclusion in the upcoming year's budget.

If the team discovers significant variances between the actual costs and income versus those planned in the parish budget (plus or minus), the team should advise the treasurer. A negative variance may be covered by a contingency budget line, or the treasurer may have to raise the matter with the wardens for resolution.

Resources

The team should summarize the monthly volunteer resources and skills required (beyond those of the team) to support the projects. The parish's volunteer coordinator will use this information to recruit the appropriate volunteers.

When all parish program teams circulate their completed plans at the start of the year, the volunteer coordinator may advise the assets management team that the required resources may not be available in the numbers or at the time planned. In these cases, the team will need to revise the plan.

Program Management Process

The assets management plan needs to lay out how the team's progress will be monitored throughout the year. Some best practices for the team's consideration follow:

1. Team Meetings
The team should meet monthly (same time each month) to review planned activities, past and future. The team meeting should be chaired by the sexton. Minutes are not necessary, but the sexton will need to keep track of commitments made during the meeting.

for follow-up purposes. The team should bring copies of their development schedule and events calendar with them to each meeting.

Team meetings should be issue-focused (e.g., issues with the development schedule/events calendar), not focused on brainstorming solutions. The meetings may then be conducted within one to one and a-half hours.

Here is a suggested agenda:

- How has the team been doing since the last meeting? Achievements should be celebrated. Problems should be learned from and used to modify subsequent events as appropriate, or used when preparing next year's plan.
- What's next? Who is working on what, according to the development schedule? How is it going? Will we be ready for the event(s)? If not, what needs to be done? Are there any cost variances?
- Are there any ideas for changes to the plan? Any new events needed but not included? If so, how might they be resourced? Are there any events that should be cancelled?

2. Program Reporting

The sexton (or designate) should report the team's status to the wardens and advisory board each month, ideally following the team's own monthly meeting if possible. The sexton may wish to schedule the team's monthly meeting to be a week or so ahead of the advisory board's meeting, so that the board receives up-to-date information.

Team reports may be quite brief (e.g., one-half to one page in length). The program update for the wardens and the advisory board should include events since the last update and results, upcoming development work and issues, and issues for the wardens' or board's action, if any.

The assets management report might be tabled only for the advisory board's information. Also, it is not necessary for the sexton to attend the board's meeting, unless there are issues for the wardens' or board's action.

In addition to the advisory board's monthly report, the sexton should prepare an annual assets management report for vestry that describes the work of the assets management team in the year ending, lessons learned, and plans for the upcoming year. The sexton should attend, in case there are questions from the vestry on the program.

3. Parish Surveys

Before the team meets to develop their plan for the upcoming year, the team should ask the parish what they thought of the assets management work this year (cleanliness of the buildings and grounds, repairs made, costs reduced, income increased, etc.). What was good? What was not so good? What was missing?

The team should use the same guidelines in the parish survey (see chapter 4) when preparing a survey of the team's work (e.g., avoidance of tick boxes, use of pot-lucks, etc.).

The team should use the feedback to plan next year's program.

Application to Your Parish

For small parishes with low-maintenance buildings and property, and with no active rentals program or capital projects on the horizon, the parish sexton role might be filled by one of the wardens (with the other warden focusing on the financial management of the parish). Even in the smallest parishes, however, assuming this amount of responsibility will pretty much rule out the warden's availability for other parish work. If the parish is looking to the same warden to lead in other ways (congregation development, outreach development, worship development, etc.), ideally the two wardens should find a parishioner to volunteer as parish sexton. In these cases, an excellent choice might be one of the deputy wardens. Being the parish sexton for a year or so will give a deputy warden the necessary knowledge and experience for when they become a warden.

For small, low-maintenance parishes, the sexton will still need a small team of volunteers to help with cleaning and repairs to the church buildings, and property maintenance. If the parish wishes to use volunteers to handle such work, the sexton should consider a rotation system to avoid volunteer burnout. Most volunteers work best in twosomes. Four teams of two (eight total) would probably be the minimum needed to spread the work—two teams of two to carry out property maintenance (grass cutting, weeding, shoveling snow) on alternate months throughout the year, and two teams of two to clean and do building repairs on alternate months throughout the year.

For large parishes, and for small parishes that require lots of ongoing repairs or capital projects, or operate an active rentals program, the assets management team structure described on pages 151–152 works best.

What's first? For starters, the leadership team should make sure there are no potential legal issues for the parish. The following proactive assets management steps apply to all parishes:

1. Appointment of a sexton and assets management team should be the wardens' first priority. (Sometimes one of the wardens will assume the role of sexton, though this is inadvisable.)

2. Once formed, the team should immediately schedule an inspection if five or more years have passed since the last one. After the inspection has been carried out, any potential liabilities that pose a danger to parishioners and renters (e.g., collapsing roof, sinking property, etc.) must be resolved by the team immediately, even if the parish has to borrow from its banker to get the work done.

3. The team should then review the parish's rental agreement—check that it includes proper provisions for renter insurance coverage and covers responsibilities for damages. If not, the agreement should be revised immediately (with help from the diocese), and re-executed by the current renters. These outstanding liabilities could bankrupt the parish, should accidents occur.

4. The team should then secure a copy of the church property deed and survey from the town or diocesan office to ensure the parish knows its responsibilities. For example, if there are any easements on parish property, the wardens should be aware of these.

5. Next, the team should review the parish bookkeeping to ensure that parish operating income and expenses are segregated from capital. If not, this should be arranged as soon as possible, and the diocesan assessment reviewed in light of these accounting changes.

6. Next, the team should review the cemetery records to ensure that records are up to date, and that the cemetery trust funds are segregated and accounted for.

With the legal and accounting issues resolved, the assets management team should then focus on how the parish assets are currently managed, looking for ways to reduce costs or improve the work being done:

7. Review the cleaning done by contracted staff. Is it being done properly? Is the contract specific? (If not, the team should update it, and get it re-signed.) Can the "regular" or light cleaning handled by the contractor be done by a volunteer team, with the contractor doing heavy cleaning?

8. Review the groundskeeping done by contracted staff. Is it being done properly? Is the contract specific? (If not, the team should update it, and get it re-signed.) Can the contractor be replaced by a volunteer team, augmented with heavy snowploughing by the contractor?

9. Review the parish's maintenance costs (electrical, heating/AC), and set up a series of projects to reduce costs (through better window and door seals, improved insulation, timed thermostats, etc.).

Lastly, the team should consider:

10. Future use of the parish rectory.

11. Capital projects (e.g., building an addition onto the parish hall, new washrooms, new meeting rooms, etc.).

Chapter 10

Staff Management

Chapter 9 discussed some ways to recruit and motivate parish volunteers. Many parishes, however, have staff who are paid, either through honorariums or salaries. These positions need to be managed by the parish leadership team in a different manner than volunteers.

Paid positions should be documented through detailed position descriptions. These must include the reporting relationships of the position, its term, criteria for performance evaluations, and detailed responsibilities. While volunteers can work into positions in the parish, paid staff cannot—their roles must be predefined by their managers (the wardens).

Also, every paid staff member of the parish must have a formal performance appraisal each year. These should be carried out in the same as any other performance appraisal in the secular world, comparing the person's work over the last 12 months to their responsibilities as outlined in the position description. Feedback from the parish will also be a factor in evaluating the person's performance. The results of the review should be documented and signed by both the staff member and their manager (usually one of the wardens).

Carrying out an interim performance appraisal every six months is also advisable to provide informal feedback, which the staff person might use to improve before their annual review. The interim appraisal need not be documented. If the wardens do not have experience in staff management, they will need to find a parishioner who does and ask for pointers about carrying out staff reviews.

Parish Members versus Non-Member Staff

Some paid parish staff are also members of the parish—they worship with other parishioners and donate to the parish's operation, outreach causes, and capital projects. As such, the parish leadership team will need to treat parish members who are also paid staff in a unique way. First, the person to whom the staff member reports (usually a warden) must clarify the difference between the person as a parishioner and a staff member. Although the person is valued on both counts, a different relationship is involved in each case. While the wardens are there to serve the parish and the interests of the parishioners (including the person in question), thereby "working for" the parishioners, paid staff of the parish work for the parish and report to the wardens. These differences need to be made clear at the outset. If the person being hired into the position cannot keep the two relationships straight day by day, they should not be considered for the position. This may be best illustrated to the staff person/parishioner by example:

Say the parish secretary, a member of the parish, is paid an honorarium by the parish to carry out secretarial tasks for the parish. In this role he or she reports to the wardens. What happens when the secretary is asked to include a controversial report in the parish newsletter? As a member of the parish, the person may (and can) object to the report. As parish secretary, however, they were asked by the wardens to include the report in the parish newsletter. The person must be able to understand when secretarial responsibilities take precedence over their right as a parishioner to object. If the person refuses to include the report in the newsletter, they are the wrong person for the job.

Here is another example (involving the same person): in the vestry meeting a point is raised to discuss the secretary's honorarium. Although the secretary is entitled to be present at vestry and to vote on the motion, he or she must recognize the potential for a conflict of interest and leave the meeting during this discussion. Again, if the person does not understand the dual relationship they have with the parish, they are wrong for the job.

Non-member staff people are much easier to manage in this context—they treat the parish as they would any other employer, and the wardens can treat them as they would any other employee in the secular world.

Honorariums versus Salaries

Managing parish staff paid by honorariums is quite different from managing those paid by salary. Honorariums are given to people in recognition that they should be compensated in some way for their work. Honorariums usually amount to a fraction of what people would normally be paid. For example, the parish secretary may put in 50 hours per month in the parish office to carry out certain responsibilities, but receive an annual honorarium of $3,000. This would equal about $5.00 per hour, which would not nearly compensate their time and efforts. Often parishes simply cannot pay full salaries. Parish staff will offer their time and effort because they care for the church and consider the job part of their ministry.

In this context, the wardens will need to treat such parish staff as they would a parishioner in some ways: acknowledging and supporting their good works for the parish. The honorarium is a way for the parish to say thank you for their efforts. There is no commitment on the part of the parish to provide the honorarium, year by year. At the beginning of each year, the wardens decide on the honorarium (or not) and the amount to be paid, based on the parish's ability to pay and the wardens' assessment of what is an appropriate thank-you amount. In most cases, annual honorariums are paid out monthly, as (quite often) the person becomes somewhat dependent on it, month by month. Honorarium positions frequently are offered to parishioners who may be struggling financially. In this way, the parish can help out in some small way as an outreach effort.

Salaried staff arrangements are much more straightforward—the hourly rate is agreed beforehand, based on the responsibilities and skills required to carry out the job. Some form of time-keeping is instituted, and the salary amount is calculated by the wardens and paid out each month. In some cases, the diocese will carry out the taxation, pension, and payroll accounting processes for the parish, and pay the salaried staff member directly, issuing the required tax forms at year-end. In the past, some parishes used honorariums to pay what would otherwise be salaried staff, in order to get around taxation accounting workloads, and pension and other benefits costs. The Canada Revenue Agency is now monitoring churches, watching for this practice.

Generally honorariums are still appropriate as thank-yous for parish volunteers doing considerable work for the parish (such as parish secretaries in many small- to medium-sized parishes). When the workload significantly increases, or the duties of the staff person become onerous, it's probably time to transfer the staff person to a salary. This guideline may also be applied to paid organists and choir directors—if the number of choir practices and services increase, or if the parish adds a junior choir to the organist's workload, it may be time to switch from an honorarium to salary. When in doubt, the wardens should contact the diocesan office for direction.

Motivating Parish Staff

Regardless of whether parish staff are members of the parish or not, or paid by honorarium or salary, it is up to the wardens to ensure that all staff are properly trained and supported by the parish leaders to whom they report, and that they are motivated and feel valued by the parish.

Unfortunately, often paid staff members are neglected. "We pay them to do the work," some might think. "What more do we need to do?" Paid staff are only human. They need to feel they are doing a good job, and receive feedback to help them improve.

In cases where the wardens do not have the time or skills to manage staff, they must transfer the management responsibility to other parish leaders who do. For example, if the parish secretary's work involves mainly book-keeping, the secretary could report directly to the parish treasurer, who may have the knowledge and skills to properly train, support, and motivate staff. The parish organist/choir director could report to the rector, for the same reasons. The parish cleaner could report to the parish sexton, and so on. However, while the wardens may delegate their responsibility for managing parish staff, ultimately they are still responsible, through the canons. They should be present during staff performance reviews, negotiate salary rates with staff, and set honorariums accordingly.

If the parish has paid staff, someone from the leadership team must be responsible for properly managing these resources. Your diocesan office may be able to help if management training is necessary.

Chapter 11

Financial Management

We have described effective ParishWorks involving the parish's leadership team, the parish's members, its volunteers and staff, its community and outreach recipients, its worship program, and its buildings and property. One important aspect of the parish's works remains: financial management.

In many cases, the parish leadership team has neither the background nor the training required to manage the parish's books: the work is similar to that of a chief financial officer for a small business. These experience and training gaps often lead parishes to neglect their financial management responsibilities, resulting in chaos as the parish tries to reconcile its books and to prepare proper financial reports for its members, the diocese, and the government.

To determine any gaps in your parish's financial management processes, it may be helpful for the parish leadership team to complete the following questionnaire, which may also be found on the enclosed CD in Microsoft Word format (see finquiz.doc):

Financial Management Questionnaire

1. Does the parish have a well-understood chart of accounts with easy to understand income and expense categories?   ____ Yes   ____No

2. Does the parish segregate its operating income and expenses from its capital transactions and its outreach donations? ____ Yes   ____No

3. Has the parish automated its bookkeeping, and if so, is the bookkeeping software easy to use?   ____ Yes   ____No

4. Does the treasurer report monthly income and expense transactions and account balances to the wardens and advisory board?
____ Yes   ____No

5. Does the parish track monthly income and expenses to its annual budget, and if so, are variances dealt with? _____ Yes _____No

6. Does the parish understand the basis for its diocesan assessment, and ensure that it is assessed only on the amounts applicable? _____ Yes _____No

7. Does the parish track and submit for GST refunds? _____ Yes _____No

8. Does the parish set aside a contingency amount each year for unforeseen expenses? _____ Yes _____No

9. Does the parish use two people to handle the cash and authorize all financial transactions (dual controls), and are audit trails clear and procedures documented? _____ Yes _____No

10. Does the parish have a three-year budget? _____ Yes _____No

11. Does the parish have a proactive cost-reduction program in place? _____ Yes _____No

12. Does the parish carry out an annual stewardship program? _____ Yes _____No

---

If the responses include two or more Nos, the parish's financial management processes need some revision. Read the entire chapter, then convene a meeting with the parish bookkeeper, auditor, treasurer, sexton, and wardens to set a plan to fill any gaps in the parish's financial management practices.

Chart of Accounts

The first step in building a good financial foundation for the parish is the proper set-up of its accounts structure. If the parish's books are not set up properly and stable, managing them will be very difficult, and the parish could soon get into serious trouble. Diocesan standards for a parish's chart of accounts may vary, so check with your diocesan office to verify that your accounts are set up in the best way. In most cases, however, dioceses tend to follow this standard:

1. *Operating (or "General") account*—used for the day-to-day operation of the parish; usually matches the parish's current account at their bank. For each payment out of the operating account, cheques are written on the corresponding current account for general expenses, and pre-authorized payments are set up for recurring payments. The operating account transactions and balances are reconciled with the current account each month. All payments out of the operating account require receipts for payment, and all payments require dual authorization. Income is from the parish's weekly service collection and other general donations. All income transactions posted into the account require dual authorization. The operating account includes a petty cash facility for the rector's discretionary fund and other small expenses of the parish. A working float is kept in the parish's current account at their bank, with excess funds invested in short- or long-term guaranteed instruments, such as money market accounts, guaranteed investment certificates, or other term deposits.

2. *Capital account*—used for capital works of the parish (see chapter 9, Capital Works); often matched by a segregated bank account, from which cheques can be written or from which transfers to the operating account can be made for capital payments. Where the capital account is matched to a segregated bank account, the capital account's transactions and balances are reconciled to the bank account each month. All transactions are subject to the same controls as for the operating account. Income is from donations, bequests, and in-memoriums specifically designated for capital works. Designated funds for specific capital works are kept as separate sub-ledgers. Funds are invested in short- or long-term guaranteed instruments, such as money market accounts, guaranteed investment certificates, or other term deposits.

3. *Outreach account*—used for outreach donations of the parish; often matched by a segregated bank account on which cheques can be written or from which transfers to the operating account can be made for outreach contributions (see chapter 8). Where the outreach account is matched to a segregated bank account, the outreach account's transactions and balances are reconciled to the bank account each month. All transactions are subject to the same controls as for the operating account. Income is from donations for outreach programs. Designated donations for specific outreach programs are kept as separate sub-ledgers. Funds are not invested, since the account runs at or near a zero balance (as outreach donations are distributed as soon as possible after collection).

4. *Cemetery account*—used for proceeds from plot purchases and payments for internments and general maintenance (see chapter 9); matched by a segregated bank account on which cheques can be written or from which transfers to the operating account can be made for cemetery maintenance payments (e.g., fencing and monument repairs, internments). The cemetery account's transactions and balances are reconciled to the bank account each month. All transactions are subject to the same controls as for the operating account. A small float is maintained in the account; excess balances are invested in short- or long-term guaranteed instruments, such as money market accounts, guaranteed investment certificates, or other term deposits.

Note: in some provinces and dioceses, the principal funds from cemetery plot sales need to be held in a trust account, often at the diocesan level. The interest on the principal balance in the trust account is used by the parish for cemetery upkeep. Check with your diocesan office if you are not clear on the accounting requirements for your cemetery funds.

Besides these four accounts, the parish may have requirements for additional accounts. For example, if the parish is operating a raffle, some provinces require the parish to create a separate accounting of the ticket sales and the disposition of the proceeds. It is best to do this in a separate account. When in doubt, however, contact your diocesan chief financial officer to check that the accounting is set up correctly. Note that the parish should maintain the minimum number of accounts required to properly control their different types of financial accounting. The more accounts the parish operates, the more work will be required to manage them by the parish bookkeeper. If the bookkeeper is a volunteer position, the parish leadership team needs to ensure that the accounting tasks are kept as simple as possible. If the bookkeeper is a paid position, the same applies—if the parish's account structure is more complex than needed, the parish is likely wasting the bookkeeper's time (and the parish's money).

While it is up to the parish to decide if they wish to match each parish account with bank accounts, the parish leadership team should think about the impact on the bookkeeper's work and the reliability of the reconciliations and financial reporting. If parish accounts are matched by bank accounts, monthly reconciliation of the bank statement will be fairly simple. If the parish attempts to minimize their banking fees by consolidating all transactions (operating, capital, and outreach) into one bank account, reconciliation will be more difficult, time-consuming, and error-prone.

While some parishes have attempted to include suspense accounting in their systems (i.e., accounts receivable and payable), most avoid doing this. It is best to operate as simply as possible on an actual accounting basis.

Likewise, some parishes have attempted to include accruals in their accounting systems, in order to level expenditures over the year. Some have also attempted to include capital depreciation. While these practices are beneficial for businesses, it is best to keep the parish's accounting methods as simple as possible—actual accounting seems to work best.

Regardless of the parish's account structure, once the system has been set up and proven itself to work, it should not be changed unless absolutely necessary. Changing the structure midstream will cause countless problems in the parish's records and the parish office. If it must be changed, wait until the beginning of a new accounting year, so that the books can be closed on the old structure and started fresh with the new structure, avoiding the need to re-enter transactions, re-reconcile accounts and re-file paper copies.

Income/Expense Categories

Within each parish account, transactions are given income and expense categories. Example: cash given as part of the Sunday collection can be to-talled each Sunday and credited to the operating account under the income category, Open Donations. If income is properly categorized, the wardens can easily see how much of the parish income is derived from cash donations each Sunday, and for the year. If income and expense categories are set up properly, they can be used to help the parish monitor its financial position throughout the year, and also simplify the set-up of next year's budget. Proper income and expense categories are also needed to allow the parish to correctly report its financial position to the diocese each year, as well as to the Canada Revenue Agency.

Parishes experience the most bookkeeping problems in setting up income and expense categories. Often parishes do not have enough categories to adequately group their financial transactions. In these cases, they cannot determine where their funds are going or where their income coming from. In the other extreme, some parishes have created so many categories that identifying each transaction with the correct category is a major piece of work. Also, with too many categories, the reports from the treasurer cannot be easily understood by the wardens, advisory board, and vestry.

While it is up to the parish to decide which categories make most sense to them, the following income/expense categories structure seems to work best. An electronic version in Microsoft Word format may be found on the enclosed CD (see categories.doc). The category numbering system used in this example is simply for reference—it need not be used by the parish. Also, the notes for each category/sub-category are for explanation/bookkeeper training only—they are not part of the income/expense category structure.

Income/Expense Categories

Operating Account

Income Categories

1. *Donations*—from parishioners. Sub-categories:

> 1.1 *Open*—cash donations from weekly collections, coffee hour donations, etc. All donations where the source cannot be identified.
>
> 1.2 *Envelopes*—cash or cheque donations where the parish's numbered envelope sets have been used. These will match the envelope secretary's records, and donors will receive tax receipts at year-end.
>
> 1.3 *PAP*—pre-authorized payment donations, as reported by the parish's bank. Donors will receive tax receipts at year-end.
>
> 1.4 *Special*—cash or cheque donations where the donor can be identified. This sub-category is used for donations from non-parishioners (through weddings, christenings, funerals, business donations, etc.). Donors will receive tax receipts at year-end.

2. *In-Memoriums and Bequests*—donations from estates, families, etc. Most dioceses omit this income from the parish's assessment, and so these donations normally are kept separate—by isolating the amounts, the parish's annual return will be easier to complete. Also, most parishes cannot budget for these donations—by isolating in-memorium donations and bequests, tracking will be clearer. Many parishes use these types of donations for their capital works. If such is the case, this category should not be included in the parish's operating account—rather, include it in the capital account (see page 178, Capital Account). Sub-categories:

> 2.1 *In-Memoriums*—donations that have a clear definition on the paying instrument (cheque) or letter of instruction . Often these donations have a designation that must be honoured by the parish. For example, if the donation is intended for "worship" (e.g., purchase of new hymn books), it must be expensed, or accounted for, in the proper category. If the in-memorium donation is designated for capital works (e.g., new organ or new church), it should not be posted here—rather, post it into the capital account. If the in-memorium donation is to be used for "the

needy" or "outreach," it should not be posted here—rather, post it into the outreach account.

2.2 *Bequests*—donations from an estate. In these cases, the treasurer needs to alert the wardens, as a copy of the will must be obtained for the parish. Also, the parish needs to know if the funds are designated (specified in the will). If designated, the income needs to be expensed to the proper category (as with in-memoriums) and to the proper account.

3. *Fund-Raising*—net income from parish fund-raising events where the proceeds are directed to the operating account. Event costs, booked to the fund-raising expense category (see 26. Fund-Raising Costs below), are first offset (as credits) by the amount of income raised. Income above the expenses is booked here.

For example: a parish dance has booked to the fund-raising expense category a pre-event cost of $1,000, say, for the DJ and refreshments. The event later makes $2,000. One thousand dollars is then booked to the fund-raising expense category (which offsets the pre-event cost), and the remaining net $1,000 is posted to this category.

Note: fund-raising events held to fund outreach programs or for capital works should be posted to the capital or outreach accounts, not here.

The parish may wish to create sub-categories for any large, repeating fund-raisers, in order to compare them with previous years' event income. Sub-categories might include (for example only):

3.1 *Bazaar*—all proceeds from the parish's annual event. This may involve a range of income transactions (e.g., bake table, rummage table, sidewalk lunch, street dance, etc.) from several teams.

3.2 *Community Fall Fair*—all proceeds from the parish's booth(s) at the fair.

3.3 *Other*—small fund-raising projects that need not be tracked individually.

4. *Rentals*—income from renters, where the rental amount is not being made as a donation to the parish. In the latter cases (where the parish does not charge the renter a rental fee, but the renter decides to give the parish a donation anyway) this income should be booked under 1.4 Donations—Special, and a tax receipt issued.

The parish may wish to create sub-categories for large, ongoing renters, or for type of rental (weddings, funerals, etc.), to help the sexton and wardens analyze the rental income in more detail, year over year. (Note: if a parish receives a large percentage of its operating income from only one or two key renters, they may have a potential risk on their hands, should one or both decide to rent elsewhere. The parish might consider trying to find additional renters to mitigate this possibility.)

Sub-categories could also help the sexton and rentals coordinator focus the parish's advertising on the type of renters that have been attracted to the parish's facilities.

5. *GST Rebates*—payments received from the Canada Revenue Agency are recorded here. These are kept separate, as diocesan assessments do not include these amounts.

6. *Interest Income*—from the bank or diocese (e.g., current account balance interest, interest from term deposits for the operating account, interest payments from the diocese on trust fund investments for the parish's operating account, other sources). Note: interest payments from capital investments should not be booked here—they belong in the capital account. If the parish has ongoing significant interest income from the diocese and/or the parish's bank, the parish may wish to use sub-categories to isolate them. This would make reconciliation to the bank and diocesan statements easier for the bookkeeper.

7. *Other Income*—income that cannot be categorized as above. Caution: "Other" accounting categories can be black holes for transactions that have not been properly categorized, and therefore will mess up the books if they are incorrectly posted here. To avoid this, make sure that all transactions going into Other categories are approved by the treasurer before they are posted.

Expense Categories
The category numbers below jump ahead, to allow for additional income categories—this makes renumbering categories unnecessary when new ones are created.

20. *Worship*—includes all expenses related to worship services. This expense category would be equivalent to the worship development team's budget/expenses for the year (see chapter 7). Worship expenses are usually exempt from the diocesan assessment, and so are segregated in order to make preparing the parish return easier. Sub-categories:

20.1 *Rector*—includes all expenses for the parish rector. Some parishes further segregate the rector's costs (e.g., stipend, pension, travel, professional development, benefits). In these cases, the sub-categories should be titled Rector: Stipend, Rector: Travel, etc.), so that the accounting system does not become a three-level system, which may be too complex for most parish bookkeepers to manage.

20.2 *Relief Clergy*—includes all expenses for priests filling in for the rector while away.

20.3 *Curate*—includes all expenses for the parish's curate (if applicable). Sub-categories might follow for all paid ministerial resources, such as assistant pastors, deacons, etc.

20.4 *Organist/Choir Director*—includes the honorarium/salary paid to the organist and choir director.

20.5 *Relief Organist*—includes all expenses for the organist filling in for the parish's usual organist/choir director while away.

20.6 *Choir Music*—expenses for music reproductions, royalties, photocopies, etc.

20.7 *Church School Supplies*—expenses for course materials reproduction, books, crafts, etc., for both the Sunday school and youth group.

20.8 *Worship Supplies*—expenses associated with the worship services, such as altar flowers, wine, Sunday bulletins, candles, etc.

20.9 *Adult Education*—expenses for Bible study groups, courses, etc., for parishioners. Includes travel expenses, if any, and instructor fees.

21. *Staff*—costs for parish staff paid on an hourly basis (requiring payroll deductions, etc.) or by honorariums. Parishes may want to include sub-categories for each paid staff position. For example:

21.1 *Parish Cleaner*—a parish volunteer, not a contractor. Cleaning contractor costs are booked to building maintenance—see 23. Property below.

21.2 *Secretary/Bookkeeper*

If the parish has only one paid staff position, simply change the category title to reflect this (i.e., change Staff to Secretary/Bookkeeper).

22. *Congregation Development*—costs associated with fellowship events, parish advertising, printing for welcome kits, posters, web site hosting, etc. This expense category would be equivalent to the congregation development team's budget/expenses for the year. The parish may wish to

use sub-categories to track advertising expenses and fellowship event costs separately. Note: fund-raising event costs should not be booked here. They belong in the fund-raising expense category (see 26. Fund-Raising Costs below). Fellowship event costs, which should not be considered fund-raisers, do not normally have income. If donations do come in during fellowship events, they can be booked to 1.1 Donations—Open.

23. *Property*—expenses for maintenance of parish buildings and grounds. This expense category would be equivalent to the assets management team's budget/expenses for the year. The parish may wish to use sub-categories to track the types of expenses by building, to determine the results of their cost-reduction programs. Example sub-categories:

23.1 *Church/Parish Hall: Water*—efforts to conserve may be reflected in the expense trends for this sub-category.

23.2 *Church/Parish Hall: Heating/AC*—gas or oil heating and air conditioning costs. Efforts by the assets management team to reduce these should be visible month by month.

23.3 *Church/Parish Hall: Hydro*—as above, efforts to conserve would be reflected in this sub-category, throughout the year.

23.4 *Church/Parish Hall: Cleaning*—contracted cleaners costs. Efforts to use renters and parish volunteers to reduce contracting cleaning costs would be apparent here.

23.5 *Church/Parish Hall: Groundskeeping*—contracted groundskeepers costs. Efforts to use parish volunteers to reduce contracting costs would show here. Note: if the parish has a cemetery adjacent to the church/parish hall/grounds, the sexton and the assets management team will need to differentiate groundskeeping costs for the cemetery grounds (which should be funded out of the cemetery account, and which is omitted from the diocesan assessment) and those for the church/parish hall. If the expenses are combined for both, the sexton should allocate them, based on the relative size of each. Or, if the amounts are small enough to make this unnecessary, simply include both in one or other of the accounts.

23.6 *Church/Parish Hall: Repairs*—non-capital costs for building repairs (e.g., resurfacing the parking lot, repointing brickwork, upgrading electrical services, etc.).

23.7 *Rectory: Water*—same as 23.1, for the rectory.

23.8 *Rectory: Heating/AC*—same as 23.2, for the rectory.

23.9 *Rectory: Hydro*—same as 23.3, for the rectory.

23.10 *Rectory: Taxes*—municipal taxes paid on the rectory property.

23.11 *Rectory: Telephone*—charges for the rectory telephone.

23.12 *Rectory: Repairs*—same as 23.6, for the rectory.

23.13 *Insurance*—premium fees for the buildings and property.

23.14 *Other*—property expenses that do not fit the above sub-categories. Note: booking expenses to Other categories can create problems. See 7. Other Income for suggested controls.

24. *Administration*—expenses associated with the parish office. The parish may want to break these down by type of expense. Example sub-categories:

24.1 *Equipment*—repairs, metered usage costs, rental fees, software up-grades. The financial management team would look at these figures to consider reduction by leasing, renting, or purchasing. Note: this category should **not** be used to post the purchase of new equipment/software for the parish. These are capital expenses, and should be expensed out of the capital account.

24.2 *Stationery*—printer ink, toner, office supplies, etc. Again, the financial management team would look for ways to reduce these costs through e-mail, parish web site content, etc. Note: paper and copying expenses related to the Sunday bulletin, and all materials for the parish's worship program, should **not** be expensed here—post these expenses to sub-category 20.8 Worship Supplies. Worship costs are not part of the diocesan assessment.

24.3 *Telephone*—charges for the parish office phone/Internet access. If charges for hosting the parish's web site are included in the telephone bill, these should be split out and posted to category 22. Congregation Development. The financial management team would look for ways to minimize the parish's telephone costs, through e-mail, service bundling, alternate carriers, etc.

24.4 *Postage*—again, the financial management team would look to e-mail and pre-authorized payments/online banking to reduce these costs.

24.5 *Other*—parish administration costs that do not fit the above sub-categories. See 7. Other Income for suggested controls on posting expenses to Other sub-categories.

25. *Financing Costs*—banking fees and interest charges to carry the parish's debts. Suggested sub-categories:

25.1 *Mortgage Interest*—the interest portion of each mortgage payment (usually monthly).

25.2 *Loan Interest*—the interest portion of each month's line of credit or other loans with the parish's bank, their diocese, or other lenders.

25.3 *Banking Fees*—for the operating account, including cheques, transaction fees, online banking service fees, etc. Some parishes debit this sub-category for banking fees associated with all parish accounts, including the capital, outreach, and cemetery bank accounts, as they do not want banking fees to reduce the donations made for capital works and outreach programs. This is quite appropriate.

26. *Fund-Raising Costs*—for expenses related to large-scale fund-raisers. For big fund-raisers, often it is more convenient for organizers to draw advances to cover pre-event costs, rather than using personal funds and being reimbursed later. All advances should be debited from this category. Once the event is over, advanced costs are reversed through a credit transaction, and the net proceeds are posted to category 3. Fund-Raising. Since advances for fund-raising costs are short-term, sub-categories are not required. This expense category should usually net to zero.

Capital Account

As noted in chapter 9, the parish's capital account could be managed by the sexton and the assets management team. While all payments would still need the wardens' approval and their signatures on all cheques paid out of the account (in accordance with the canons), the assets management team could plan campaigns to replenish the account and fund capital projects.

The category numbers below jump ahead, to allow for additional expense categories in the operating account—this makes renumbering categories unnecessary when new ones are created.

Income Categories

40. *Donations*—donations from all sources, designated for capital works. If the parish decides all bequests and in-memorium donations will be credited to their capital account, sub-categories 2.1 and 2.2 would be omitted from the operating account and would be included here (40.2 and 40.3). Also, designated donations will need to be segregated to ensure that those funds are kept separate. For example, capital donations specified for the purchase of a new organ would need a donations sub-category, Organ Fund. Example sub-categories:

40.1 *Undesignated*—capital donations that have no designated use. The sexton and the assets management team would propose uses for these funds, based on parish priorities.

40.2 *In-Memoriums*—refer to sub-category 2.1, above.

40.3 *Bequests*—refer to sub-category 2.2, above.

41. *Interest Income*—interest earned on capital account balances and term deposits. Includes any interest on capital funds held in trust by the parish, diocese (for the parish), or any other source. Some parishes use capital interest to help cover operating expenses. In these cases, the interest payments would be transferred to the operating account (category 6. Interest Income). Otherwise, the interest income is included in the capital account to help cover the parish's capital works. Note: some bequests will stipulate that not only the principal amount, but also the interest earned from it, should be designated for a particular parish expense. Before the parish assumes they can move capital interest payments to their operating account (or expense it on a capital work of their choice), the wardens must check the particulars of the associated bequest.

Expense Categories

The category numbers below jump ahead, to allow for additional income categories—this makes renumbering categories unnecessary when new ones are created.

50. *Capital Payments*—capital expenses. If the parish has multiple capital works underway, each project should have its payments sub-categorized here. Example: payments on the new organ should be debited from the New Organ sub-category, while payments made to the contractor for the new church addition should be debited from the Church Addition sub-category. In these cases, the parish will also want to have an Other sub-category, for small capital works that the sexton can report on, as a financial report footnote, or some such.

Some parishes issue cheques only out of their operating account (in order to save current account costs for the capital and outreach bank accounts). In these cases, they post a transfer from this category to an income category in the operating account. Note: this type of accounting is more complicated for parish bookkeepers, and subject to mistakes—the parish should consider avoiding such accounting. Also, when auditing the parish's financial records at year-end, tracing inter-account transfers is always difficult. The banking fees for chequing privileges are well worth it, for both the capital and outreach accounts.

51. *Banking Fees*—bank charges on the capital account. As noted above, some parishes pay these out of their operating account. In these cases, this category would be omitted.

Outreach Account

As noted in chapter 8, the outreach account could be managed by the parish's outreach development team. While all donations to the recipients (cheques issued out of this account) would still need the wardens' approval and their signatures, the outreach development team would still plan campaigns to replenish the account and fund outreach programs.

All donations—in and out—of parish outreach programs must be segregated from the parish operating account, since the funds do not belong to the parish. Outreach donations are made by parishioners for use outside their parish—for those in need in their community and beyond. This key point needs to be understood by everyone in the parish, especially those who process outreach donations. Outreach donations are exempt from the diocesan assessment, and so are segregated in order to make preparing the parish return easier.

The category numbers below jump ahead, to allow for additional expense categories in the capital account—this makes renumbering categories unnecessary when new ones are created.

Income Categories
60. *Donations*—all donations (designated or otherwise) for outreach purposes. Many outreach donations are designated for specific programs (e.g., the Primate's World Relief and Development Fund, Anglican Appeal, the parish's local food bank program). For designated donations, the parish should use sub-categories within the donations category, to keep track of which donations go where. Sub-categories should include Undesignated, where donations with no designations are credited. The outreach development team would then decide the disposition of these undesignated donations, according to their outreach development plan for the year.

While the outreach bank account could incur small amounts of interest income, this is not likely, as outreach donations should be distributed as soon as possible once they are received (no less frequent than monthly). Some parishes make the mistake of holding donations for months or years, until they can make a larger donation (and make a bigger impact). In most cases, though, the needs of outreach programs are dire, and donors' gifts should reach them as soon as possible.

Expense Categories

The category numbers below jump ahead, to allow for additional income categories—this makes renumbering categories unnecessary when new ones are created.

70. *Contributions*—payments to outreach programs. As above, the parish's specific outreach programs should each have a separate sub-category to ensure that payments are made properly. For example, the parish would have a separate sub-category for the Primate's World Relief and Development Fund.

71. *Program Costs*—costs to run the parish's local outreach programs (e.g., costs for printing posters, mailing costs, event expenses). Many parishes decide to absorb outreach program costs within their operating account—to ensure that 100% of the outreach donations reach those in need. In these cases, the parish will need to add an outreach program costs expense category to their operating account. If the parish wishes to deduct outreach program costs from outreach donations, it is important to note these can be deducted only from undesignated donations—designated gifts must go to the outreach program as specified. Also, if outreach program costs are deducted from donations, the outreach development team should mention this in their outreach program material, so that donors know this.

72. *Banking Fees*—bank charges on the outreach bank account. As noted above, some parishes pay these out of their operating account. In these cases, this category would be omitted.

73. *Diocesan Assessment*—based on a formula used by the diocese, the parish is assessed for an annual amount, usually paid each quarter or each month. Most parish assessment proceeds are used to fund diocesan outreach programs, and to pay the diocesan portion of national outreach programs, including the Primate's World Relief and Development Fund and Anglican Appeal. The parish normally pays the assessment from their operating account balance. In this example, a transfer would be made each quarter or each month from the operating account to the outreach account, and a cheque issued to the diocese from the outreach account.

74. *Synod*—the parish sends representatives to the diocesan synod. Synod is considered an outreach program, as it discusses outreach programs in the diocese, refugee justice and advocacy, and support to partner dioceses and parishes. The fees for each representative are debited from this category. Normally parishes transfer synod fee funds from the operating account, then produce cheques payable to the diocese from the outreach account.

Cemetery Account

As noted in chapter 9, the cemetery account could be managed by the parish sexton. While all payments would still need the wardens' approval and their signatures on all cheques paid out of the account (in accordance with the canons), the sexton could oversee the status of the account to ensure that sufficient funds are available for the required cemetery maintenance.

The category numbers below jump ahead, to allow for additional expense categories in the outreach account—this makes renumbering categories unnecessary when new ones are created.

Income Categories
80. *Plots*—income from plot purchases.

81. *Other*—income from other sources. This might include donations, interest income from cemetery funds held in trust, etc.

Expense Categories
The category numbers below jump ahead, to allow for additional income categories—this makes renumbering categories unnecessary when new ones are created.

90. *Burials*—costs of internments and initial placement of monuments.

91. *Maintenance*—relevelling/repairing monuments, fence repair, relevelling grounds, grass cutting, etc.

The category structure shown here is a two-level system. For instance, while Donations is a category on its own, at the next level it has four sub-categories: 1.1 Open, 1.2 Envelopes, 1.3 PAP (Pre-Authorized Payments), and 1.4

Special. To illustrate, the wardens, treasurer, advisory board, and vestry will certainly want to know the donations so far this year. The Donations category will keep these amounts segregated so that the total will be reported each month. By having sub-groupings within Donations, however, the treasurer can also report the total Open donations versus Envelopes donations versus total Pre-Authorized Payments versus total Special donations. In this way, the parish leadership team can see the effect of the PAP program on givings, and see how much is still given as open offerings (and perhaps try to move these donors to envelopes or PAP).

While many small parishes have elected to go with a single-level category system, medium- and large-sized parishes could easily use a two-level system. If your parish chooses a single-level system, make sure that your higher-level categories will give you the breakdowns needed to fully analyze your parish's income and expenses. For example, you may decide to aggregate all parishioners' donations under Donations, but in order to better track building costs, you might decide to break down the Property category into sub-categories as shown above (see 23. Property).

The major benefit of a two-level system is that your parish bookkeeper or treasurer can provide different income/expense reports to different people in the parish, depending on their needs. For example, the sexton would want to see totals for building utilities segregated, to compare the parish's costs for oil heating, say, with electricity; the wardens would want to see the totals for the various fund-raising events held, to learn which types were more successful; the advisory board and vestry, on the other hand, might wish to see a more simplified report, with only the higher-level categories shown.

While the above categories and sub-categories may look like a lot, consider the version of the income/expense report that the advisory board and vestry will receive. Assuming the report focuses on only the higher-level categories, the operating account will show seven income lines and seven expense lines; the capital and cemetery accounts will show two income lines and two expense lines; and the outreach account will show one income line and five expense lines. This would be quite simple to read for most advisory board and vestry members.

The categories and sub-categories suggested above should give your parish a good head start in building an accounting structure, or a way to check current categories against what might be needed. And no doubt, other income and expense categories and sub-categories, particular to your parish, could be added.

With the above income/expense categories in place, the parish bookkeeper will be able to post all donations and other income payments to the appropriate income category, and process payments out of the appropriate expense category—if proper procedures exist. Some form of procedure manual should be produced by the parish treasurer to ensure that these accounts, categories, and sub-categories are fully understood. It may be helpful to include the notes from this chapter.

Even with a pre-established set of accounts and income/expense categories with bookkeeper's procedures in place, parish bookkeepers will still have a hard time keeping up with the parish's financial transactions, unless the parish invests in some form of accounting automation. Automation is discussed later in this chapter (see page 198).

Controls/Audit Trails/Reconciliation

Once the account structure and income/expense categories are set, how is the parish to process its financial transactions? Here are some basic accounting controls that every parish should follow:

1. *Dual Controls.* Handling of cash and authorizing payments should be done by two parishioners, whenever possible. This ensures that the financial accounting has been double-checked and that responsibility is shared. For instance, when the Sunday collection is counted (especially the open cash), two parishioners should be involved. Likewise, depositing the collection at the bank should be carried out by the two parishioners who counted the collection and sealed the bank deposit envelope. In this way, there is no break in the control flow. For example, if two parishioners did the collection count, then handed off the collection to the parish bookkeeper, say, to do the deposit, control would be broken. All cheques issued by the parish should have two signatures (both wardens, normally). Note: in some parishes, wardens will pre-sign blank cheques, and have the parish bookkeeper fill them in later. This is highly inadvisable—pre-signed cheques, in the wrong hands, could be made out to any amount for any payee. Would you leave blank, pre-signed cheques lying around for your own personal chequing account?

All parish procedures and processes involving financial transactions should have dual controls in place.

2. *Receipts.* All parish payments require receipts, no matter how small the amount. This ensures that there is an audit trail of each payment, and that the parish's financial records can pass its annual audit at year-end. In cases where people donate professional time or materials to the parish in return

for tax receipts, these procedures still should be followed (this is where parishes most often break the rules and get into accounting and audit nightmares). Example: a parishioner who is a plumber donates 16 hours of labour to install a new kitchen sink and bathroom fixtures, and then wants a tax receipt for the value of their time. In this case,

- the parishioner must bill the parish for the value of the work done (through a bona fide invoice);
- the bookkeeper must issue a cheque payable to the parishioner for the amount billed;
- the parishioner must sign back the cheque to the parish as a donation; and
- in receiving the donation, the bookkeeper can then give the parishioner a tax receipt (or add the donation to the parishioner's year-to-date givings ledger, as with any other Sunday service donation).

This transaction must also be reflected correctly in the parish's books:

- a debit transaction should be posted to the appropriate expense category for the amount of the invoice;
- the transaction reference number should be recorded on the internal ledger (manual or automated) and on the invoice;
- the donation amount should be posted to the appropriate income category for the amount of the donation; and
- the transaction reference number should be recorded on the internal ledger (manual or automated) and on the endorsed cheque.

To give you an example of how dual controls and receipting works well in a parish, let's consider a "model" Sunday service collection process. Two volunteers (usually the sidespersons) collect, count, and bank the collection. Since there are no receipts for these Sunday collection income transactions, the parish has created a weekly collection form, which serves as the receipt. The verified (empty) collection envelopes and photocopied cheques are also used as individual receipts from each donor.

A sample weekly collection "receipt" form follows, and a brief description of its use. An electronic version in Microsoft Word format may be found on the enclosed CD (see collform.doc).

Operating Account Donations:

Operating Cash Total: $_____
Operating Cheques Total: $_____
Operating Envelopes Total: $_____
Operating Donations Total: $_____
(matches operating account bank deposit)

Memorial Donations *(include sources and designations, if any, for each):*

_____: $_____
_____: $_____
Memorial Donations (Undesignated) Total: $_____
Memorial Donations Total: $_____
(matches capital account bank deposit)

Outreach Donations *(include designations for each, if specified):*

_____: $_____
_____: $_____
Outreach Donations (Undesignated) Total: $_____
Outreach Donations Total: $_____
(matches outreach account bank deposit)

Signed,   **Signed,**
Sidesperson 1:   **Sidesperson 2:**

_____ _____

After the Sunday services, the two people assigned to count the collection and bank the proceeds use the above form to help the bookkeeper record the parish income. The open offering (cash), special offerings (cheques), and envelope offerings are totalled. The sidespersons include the verified amounts on each envelope and co-sign them, then give the empty envelopes to the parish's envelope secretary to update the envelope holders' records.

The sidespersons photocopy the special cheques, so that the bookkeeper can issue and mail individual tax receipts to the donors (as they are not regular attendees).

If there are any in-memorium donations, the sidespersons note the details (and designations if any) and photocopy the cheques. If the parish includes in-memorium donations in their operating account, the cheques are included in the operating account deposit. If they are to go into the parish's capital bank account, the sidespersons make up separate deposit slips for this.

The sidespersons then fill out a bank deposit slip for the operating account's cash and cheques, co-sign it, and place all operating account cash and cheques in a bank deposit envelope. (The same for capital account deposits.)

If there are outreach donations, the sidespersons total the amounts for each designated program and record them on the form. Undesignated donations are likewise noted. The sidepersons photocopy all cheques and forward them to the bookkeeper for tax receipts or for adding the amounts to the parishioners' year-to-date donations ledger. The sidespersons then fill out a deposit slip for the parish's outreach account, and place all outreach donations (cash and cheques) in the deposit envelope.

The sidespersons co-sign the weekly collection form, and forward it to the bookkeeper along with the photocopied cheques, for updating the internal books of the parish. The empty (but verified) envelopes are forwarded to the envelope secretary.

Both sidespersons take the deposit envelope(s) to the bank (night deposit box).

In this way, dual control has been maintained throughout the counting and deposit process, and the parish bookkeeper and envelope secretary have the information they need to update their records, without having to deal with the cash and cheques.

Note: parishes should use their bank's drop box to deposit the Sunday collection immediately after the deposit envelope is sealed. Leaving the collection in the parish office for later deposit at the bank—Monday morning, for example—is an invitation for theft (which has occurred in parishes that have used this risky process). The wardens must ensure that the Sunday collection gets banked as soon as possible after it is received.

3. *Audit Trails.* All transactions posted to the parish's books and passed through its bank accounts need a consistent reference number. This unique number must be recorded on payment receipts, on the internal account ledger (manual or automated), and on the bank's cheques. For deposits, copies of the weekly collection form (or whatever the parish uses to manage this) must be kept on file to reference deposit transactions made to the parish's internal ledgers and bank accounts. All transfers (from one account to another) must have reference numbers on both accounts (for both outgoing and incoming transactions).

To give an example of how audit trails could be maintained through the various processes and accounting systems used by a parish, let's consider how parishes match up payment transactions flowing from receipts for payment, through the parish's internal accounting records, to the banking system. To keep the three in sync, and to ensure dual controls on payment authorizations, some parishes have designed payment control forms. A good example follows (see payauth.doc on the enclosed CD):

Payment Authorization

Reference No. ☐

Payee: _____

Invoice No./Date: _____ *(as appears on the receipt)*

Payable From: _____
                parish account name/(sub)category

Amount: $_____ GST Refundable: $_____

Payment Memo Line: _____

Authorized By 1: _____ Authorized By 2: _____

Input By/Date: _____

Cheque No./Date: _____

The parish bookkeeper fills in the payee's name from the invoice/receipt, along with the invoice number (if supplied) and billing/receipt date. This ensures that the payment authorization can be tracked to the originating invoice/receipt. The bookkeeper fills in which parish account the payment should be debited from, and under which category/sub-category. The book-keeper also fills in the payment amount from the invoice, and calculates and records the parish's GST rebate amount, if applicable. The bookkeeper includes a payment memo, if required. The payment authorization and the invoice/receipt are provided to the wardens for their authorization (two sig-natures—dual control) to pay. The wardens also verify that the bookkeeper has selected the correct parish account and expense category to process the payment.

When the payment authorization and the invoice/receipt are returned from the wardens, the bookkeeper writes the cheque and includes the cheque number and payment date on the payment authorization. This ensures that the internal transaction can be reconciled to the bank transaction. The book-keeper also includes the payment memo on the cheque. The bookkeeper then enters the payment on the parish's account ledger (manual or automated) and includes their name, the date of the entry, and the internal transaction number on the payment authorization. This ensures that the payment authorization and invoice/receipt can be matched to the parish's internal accounting records. The bookkeeper also writes the internal transaction reference number on the cheque. This ensures that the bank's transaction numbers will cross-reference the parish's. The bookkeeper also records the internal transaction number and the GST refund amount in the GST refund ledger, so that the Canada Revenue Agency return can be easily completed when required. The bookkeeper then files the payment authorization (in internal reference number sequence) in the parish's filing system. This en-sures that the originating invoice and payment authorization can be easily retrieved if needed.

In many cases, the bookkeeper might fast-track the process for recur-ring payments, where there is no question of which account and expense category to use, and when the payment is not in question (example: the monthly organist's honorarium). In these cases, the bookkeeper completes the cheque at the same time as the payment authorization, so that the war-dens sign both at the same time.

4. *Reconciliation*. All transactions passing through the parish's internal accounts must be reconciled each month to the parish's bank account statements. The monthly closing account balances on the parish's bank

statements must match the closing balances of the parish's internal account records. (This is the same process most of us use to balance our personal chequing accounts each month.)

If the bookkeeper has included the cheque number for each payment in the parish's internal accounting ledger (manual or automated), reconciliation will be much easier, as the bookkeeper can compare cheque numbers on the bank statement and in the ledger. The bookkeeper simply ticks off the cheque numbers and amounts on the bank statement that correspond to the cheque numbers and amounts of the expense transactions shown in the parish's internal ledger. Outstanding cheques may be simply moving through the banking system. However, if any have been outstanding for more than 20 days from the time of mailing, the bookkeeper should alert the treasurer, who should follow up with the payee.

If there are payments on the bank statement that the parish did not make, the bookkeeper should contact the parish's account manager at the bank. (Same with deposits not reflected in the bank statement or amounts that do not match.)

It is critical that reconciliation be done as soon as the bank statements are received by the parish. If not, reconciliation becomes a more difficult job, and it will be more difficult for the bank to track down missing entries as time goes by.

When the bookkeeper has completed the reconciliation, it should be given to the parish treasurer to verify (dual control) and co-sign.

Note: banks' current account statements are notoriously late in getting to the parish through the mail (up to three weeks after month-end). This makes the bookkeeper's reconciliation task much more difficult, as there will be almost an additional month's payments and deposits outstanding when the statement arrives. To ease this problem, the parish leadership team should seriously consider getting the parish set up to use online banking services. Month-end closing statements can usually be printed online in the parish office on the month-end date. Also, outstanding cheques can be tracked online by the bookkeeper. In most cases, online banking services are offered to parishes by their bankers at no charge. These facilities can certainly reduce the bookkeeper's workload. If the bookkeeper is a paid position (by the hour), the parish will save money by subscribing to this service.

The Envelope Secretary

Most parishes have a volunteer envelope secretary who keeps track of each donor's givings for the year and issues tax receipts at year-end, along with quarterly statements of the donor's year to date givings. (The year-to-date statement process is *very important* for the parish—often parishioners will lose track of where their year-to-date donations are at, relative to where they want to be in their givings/their pledge for the year. *The receipt of a quarterly statement will result in a "catch-up" of donations from parishioners who would not otherwise think to do it.*)

The envelope secretary receives the envelopes from the Sunday collection (with the donation amount already verified by the counters), as well as photocopies of any loose cheques in the collection. Using a manual or automated donor accounting system, the envelope secretary matches the envelope number to the corresponding donor record, and records their donation amount and date in the accounting ledger.

Some parishioners do not like to use parish envelope sets—they prefer to donate by (loose) cheque or cash in a non-numbered envelope that includes their names. In these cases, the envelope secretary will create a donor number in the accounting system (as if the donor had used a set of envelopes) and add these donations to their records.

Also, the envelope secretary will receive a monthly statement of PAP donors from the parish's bank. PAP donors are also given donor numbers. They are matched by name with the PAP deposit report from the bank, and their donations are recorded in the donor accounting system. The envelope secretary bundles each Sunday's envelopes and cheque photocopies along with the monthly PAP report, and files them in date order in the parish's files.

At year-end (in January), the envelope secretary produces a manual or automated statement of givings for each donor, and an official tax receipt, and mails these to each donor. (It is important that the rector include a thank-you letter with each statement, indicating the differences their gifts made in the parish last year, with examples.)

Some parishes have given the responsibilities of envelope secretary to the parish secretary/bookkeeper. *If so, the parish should rethink this decision*. Ideally the envelope secretary's responsibilities should be handled by a separate person for several reasons:

1. The envelope secretary's workload tends to be fairly light, even in large parishes. This allows the position to be held by a parish volunteer. If the parish secretary/bookkeeper is a paid position, their workload should not be increased by donor recordkeeping, thereby needlessly increasing staff expenses for the parish.

2. The parish secretary/bookkeeper is in contact with many parishioners on

many occasions for many reasons. Knowledge of the parishioner's annual givings could influence their treatment of the parishioner, and negatively affect their working relationship.

3. The recordkeeping done by the envelope secretary is highly confidential. It is much easier to ensure confidentiality when the work is restricted to one person who has less daily contact with church members.

Note: several parishes have invested in donor recordkeeping software, to help the envelope secretary keep track of weekly givings and to generate interim statements and year-end tax receipts. In many cases, these have been subsequently abandoned, as they tend to be overly-complex for the relatively simple tasks involved. Unless the software is fairly straightfoward or the parish is very large, you may want to go with a manual system for this work.

The Anglican Book Centre has a very effective (and inexpensive) manual control form for envelope secretaries—it includes self-duplicating slips for each donor, which can be filed in a binder for the parish. The underlying four copies can be removed at each quarter to serve as the donor's interim statements, with no additional preparation. The last copy is the year-end tax receipt (stamped with the parish address and charitable organization number); the original is filed in the parish office when the tax receipts are mailed out. This manual system, however, will not give the envelope secretary an easy way of reporting average weekly givings to the treasurer and wardens. However, for small- to medium-sized parishes, this calculation would not take a lot of time (with a calculator to help).

A computer spreadsheet (Microsoft Excel or Lotus 123, for example) would also do the job. The envelope secretary would use one row per donor and one column for each week of the year; and would key the amounts into each week's cell. This would give the envelope secretary a way of automating the calculation of average weekly givings. However, the interim and year-end statements would need to be manually produced.

For larger parishes, doners could be setup on the automated accounting system as "customers" of the parish. Weekly donations could be recorded as "purchases" and donor ("customer") statements could be automated. In this way, the parish could include both their payments and donations recordkeeping on one system.

Reporting

While the internal financial reporting preferences of each parish may differ, some minimum standards should be followed. Under the canons, the wardens are responsible for monitoring the financial records of the parish, and ensuring its financial health. To do this, they must review—every month—income and expense transactions and account balances with the parish treasurer. The secretary/bookkeeper will need to produce at least two reports: an income and expenses report and a trial balance report for each account the parish maintains. Using the examples in the previous sections, this would mean two reports for each of the parish's three or four accounts, or eight reports in total. Given the associated workload to produce these, the parish should seriously consider automating their accounting processes if they have not already done so. This is discussed in detail in the automation section following.

1. Monthly Income/Expenses Report

An income/expenses report will need to be produced for each parish account (operating, outreach, capital, cemetery). At a minimum, the "actuals only" report should include the past month's income and expenses by sub-category and be totalled by category. Totals for all income and expenses should be included as well as the net of income and expenses. To the right of the monthly actuals, the year-to-date actuals for the same sub-categories, with category and income and expenses totals and net, should also be included.

Better (actuals versus plan): in addition to the above, the report should also include the budget amounts for the past month, for each sub-category with totals for categories, income, expenses, and net. Beside last month's budget amounts should be a variance column (the difference between the month's actuals and budget) for each sub-category with totals for categories, income, expenses, and net. The actual versus plan version of the report should also include the year-to-date budget amounts for each sub-category, with totals for categories, income, expenses, and net, along with a year-to-date variance column (the difference between the year-to-date actuals and year-to-date budget amounts) for all sub-categories and category, income, and expense totals and net.

A sample report follows:

Monthly Income/Expenses Report for *(last month)*
Operating Account

	Month			Year To Date		
	Actual	Budget	Variance	Actual	Budget	Variance
Income						
Donations						
Open	$$	$$	$$	$$	$$	$$
Envelopes	$$	$$	$$	$$	$$	$$
PAP	$$	$$	$$	$$	$$	$$
Special	$$	$$	$$	$$	$$	$$
Total Donations	$$	$$	$$	$$	$$	$$
Fund-Raising						
(etc.)	$$	$$	$$	$$	$$	$$
Total Income	$$	$$	$$	$$	$$	$$
Expenses						
Worship						
Rector	$$	$$	$$	$$	$$	$$
Curate	$$	$$	$$	$$	$$	$$
Organist	$$	$$	$$	$$	$$	$$
Supplies	$$	$$	$$	$$	$$	$$
Total Worship	$$	$$	$$	$$	$$	$$
Staff						
(etc.)						
Total Expenses	$$	$$	$$	$$	$$	$$
Net:	$$	$$	$$	$$	$$	$$

For each large variance (actual to budget), the treasurer will need to explain the reason to the wardens, and describe an action plan to get the actuals back in line to the budget. If there is no suggested plan, the treasurer should highlight the situation for the wardens' decisioning. (This could take the form of dropping some discretionary parish expenses to make up the difference, initiating some fund-raising events, etc.). If the variance cannot be resolved by the wardens, they should consider taking the issue to the advisory board for their advice. If all else fails, the wardens may have to take the matter to a special vestry, to revise the vestry-approved budget for the year.

The parish sexton should also receive a copy of the report, so that he or she can take it back to the assets management team, to plan for the next round of property and building maintenance cost-cutting initiatives, and to monitor the capital account (see chapter 9).

The parish outreach team leader should also receive a copy of the report for the outreach account, so that he or she can take it back to the outreach development team, to monitor donations received versus the year's outreach goal, to determine if additional reminders need to be made. The report will also help the team decide when they can make donations to the outreach program recipients (see chapter 8).

2. Monthly Trial Balance Report

In addition to the income/expenses report, the secretary/bookkeeper will need to produce a trial balance for each parish account (verified to match the bank's record of the balances being reported).

At a minimum, include for each account the opening balance for the month, total credits, total debits, and closing balance. This includes all parish cash accounts (as described above), as well as the parish's loan accounts (mortgage, line of credit, diocesan loan, etc.).

A sample trial balance report follows:

Monthly Trial Balance Report for *(last month)* Operating Account

	Current Account	GIC # 123	Line of Credit	Totals
Opening Balance	$$	$$	$$	$$
Credits	$$	$$	$$	$$
Debits	$$	$$	$$	$$
Closing Balance	$$	$$	$$	$$

Better: the above, plus sub-total balances for each of the asset types in each account—for instance, cash balance, short-term deposits (i.e., money market funds), and long-term deposits such as GICs, along with a maturity schedule.

Best: the above, plus (using past history of the account balances) a trend-line of the account balance over the last five years. This way, the parish leadership team can see the overall trend for their accounts and take actions to change it, if necessary.

With reference to the report, the treasurer should be in a position to highlight upcoming expenses that might take one of the account balances into a negative position or a very low float amount. In these cases, the treasurer should have ideas to cover it (e.g., transfers from other accounts, drawing down the parish credit line, deferring some upcoming discretionary expenses, etc.). As with the above report, if the situation cannot be resolved by the wardens, they should turn to the advisory board or vestry for ideas and decisioning.

3. Donations Report

In addition to the above financial management reports for the wardens, a quarterly donations report, prepared by the envelope secretary from the donors ledger, would be helpful. It would include

- for envelope holders—current number of envelope donors versus number of envelope donors last year; average weekly donation this year versus last year;
- for PAP donors—current number of PAP donors versus number of PAP donors last year; average weekly donation this year versus last year; and
- for all donors—current number of envelope + PAP donors versus number of envelope + PAP donors last year; average weekly donation this year versus last year.

A sample donations report follows:

Quarterly Donations Report *(date)*
Operating Account

	Quarter Ending	Year-End (last year)
No. Envelope Holders:	nnn	nnn
Average Weekly Donation:	$$	$$
PAP Donors:	nnn	nnn
Average Weekly Donation:	$$	$$
All Donors:	nnn	nnn
Average Weekly Donation:	$$	$$

From this report, the treasurer and wardens would see the differences in givings between the two payment options, and emphasize the more successful one to the parish (in most cases, PAP). Also, the treasurer could print the total donor statistics in the service bulletin, along with some equivalent expense statistics (such as the average weekly costs to run the parish), with an appeal to increase givings, as appropriate. (This is a very effective way to educate parishioners. If they see average weekly givings at $1,000, say, and average weekly expenses at $1,200, say, they can certainly see how they need to make a difference.) In these cases, a simple message might be: "If you are under the average, maybe the average should be your goal," or, "If you are an 'average' giver, maybe you want to be above average."

4. Annual Returns

Every parish is required to report its financials to the diocese and to the Canada Revenue Agency (CRA) each year. While the accounting system cannot print this information in the formats needed, it can produce the data the treasurer and wardens need to prepare

- the parish's annual parochial return for the diocese. If you are not sure of the format of the report and the information needed, contact the chief financial officer (CFO) at your diocesan office;
- the parish's annual T3010 for CRA. This ensures that the parish continues to be registered as a charitable entity. Again, if you are

not sure of the information needed and the form's timing, contact the diocesan CFO;

- the parish's annual GST34 for CRA. This ensures that the parish is registered to receive GST rebates. Again, if you are not sure of the information needed and the form's timing, contact the diocesan CFO;
- the parish's quarterly GST66 for CRA. This is the parish's GST rebate claim. Again, if you are not sure of the information needed and the form's timing, contact the diocesan CFO. (The GST66 can be submitted monthly or annually. Most parishes, however, can wait for quarterly rebates rather than go to the effort every month. Waiting until year-end may tie up the funds due to the parish for too long.)

In addition to the CFO's help, you can print the CRA forms and procedures from the CRA web site: <cra-arc.gc.ca/tax/charities/publications_list-e.html>.

Note: some provinces also provide rebates on provincial sales and services tax. Check with your diocesan CFO to determine if your parish is eligible, and which forms should be used.

Although the parish leadership team will likely want to see a variety of reports, the above reports—monthly income/expenses, monthly trial balance, donations, and annual returns—should be considered mandatory for proper financial management.

Automation Options

The Parish Computer

Some small parishes do not yet have a computer in their offices, although they could, and probably should. Cost need not be a major factor—many Canadian banks and large retail companies regularly upgrade their computers with newer models and, as a community service, donate their old computers to non-profit organizations. A parishioner connected to a bank or one of these firms might ask on behalf of the parish to obtain a computer. Or the diocese may also offer inexpensive ways of getting one. Give them a call.

Most parishes do not need a top-of-the-line computer to handle normal parish work. The following criteria would be reasonable:

- built-in modem (for Internet access, for e-mails, and web site hosting);
- one gigaHertz (or more) processor (internal speed);

- five gigabytes (or more) hard drive (for data storage space); and
- floppy disk or or USB memory chip (for offsite file back-ups).

In addition, the following computer devices could be added onto the donated computer through purchases:

- 15-inch (or more) monitor (smaller might cause eyestrain for the secretary/bookkeeper); and
- laser printer (impact printers would be too slow and of poor quality).

Donated computers do not come with software—the parish will need to purchase it. Most parishes and parishioners use the Microsoft Windows operating system, with Microsoft Office application software. In the latter case, Office includes several applications—the more you buy, the more expensive your version of Office. The secretary/bookkeeper will need Microsoft Word (for word processing) and Microsoft Excel (for spreadsheet preparation). Other Office applications include Access, a database application, which might be helpful to store information about parishioners' skills and interests, though its use does require some computer savvy. (PowerPoint, a presentation slides application, is also available, but probably not needed in most parishes.)

In addition, the parish computer will need telecommunications software for Internet access. Normally this is supplied at no cost by the Internet service provider selected by the parish. The software is simply loaded onto the computer by the secretary/bookkeeper.

Lastly, the parish may want to add some basic desktop publishing software to the parish computer, to allow the secretary/bookkeeper to use clip art and graphics to liven up the weekly service bulletin and parish newsletter. These products are quite inexpensive.

To decrease parish administration costs (stationery, photocopying, and postage), the financial management team should make maximum use of e-mails and the parish's web site to distribute parish information. Ask parishioners to give the secretary/bookkeeper their e-mail addresses, if these are not already on file, and have the secretary/bookkeeper e-mail parish newsletters, meeting minutes, etc., whenever possible. (When the congregation development team builds the parishioner inventory [see chapter 4], e-mail addresses should be part of the information they gather.) Some parishioners with e-mail could be asked to print copies of bulletins and newsletters for neighbouring parishioners who do not have e-mail.

The parish web site should feature upcoming events, the parish newsletter, the service bulletin, etc., which will further decrease administrative costs such as printing and postage.

These tools will also decrease the work effort of the secretary/bookkeeper. If this is a paid position, staff costs will likewise be reduced.

Because the parish computer holds confidential information, the secretary/bookkeeper should use a "power-on" password and a "time-out" password, which are shared with only the wardens and treasurer. Sometimes team leaders will need file copies to carry out analysis of their program's effectiveness. In these cases, the team leaders should obtain the wardens' permission. Then the secretary/bookkeeper will make copies on diskettes, CDs, or memory chips. Also, the secretary/bookkeeper should make file back-ups every week, and store the back-up copies somewhere other than in the parish office (in case of fire). Some secretary/bookkeepers take the back-up copies home when they leave for the day and return them when it is time to do another back-up.

Accounting Automation

While some small parishes can probably manage their financials using a manual ledger, they may want to reconsider, given the accounting and reporting requirements outlined in this chapter. It does not take many financial transactions each month for a parish secretary/bookkeeper to become loaded down with accounting work. If you have more than 15 or so payments per month and more than 10 income transactions per month, consider automating the parish accounting process, especially if the secretary/bookkeeper is a paid position. Fairly inexpensive accounting software applications can significantly reduce the secretary/bookkeeper's workload (and costs).

Many computer-based accounting packages will operate using the capacity of a PC described above. These include AccPac, Simply Accounting, Quicken, etc. When the financial management team decides to automate their accounting system, they should first contact their diocesan CFO for recommendations, then go shopping for the package that best suits the parish's needs. The parish secretary/bookkeeper should be included on the shopping trip. Most computer stores have these packages and can demonstrate them for you.

Before you go shopping, however, prepare a list of the mandatory features you will need, and (on a sub-list) some of the "nice-to-haves." Here are some considerations for the team:

1. *Supplier Questions*
   - Will the application run under the current version of the operating system we have, or do we need to upgrade? If so, what would be the additional cost for this?

   - Will the application run on the computer hardware we have, or will we have to upgrade? If so, what will be the additional costs for this?

   - How intuitive is the application? Does its design make it simple to use—will the secretary/bookkeeper be able to use it with minimal training? Note: while the application may have a built-in tutorial, do not make the assumption that it will be easy to use. If the application really is easy, the tutorial would not likely be needed.

   - What is the level of application support? Is there a 24-hour help desk? A 1-800 number? Are there additional costs to use it?

   - What is the application warrantee period? If it breaks, will someone come onsite to fix it? What will this cost?

   - How long has this version of the application been running? Will we be guinea pigs? Are there users close by we could call for their opinions of the product, or visit, to see it in action? (The financial management team should do this as a matter of course, before buying. Check with other parishes in your area to learn if any have the package you are considering, and go see how it works for them.)

   - How much is the package (all-in)? Is there an annual license fee as well?

   - How are database back-ups done? Are they part of the application, with user-friendly prompts?

2. *Mandatory Application Features*
   - Does the product allow for multiple accounts? Is there a limit on these? (If not, you will probably have a dead-end product on your hands—move on to the next one.)

- Does the product allow for income and expense categories named by the user? Is there a limit on these? (Again, the parish needs to be able to control these and name them. If not, move on.)

- Compare the "credit" transactions in the application to the income transactions you are currently processing. Does the application cover all the information elements in the income transaction? If not, can they be easily added? (Key elements are mandatory, or move on. However, some might be able to be input into "memo" or "description" fields in the application—check them out before you reject the application.)

- Compare the "debit" transactions in the application to the expense transactions you are currently processing. Does the application cover all the information elements in the expense transaction? If not, can they be easily added? Note especially, where the secretary/bookkeeper would key in the bank cheque number on debit transactions. If there is no place for this (or it cannot be used as a "search" field—i.e., if the secretary/bookkeeper wants to find the internal transaction for a particular cheque number), how do they do it? (Same for credit transaction fields—check out otherwise superfluous fields in the application; often they can be made to work. If not, move on to the next product.)

- Does the product have a reconciliation feature (whereby the secretary/bookkeeper electronically ticks off cleared cheques)? Does the product then highlight outstanding payments? If not, how would the parish do this? (Highlighting outstanding, or unreconciled, payments is a key requirement—see how the application might be "tweaked" to provide this, if it is not obvious at first—sometimes there is an answer. If not, move on.)

- Does the product allow for input of annual budget amounts for each income/expense category within each account? In reporting the monthly and year-to-date actual income and expenses, does the application also compare them to the monthly and year-to-date budget amounts and produce variance reporting? If not, how would the parish do this? (If there is no budget accounting in the package, move on.)

- Can the product provide reports the parish will need (income/expenses and trial balances, at a minimum)? It is not likely that the product's reports will have the same format as you use today. Have a closer look at them—can the parish adapt to the new formats? Do they make sense? (Many software packages come with "report writers," whereby the user can custom-build the report. Check if the package includes this feature—ask the salesperson to build the report you need during the demo.)

3. *"Nice-to-Have" Application Features*

When two or more packages seem to tie on price, support, mandatory functions, etc., the evaluation team may want to use the "nice-to-haves" list to help decide which product the parish should acquire. Here are some thoughts on nice-to-haves:

- Has the product been improved by the vendor over time? Will there be new releases in the future? What is the upgrade cost? Is it mandatory? How difficult have they been?

- Can the reports be e-mailed (to the treasurer, wardens, advisory board) within the application?

- Does the product have multi-year tracking (to track parish trends over the last five years, for various categories)?

- Does the product support donor recordkeeping in some fashion? (Could it also be used by the envelope secretary?)

- Does the product support capital project expense management? (Could the sexton use it to track large capital projects?)

- Does the product allow for export of data to other software (e.g., Microsoft Excel or Word)? (Could the secretary/bookkeeper transfer transactions or balances data to spreadsheets, to e-mail to the treasurer and wardens?)

Note: several of these packages have automated reconciliation sub-systems built in—for example, the package downloads an electronic version of the monthly bank statement from the parish's bank and automatically compares each outstanding debit and credit transaction in the application to transactions in the bank's file. It looks slick in the product glossies—however, many parishes have found that setting up and executing the process between the bank and the parish computer was too complex, and have gone back to the electronic "tick back" method. Do not get overwhelmed by this feature.

When the parish acquires the new accounting application, give the secretary/bookkeeper sufficient time to become familiar with it. This is best done by having them open "practice" accounts and categories, and putting fake transactions through the system, to see how it works and to look at the reports that come out. When the training is over, the secretary/bookkeeper can delete all the practice data, then start to build the real accounts, categories, etc.

The best time to adopt a new accounting system is when the new accounting year starts. This way, the secretary/bookkeeper need not input past transactions to get the current year's books right. If at all possible, the parish leadership team should schedule the new system installation for January 1, or soon after. The later the conversion happens, the more historical transactions must be (re)input to ensure the books are correct.

It may be a good idea to test the new application, especially when the old system is manual, by running both the old and new systems in parallel, to check whether the parish's transactions will be processed in the same way as before. In these cases, the parish leadership team should consider providing additional support to the secretary/bookkeeper, as the workload will double during the parallel period. Also, the parish should try to minimize the duration of parallel operations—run these only to the point where the parish is confident in the new system. Normally a week will be sufficient to test and become familiar with a new system.

With the new system up and running, parishes sometimes make a grave error—they leave administration of the system to only one person, the secretary/bookkeeper. But what if that person becomes ill or resigns? Who will take over? To prevent calamity, as soon as the new system stabilizes, the secretary/bookkeeper should train a back-up person to understand how the new system operates, and keep that back-up person current.

Expense Management

Chapter 9 described how the parish sexton and assets management team could manage expenses associated with parish buildings and property. Other parish expenses, such as administration, financing, and staff costs, could (and should) be managed by the treasurer and the financial management team. This team includes the secretary/bookkeeper and other volunteers interested in the finances of the parish. If the sexton and the assets management team do not take on the expense management of parish property and buildings, this responsibility will fall to the parish treasurer and the financial team. (See chapter 9 for expense reduction tips.)

1. Administration Expenses

Paperless Operations. Use of e-mail and the parish web site to distribute information will significantly decrease costs for stationery, postage, and photocopying. As well as saving money, these forms of communication demonstrate good stewardship of parish resources.

Equipment. Investigate contracts for the parish's office equipment. Is leasing the most cost-effective approach? Is metering photocopiers a viable process? Can expense reductions be made here, by renegotiating service contracts or by replacing equipment? Check downtime history and repair costs—is it time for replacement? (If the financial management team elect to replace equipment, new equipment should be funded out of the parish's capital account.)

Telephone. Check the telephone bill—are Internet and other services bundled to reduce costs? Would adding web hosting reduce other charges? Is the current carrier offering the best price—have others been asked for a quote?

Banking Fees. Can the secretary/bookkeeper make more use of PAPs to cut down on the cost of cheques and to reduce their own workload? Can the secretary/bookkeeper use online banking services to cut down on workload and be more effective?

2. Financing Expenses

Consider the parish's financial structure—can high-cost lines of credit be rolled into a conventional loan? Can the parish borrow from itself—i.e., borrow from long-term capital deposits to cover operating deficits? Has this possibility been explored with the diocese's chief financial officer? Can the parish borrow from the diocese more advantageously than from the bank? Might a parishioner lend the parish funds for a special need, and be paid back only the principal (the interest being a tax receiptable donation)? Can the mortgage be renegotiated at a lesser rate, even considering the penalty fees? Can the parish use its leverage (i.e., large GIC deposits) to have current account banking fees waived? The possibilities are there—the financing expenses you save the parish can be put to far better uses.

3. Staff Expenses

Have you read chapter 5? Go through the parish membership list to see whether any volunteers might be found who could replace paid parish staff or reduce their workloads, thereby reducing costs.

Organist/Choir Director. Many parishes hire their organist/choir director on an honorarium, which is increased from time to time as the years go by. While it is assumed in many parishes that the honorarium represents only a fraction of what the organist could be making at an hourly rate, this is worth validation. Has anyone calculated the hourly equivalent rate of the organist/choir director lately? Maybe the parish had a junior choir when the organist was hired, and it has since disbanded? Maybe the choir practises only once every second week, rather than weekly, as before? When you know the average monthly hours worked by the organist/choir director, divide by the monthly honorarium amount. Determine if the hourly equivalent rate is competitive in the marketplace. (If you are not sure of what organists are paid in your area, contact your diocesan office.) If the rate is out of line, raise the issue with the wardens, suggesting an adjusted amount and why.

Perhaps, too, a parish volunteer could replace the paid organist. Check the parish membership list—are there any organists? Also check with your diocesan office—are there organists who could do as good a job (or better) at a lower rate?

Secretary/Bookkeeper. Review the work done by the secretary/bookkeeper. Is the accounting application being used effectively? Are reports being prepared manually that could be generated from the system? Is the processing of financial transactions as efficient as possible, or could some steps be omitted or automated? Could some work be assigned to parish volunteers? Is the secretary/bookkeeper being used as a "do-everything" person, driving up the number of hours they work? Is the online banking system being used? Have all recurring payments been set up as PAPs?

When all work-reduction opportunities for the secretary/bookkeeper have been implemented, recalculate their hours worked. You might be able to reduce their salary or honorarium.

Stewardship Campaigns

The flip side of parish expense management is appropriate parish steward-ship. While some parishes have very generous members and are satisfied to have stewardship remain a background topic, many parishes could take stewardship more seriously by reminding their membership of the callings of their faith, not only for outreach but for support of their parish—its rec-tor and its operation.

How do you know if parishioners are taking stewardship seriously? Most dioceses have compiled statistics from the annual parochial returns, including average weekly givings per family, average annual family income for each parish's area (from Statistics Canada), and the average percentage of givings to income per family for each parish, and for the diocese as a whole. While one cannot say what the percentage ought to be for each par-ish family, certainly it is possible to compare your parish's average to other parishes of your size.

If your parish is below the diocese's average in terms of giving, have a look at the parishes who are above the average—consider calling them and trying to find out why their parishioners give at levels higher than yours. If you feel your parish might need a stewardship wake-up call, consider launching a stewardship campaign.

While the stewardship campaign of each parish is and should be unique, some best practices have proven quite successful in the past:

1. *Define Your Goal*. What do you believe should be the parish's "proper" stewardship level, compared with the annual donations received to date? Why do you think this? Is the level realistic, given the parish's history and its current membership? Is it realistic to assume the parish can move to the proper level in one year—or would this involve a culture change in the parish, which could take four to five years to bring about? What does the proper level mean to each parish family—how much more will they be asked for?

2. *Define Your Image*. What might inspire current donors to dig deeper? What has changed? In this consumer-based society, what might inspire parishioners to give more for the same "services"? Or does the parish need to change its "offerings" as well? What faith-based messages will be at the heart of the campaign?

3. *Define Your Timing*. When will the campaign be launched? (The best times are April to May and October to November, when most parishioners have returned from vacation or time away.) Make sure the campaign will not

compete with any capital or outreach campaigns in the parish. If the outreach development team or assets management team is also planning a campaign this year, integrate all campaigns and carry one consistent message.

Is the campaign a one-time event for this year, multi-year (to reach a set annual goal at the end of the final year), or annual (repeating every year)? Each involves a different campaign structure.

One-time campaigns usually have a modest goal, and are intended as wake-up calls to move the parish to where it should be. They are minor "course corrections"—the assumption is that, following the campaign, the parish will not need subsequent reminders to stay on course.

Multi-year campaigns require significant culture changes within the parish, in order to move the parish to where it should be. Over the duration of the campaign (say, five years), specific goals are set for each year; the campaign content and approach are quite different for each year, as the parish changes through the campaign period.

Annual campaigns are intended for parishes that likely will reach the goal in the first year, but then need annual encouragement to maintain their givings level. These campaigns tend to be low-key reminders, assuming the target is met the first year.

4. *Get Advice.* Your diocesan office has lots of information gathered from other stewardship campaigns in your area, as well as materials. Call and ask them to help your team. Also, contact any parishes the diocese points to as having had successful campaigns. Find out what worked, what didn't.

5. *Don't be Afraid to Ask.* For unknown reasons, we Anglicans often treat stewardship as a taboo subject, and anyone promoting it as an enemy. Your campaign approach, message, and materials will need to cut through this attitude. While the diocese and other parishes will have suggestions, successful approaches will appeal to

- *faith-based giving*—using Christ's example and our calling to live our faith. The rector could provide sermons on this theme, with many examples;
- *consumer-based giving*—asking parishioners to give according to the value they (and their children) receive from the parish. Digging deep to understand what they really get will reveal much more than they assume at first—a self-assessment questionnaire may be helpful. Campaign materials could "market" some parish programs, etc. (refer to chapter 4, and consult with the congregation development team); and

- *ownership-based giving*—this church was built by your predecessors for you; it is now your church and needs you now; you need to pass it on to your children. Your campaign materials could include some historical images of the parish, including the key founders.

You may decide to base your campaign on all of these platforms, to reach all of your parishioners. If so, take care creating the campaign message—if it is not crisp and clear, the campaign will fail.

6. *Educate Your Donors.* If donors do not understand the need, they will not respond. The campaign materials should recap parish expenses (in the simplest way possible) and the extent to which current sources of income cover these. Many parishioners assume that the rector and church building maintenance are paid for by the diocese (!). Parishioners should clearly understand that the parish sinks or swims on its own—and that it must also extend help to others, over and above its own needs, through outreach and the diocesan assessment.

7. *Ask Everyone.* Every parish has members who are seldom seen in the pews each Sunday—between 20% to 40% of total membership. Do not make the assumption that they are any less financially committed to the parish than the frequent attendees. Ensure that your campaign includes a face-to-face discussion with everyone.

8. *Repeat for Newcomers.* Newcomers may have missed the message—redeliver it as necessary. (Consult with the congregation development team to access information for newcomers—see chapter 4.)

9. *Adjust as You Go.* In multi-year campaigns, assess the year ended. Make adjustments to the campaign, emphasizing those aspects that struck a chord, and omitting those that fell flat.

10. *Celebrate and Thank as You Go.* Communicate the progress of the campaign to all, and frequently. Define interim milestones in your plan that can be causes for celebrations in the parish. Never forget the six most important words in all stewardship campaigns—***thank you, thank you, thank you.***

Creating the Parish Budget

Why are budgets necessary? Families budget to make sure they live within their means. To create a budget, most families take their monthly net income, subtract that month's essential expenses (rent, mortgage payment, groceries, car payments, transit fees, parking, insurance, etc.), subtract their monthly savings (children's education fund; RSPs, life insurance), and arrive at their discretionary funds for the month. Sometimes, when there is a lump sum payment due (for example, municipal taxes or a dental bill), discretionary funds for that month may drop to zero, or even negative. On the whole, most families budget month by month, to be slightly ahead each year.

Creating a parish budget isn't much different. We do it to ensure that the parish is operating within its means. This is proper stewardship of our ParishWorks.

However, many parishes go through the process with very little thought. Some take the current year's actuals, add an inflation rate, and that is next year's budget. Others take their annual budget numbers and divide by 12, to arrive at their monthly budgets, despite the fact that many expenses are known to spike in specific months and that income goes down in summer months. Then the parish wonders why, halfway through the year, they are not within their budget amounts, and they end up in a financial crisis. If we did our family budgets with the same lack of effort or concern, many more of us would be seeking financial assistance.

While the canons stipulate that setting the parish budget is the responsibility of the wardens, most often the creation of the first draft remains with the parish treasurer and the financial management team. The treasurer and financial management team need to take the time to prepare parish budgets that are realistic and complete. Budget amounts should be set for each income and expense sub-category, for each month of the upcoming year.

The team should include the congregation development team leader (for the operating account's donations sub-categories), the parish sexton (for the operating account's property and buildings sub-categories and for the capital account sub-categories), and the outreach development team leader (for the outreach account sub-categories). The team needs to start drafting the budget in November, so that the wardens and advisory board have time to review it, and make any necessary revisions, before it is distributed at least two weeks in advance of the annual vestry meeting in January.

How should the team proceed? Let's look at the sample income and expense sub-categories from the previous section:

Operating Account

Income Categories

1. *Donations*

Consider the following when drawing up the donations budget:

- *Parish Growth.* Will the parish grow in its membership next year? If so, by how many net families? (Keep in mind that the parish will lose families through moves, etc.) The congregation development team leader needs to give the budget team the net increase—take the average annual donations per family for the current year and multiply by the number of net new families for next year. Add this amount to the donations estimate for next year. Note: if the parish will see a net loss of families next year, multiply the number by the average annual family donations of this year, and subtract the total from the budget income for next year. The budget team can adjust the sub-categories by the estimate, based on their best guess of how many of the new families will use envelopes versus PAP.

- *Stewardship.* Has the parish had a significant stewardship drive this year or is one planned for early next year? If so, what is the financial management team's estimate of increased givings for next year? Add this to the current year's actuals, in the envelopes and PAP sub-categories in the same ratio as the current year's actuals to date.

- *Monthly Estimates.* Look at last year's monthly income—or better yet, income from the last three years. What percentage of the total did each month represent? Use these monthly percentages to calculate next year's monthly estimates. Example: by averaging the last three years' income by month, the budget team has found that in January the parish receives 10% of its annual donations, whereas in February it normally receives 8%. To set the monthly budget amounts for next January, multiply the total expected by 10%; for February, multiply the total expected by 8%. Use the same formula to determine the remaining monthly budget amounts for next year.

Here are some suggestions to calculate amounts for the sub-categories:

1.1 Open—cannot be budgeted. A prudent approach is to simply repeat the current year's actual for next year—unless the stewardship campaign will be trying to switch open donors to envelopes/PAP in a big way. In that case, estimate what percentage will switch, reduce the Open estimate for next year by that amount, and raise the percentage for Envelopes and PAP.

1.2 Envelopes—split with PAP, as noted above.

1.3 PAP—split with Envelopes, as noted above.

1.4 Special—cannot be budgeted (set at $0). If any income fits this sub-category next year, it may be used as a contingency for the parish's financial plan.

2. *In-Memoriums and Bequests.* Look at the current year's actuals. Were there significant donations that the parish really should not count on next year? If so, reduce the current year's actuals by this amount, and use the result for next year's budget. The split between the two sub-categories does not really matter.

Note: if the sexton plans to move in-memoriums and bequests to the capital account next year, ensure that the budget reflects this change.

Unlike donations from the congregation, these income categories cannot be predicted month by month. The best way to project monthly estimates is to consider the previous year's actual total, then divide by 12 to arrive at next year's.

3. *Fund-Raising.* The financial management team should look at fund-raising plans for next year, beyond any stewardship campaigns. Will fund-raisers increase in the coming year? Will they cost less to fund (i.e., will the net be higher)? Will they be better advertised/better attended?

Note: if a stewardship drive is planned for the coming year, the team should understand that special fund-raisers may bring in less income than those carried out in the current year (if there was no stewardship campaign carried out in the current year), unless the planned fund-raisers will tap into the broader community, rather than simply re-asking parishioners for more. If so, increased fund-raising income could be budgeted, even when an aggressive capital or stewardship campaign is underway. If the financial management team has planned specific fund-raisers for next year, and projected income from them, these should be itemized in the parish budget (as Fund-Raising sub-categories), so that the wardens, advisory board, and vestry can see how the overall fund-raising budget amount will be reached.

To arrive at monthly estimates, consider when next year's large fund-raisers are scheduled, and include the estimates in the proper months. For the remaining (smaller) events, add all projected income, divide by 12, and spread the income throughout the year.

4. *Rentals.* The financial management team should check with the sexton and the assets management team to find out what plans are underway for next year's rentals. If the sexton plans to switch the usage of parish facilities from income to outreach, the budget must project the drop in next year's income. If the sexton plans to increase rentals income through a more aggressive advertising campaign, improving the facilities, freeing up more rentable facilities, reducing fees, or a combination of these initiatives, the budget must also reflect the increased income as estimated by the sexton.

If the assets management team plans to focus on specific renters, the budget should include each renter as a sub-category, so that the wardens, advisory board, and vestry can see how the increase in rentals income will come about.

For monthly estimates, consider if there are any large-income renters that use the parish facilities at specific times of the year. If so, place their estimated income in the appropriate months. For all other small or year-round renters, total the projected income, divide by 12, and spread the income throughout the year.

5. *GST Rebates.* Unless the parish plans to spend a great deal more on taxable supplies and services next year, the same rebate amount from last year's actuals should be used for next year's budget.

For monthly estimates, determine when the parish received last year's rebates, and place these figures in the appropriate months for next year.

6. *Interest Income.* The financial management team must know if parish assets will be significantly increased or reduced next year. If the sexton and the assets management team have a large capital project planned for next year, for instance, the parish's principal investments will likely be reduced, with an associated reduction in interest income. However, if nothing significant is planned for next year, the budget for next year's interest income should equal this year's actual.

For monthly estimates, check during which months interest payments were received last year, and place these figures in the appropriate months for next year. All other interest payments can be totalled, divided by 12, and spread throughout the year.

7. *Other Income*—cannot be budgeted (set at $0). Again, any income posted here next year may serve as contingency funds.

Expense Categories

20. *Worship*—each sub-category below should be included when preparing this portion of the parish budget:

20.1 *Rector*—consider each sub-component (e.g., stipend, pension, travel, professional development, benefits). The diocese will issue an annual guideline to parishes on next year's clergy stipend, travel, etc., which the parish should refer to when preparing the budget. For the rector's stipend, the wardens may be considering an increase above the diocesan guideline, based on the incumbent's work over the past year and funds expected to be available. This should be discussed with the wardens, and included in the budget, as appropriate. Also, the rector's travel allowance should be considered: will there be more visitations next year? Other rector costs are based on the stipend, and can be calculated by the financial management team. Monthly estimates can be arrived at by dividing the total by 12.

20.2 *Relief Clergy*—will the rector be away more often next year, or will relief costs be the same as for last year? Does the rector know when he or she will be away next year? If so, place the relief estimate in the appropriate month(s). Otherwise, divide the total by 12 for monthly estimates.

20.3 *Curate*—will the parish be adding a curate to the clerical team next year, part-time or full-time? Will the parish be losing their curate next year? Or will next year's costs be the same as this year's? The estimate can be divided by 12 for monthly figures.

20.4 *Organist/Choir Director*—will the parish increase the honorarium amount, based on the organist's workload this year? Will the parish be replacing their more expensive organist next year with a less expensive parish volunteer? Or will the choir carry on next year as they have this year? In this case, can this year's actual amount be used as next year's budget amount? The estimate can be divided by 12 to obtain monthly figures.

20.5 *Relief Organist*—will the organist be away more next year than this year, or can this year's actual be used for the budget? Does the organist know when he or she will be away next year? If so, place the relief estimate in the appropriate month(s). Otherwise, divide the annual amount by 12 to obtain monthly figures.

20.6 *Choir Music*—is the choir director planning to significantly expand the choir's selections? Or will costs for music reproductions, copyright fees, etc., approximate the same costs as this year's? Divide the total estimate by 12 to obtain monthly figures.

20.7 *Church School Supplies*—will the same number of children/youth be present next year? Will the same number of classes be held? Will the same materials/venue be used? The Sunday school superintendent and youth group leader will need to let the financial management team know what is being planned for next year, to ensure the budget reflects this. When will the Sunday school/youth group materials be purchased? Place the estimates in the proper month(s).

20.8 *Worship Supplies*—will the parish be reproducing some of the hymns and service content in their bulletins next year (thereby driving up stationery and photocopy costs)? Will there be more newsletters next year? Will the parish be reducing paper and photocopy costs next year through e-mails and web site use? For monthly figures, divide the total estimate by 12.

20.9 *Adult Education*—will the parish offer more (or fewer) courses next year? Will these take place in a parish building or elsewhere? Include travel/lodging costs. Will there be additional facilitator costs or travel? Is the timing of the events known for next year? If so, place the estimates in the appropriate months. If not, divide the total estimate by 12 to obtain monthly figures.

21. *Staff*—will paid staff expenses be reduced through increased use of parish volunteers? Will honorariums need to be increased or decreased? Are any contracts involved?

The financial management team must budget for each paid position to ensure that the wardens, advisory board, and vestry understand any changes. For monthly estimates, consider if any paid staff will be reducing their hours in the summer or at other times of the year, and if so, adjust the monthly figures accordingly.

22. *Congregation Development*—the congregation development team leader should provide the financial management team with the specifics for next year: will parish advertising costs remain the same, or will these be increasing/decreasing? Will there be more/fewer fellowship events next year? Will these events be self-funding? For those fellowship events that require a budget, the team should create a sub-category for each. Monthly figures can be obtained by dividing total estimates by 12.

23. *Property*—the sexton should provide the financial management team with next year's assets management plan. Each sub-category below should

be included in the budget, so that the wardens, advisory board, and vestry will know how the budget amounts were arrived at:

23.1 *Church/Parish Hall: Water*—will next year's cost approximate this year's, or will efforts be made to cut back on usage (through reduced lawn watering, etc.)? Are water billings monthly or quarterly? Place figures in the appropriate months.

23.2 *Church/Parish Hall: Heating/AC*—are significant improvements in the buildings' energy efficiency planned, through resealing, double-glazing, timed thermostats, etc.? Will there be less expensive contracting? Or has the assets management team done all they can, and will next year's costs be the same as this year's *plus* any anticipated cost increases from suppliers? For monthly estimates, look at the parish's costs for the last three years. Calculate the percentage of the average annual total for each month, then use these percentages to calculate next year's monthly estimates. Example: by averaging the heating/AC totals for the last five years, the budget team has calculated that 12% of the heating/AC costs are incurred in January and 10% are incurred in February. To determine next year's budget amount for January, multiply the yearly estimate by 12%. For February, multiply the yearly estimate by 10%. Use the same formula to determine the remaining monthly budget amounts for next year.

23.3 *Church/Parish Hall: Hydro*—as above, next year's efforts to conserve would be reflected in this sub-category. For monthly totals, use the same approach as for 23.2 Heating/AC above.

23.4 *Church/Parish Hall: Cleaning*—will contracted staff be (partially) replaced by parish volunteers? Will more maintenance be needed? Will less expensive contract staff be used? For monthly totals, look at the previous years' actuals: does the parish carry out less cleaning during the summer? What percentages by month represent the total? Use these percentages to calculate next year's monthly estimates, as for 23.2 Heating/AC above.

23.5 *Church/Parish Hall: Groundskeeping*—will contracted staff be replaced by parish volunteers (partially)? Will more maintenance be needed? Will less expensive contract staff be used? For monthly totals, look at the previous years' actuals. Does the parish need less groundskeeping during the spring and fall? What percentages by month represent the total? Use these percentages to calculate next year's monthly estimates, as for 23.2 Heating/AC above.

23.6 *Church/Parish Hall: Repairs*—what repairs are included in the assets management team's plan for next year? What is the added contingency amount? Does the team know when the most expensive maintenance projects will be done? If so, put the estimates in the appropriate months. If not, divide the total estimate by 12 to obtain monthly figures.

23.7 *Rectory: Water*—same as 23.1, for the rectory.

23.8 *Rectory: Heating/AC*—same as 23.2, for the rectory.

23.9 *Rectory: Hydro*—same as 23.3, for the rectory.

23.10 *Rectory: Taxes*—what are the projected taxes, based on the municipality's estimate? Are taxes due quarterly? If so, place the estimates in the appropriate months. If due monthly, divide the total estimate by 12.

23.11 *Rectory: Telephone*—budget this year's actual amount plus the inflation rate for next year. Divide the total estimate by 12 to obtain monthly figures.

23.12 *Rectory: Repairs*—same as 23.6, for the rectory.

23.13 *Insurance*—what will be the projected premium, based on the company's estimate? When is the premium due? Place the estimate in the appropriate month.

23.14 *Other*—cannot be budgeted (set at $0). Expense contingencies should be built into the individual sub-categories.

24. *Administration*—both the financial management team and the congregation development team leader should estimate administration expenses, in light of next year's growth and communications plans. Include each sub-category below:

24.1 *Equipment*—will the parish be renegotiating service agreements/rates? Will usage go up (additional membership/events/communications) or down (e-mail/web site/decreases in membership)? Are expenses averaged monthly, or are there cost spikes? Place the estimates in the appropriate months.

24.2 *Stationery*—will usage go up (additional membership/events/communications) or down (e-mail/web site/decreases in membership)? Divide the total estimate by 12 to obtain monthly figures.

24.3 *Telephone*—will charges go down, based on more effective leverage of the parish's carrier(s)? Or up, due to increased usage? Divide the total estimate by 12 to obtain monthly figures.

24.4 *Postage*—will charges go down (e-mails/web site) or up (more members/better communications)? Will there be mass mailings at specific times during the year? If so, place the estimates in the appropriate months. Otherwise, divide the total estimate by 12 to obtain monthly figures.

24.5 *Other*—cannot be budgeted (set at $0). Expense contingencies should be built into the individual sub-categories.

25. *Financing Costs*—the financial management team should estimate these costs, based on their plans for next year and with input from the sexton, taking into account any property improvement plans. The sub-categories listed below should be included to help the wardens, advisory board, and vestry understand how the amounts were arrived at:

25.1 *Mortgage Interest*—does the term expire next year? If so, what is the bank's best estimate of rates? If not, what will be the declining interest portion throughout the year? Place the estimates in the appropriate months.

25.2 *Loan Interest*—for term loans, are there any expiries next year? If so, what are the estimated rates for renewal? What is the team's estimate for line of credit usage, and the bank's estimated interest rates for next year? Will the team be restructuring parish debt to minimize interest charges? If so, what is the bank's estimate for next year? Place the estimates in the appropriate months.

25.3 *Banking Fees*—will the team be leveraging the parish's banking relationship to minimize (or eliminate) these fees? Will increased use of PAPs decrease transaction and cheque fees? Will there be a consolidation (or distribution) of accounts next year? Divide the total estimate by 12 to obtain monthly figures.

26. *Fund-Raising Costs*—should be budgeted at $0, based on the objective that none of next year's fund-raisers should cost the parish.

Capital Account

The sexton will need to provide the estimates for the budget for this account, based on the assets management team's capital works plan and capital campaign for next year.

Income Categories

40. *Donations*—unless the assets management team is planning capital fund-

raisers and/or a capital campaign next year, the budget should assume the actuals from this year, unless extraordinary donations were made this year, in which case budget amounts should be reduced accordingly. The monthly estimates should reflect the planned timing of the fund-raising events and/ or the capital campaign donation flow start-up, and the monthly average thereafter.

41. *Interest Income*—if no significant capital works are planned for next year, the budgeted interest income should reflect this year's actuals. Otherwise, calculate the interest income based on the reduced capital amounts on deposit. Place amounts for interest payments in the appropriate months, or if received monthly, divide the total by 12 to obtain monthly figures.

Expense Categories

50. *Capital Payments*—the sexton estimates capital expenses for next year (both large and small) and budgets them here. To help the wardens, advisory board, and vestry understand the makeup of these expenses, the sexton should create a sub-category for each capital project, with its own budget amounts. For monthly estimates, specify when payments will likely be due, and their amounts.

51. *Banking Charges*—same as for this year. Divide the total by 12 for monthly figures. Note: if the parish is planning a large capital project (e.g., a new church or addition), the parish may need bridge financing to cover the project while the fund-raising proceeds come in. In these cases, bridge financing should be treated as a sub-category in those months when it will be needed.

Outreach Account

The outreach development team leader will need to provide the financial management team with next year's estimates of the outreach team's outreach appeal and the donation timings. While budgeting for this account is less critical to the parish than others (in that the outreach account will always net to zero—donations in will always equal donations out), it is important that the parish know the outreach goals set for next year.

Income Categories

60. *Donations*—the outreach development leader must provide the starting point for donations in, and the monthly estimates thereafter. The financial management team should place the estimates in the appropriate months.

Expense Categories

70. *Contributions*—payments to outreach programs will flow when donations are received, and will net the outreach account to zero. The financial management team can do this cash-flow estimate, based on donation in-flows and their monthly amounts.

71. *Program Costs*—if outreach program costs will be deducted from the outreach account, the budget must reflect this. The cost estimates, and when they are expected, should come from the outreach development team leader. The financial management team should place these estimates in the appropriate months. If the parish funds the outreach program costs from the operating account, the estimates go into the corresponding category in the operating account.

72. *Banking Charges*—use last year's actuals and divide the total by 12 for monthly figures. Again, these may be paid out of the operating account for some parishes.

73. *Diocese Assessment*—according to the diocese's assessment for next year, the financial management team should divide the amount by 4 (if quarterly payments) or 12 (if monthly), and place the expenses in the appropriate months.

74. *Synod*—according to the diocese's schedule for next year, and the parish's number of delegates who will be attending, place the estimated costs in the appropriate months.

Cemetery Account

Since plot purchases, burials, and maintenance cannot be planned for by month, the best approach is to take last year's actuals and divide by 12 to calculate monthly figures. Each sub-category (e.g., plot purchases, burials, maintenance) should be included in the budget.

The Finished Budget—Staying on Track

When the financial management team has completed the budget, and has reviewed it with the wardens and advisory board, and has had it passed by vestry, the budget should then be input to the manual or automated ledger of the parish by the secretary/bookkeeper. This is a rather big job—if the secretary/bookkeeper is normally very busy with the day-to-day running of the parish office. The financial management team should arrange (volunteer) office help while the secretary/bookkeeper does the initial set-up of the annual budget.

Once set up, the secretary/bookkeeper can use the monthly budget estimates to track actual income and expenses. Large differences will act as early warnings to the secretary/bookkeeper, who could inform the treasurer as they occur. This will allow the treasurer (and the wardens, if necessary) to take corrective action as events unfold, rather than later, when the parish may not easily recover. Each month, the secretary/bookkeeper should produce an income and expenses report that includes the monthly budget estimates and any variances to the corresponding actuals. The treasurer and wardens could then use the information to address variances in the advisory board meeting, as necessary.

A parish with a well-prepared budget, such as the one outlined above, and a process to manage and monitor its finances, will operate much more smoothly and show good stewardship of the parish's financial resources and its ParishWorks.

When the parish has had several years' experience of monthly budget management (including variance management), the financial management team could undertake to create a **three-year financial plan** for the parish. With respect to the parish's long-term goals, the financial management team could create a budget that moves the parish to where it wants to be over time. For example, if the parish is trying to pay off its mortgage, the three-year plan would include a capital campaign to accomplish that, year by year. (The long-term plan would also include gradual reductions in parish costs.) Another example: the parish is undertaking an aggressive congregation development program to increase its membership over the next three years, plus an aggressive three-year stewardship campaign. The financial management team would create a three-year plan showing the gradual increase in parish income year by year.

From these three-year plans, an annual budget could be prepared. At every year-end, the financial management team would check actuals against the three-year plan to help determine any adjustments needed to get the plan back on track. Ideally every parish should aim for this more strategic level of financial management—however, it cannot jump to this stage until annual monthly budget tracking has been mastered.

The Financial Management Team

While the canons specify that the financial management of the parish rests with the wardens, this task (plus all the other responsibilities of the wardens) is usually too much for two people to carry. In most parishes, wardens delegate some of their financial management responsibilities to parish treasurers, secretary/bookkeepers, and others. While the treasurer and secretary/bookkeeper and other members of the parish's financial management team carry out their agreed duties, it is important they understand that the ultimate responsibility for financial management of the parish still rests with the wardens. All too often, well-meaning treasurers or secretary/bookkeepers have forgotten this point in the process of doing the day-to-day work, and have gone off on their own to commit the parish to income or expenses that the wardens have had no involvement in. Likewise, in some parishes the wardens become so distanced from the day-to-day financial operations of their parish that they lose track of what is happening.

Having said that, the financial management team can do a lot for a parish to keep it on a financial even keel. While the responsibilities of a parish's financial management team may vary, here are some considerations:

- set-up and maintenance of the parish's financial records and reporting, including controls, procedures, and automation;
- set-up and maintenance of the parish's bank accounts, financing, and investment structures;
- expense management;
- fund-raising initiatives, including parish stewardship campaigns;
- set-up of paid staff remuneration levels; and
- creation of the parish's annual draft budget, with input from the parish sexton, outreach development team leader, and congregation development team leader.

Who might make up the financial management team? For starters, the parish treasurer should chair the team and lead it in its work. Other key members would be the parish secretary/bookkeeper, the envelope secretary, the stewardship coordinator, and the fund-raising events coordinator. The team should meet each month to review the results of the previous month's work, and to plan the work of the forthcoming months. The team should have annual goals for expense management (reductions), automation, banking improvements, fund-raising targets, and raising overall stewardship levels.

The Financial Management Plan

It would be helpful for the team to create an annual financial management plan. This plan would not only guide the team throughout the year, but would be used to inform the parish of the team's plans. Other team leaders (especially the sexton, outreach development, and congregation development) would also appreciate having the information, to ensure that their plans will match.

The team should meet each year in the fall to plan their ParishWorks for next year. The team would estimate,

- if acquiring new accounting software next year, the software costs, computer hardware upgrades, professional support costs, additional staff costs for the conversion period, and ongoing maintenance costs, as well as reduced staff costs, banking and interest fees, and stationery costs;
- capital costs for new office equipment (if planned—computer, photocopier, fax machine), as well as changes in maintenance costs for the upcoming year;
- reductions in stationery, photocopier usage costs, and postage through increased use of e-mail and web site content improvements;
- reductions in banking and interest fees through initiatives to consolidate debts, renegotiate rates and fees, and accounting automation;
- reductions in staff costs through increased use of volunteers; and
- increases in parish income through more cost-effective and more frequent fund-raising events and/or through a stewardship campaign. (Note: if the team is planning a multi-year stewardship campaign launch in the upcoming year, the campaign should have its own separate plan. The plan should be included in the overall financial management plan as an appendix.)

When the team has completed the plan to their satisfaction, the treasurer should provide copies to the wardens, treasurer, and advisory board for their feedback and approval. The plan would then be included in the vestry package for vestry approval. The treasurer should attend vestry to motion adoption of the plan, and to respond to any questions.

The following template has helped other parishes' financial management teams to successfully build their plan. To use this template, read the italicized notes in each section, then replace these notes with the content of your plan. An electronic version in Microsoft Word format may be found on the enclosed CD (see finplan.doc).

Financial Management Plan

For

Parish Name

Table of Contents

Program Team/Scope

The Team. *List the members of the financial development team, their phone numbers, street and e-mail addresses; their role(s) within the team (e.g., their special interests, talents, passions); and their time available to support the team's work. Include the organization of the team, if it might prove helpful to the readers of the plan.*

Program Scope *for the year. List the team's scope boundaries. These may include financial limitations, workload limitations, timing limitations (e.g., certain program events must occur at specific times or dates), the parish's expectations of the team for the year being planned.*

For the financial management team, consider the following scope attributes:

- *the number of volunteers likely available to do the work of the team during the planning year, and the hours per week/month they have available to do the work. They will be particularly needed for fund-raising events and stewardship campaigns. For ongoing volunteer positions needed to replace paid staff time, and the estimated hours for the year, give estimates separately for each of the team's volunteer focal points: secretarial duties, accounting entries input, reconciliation, etc.; and*
- *the expense budget lines available to the team for next's year's work. This should include each parish budget line for which the financial management team is responsible: stationery, office equipment, staff, telephone, postage, financing costs, fund-raising costs.*

Program Objectives for 20__

The objectives of the financial management team for next year include the team's and the parish's expectations. The objectives should be specific and measurable. Use objective statements that will move the parish from where it is today to where it will be by year-end. Include how the changes will be measured at year-end (i.e., How did we do?).

Example of a poor financial management objective: "Increase fund-raising income next year."

Example of a strong financial management objective: "Increase fund-raising income by 20%, generating an additional $10,000 income for the parish. This will be done by reducing the costs of fund-raising projects, eliminating those that do not have a good return, initiating others that have better potential, increasing the number of events, improving internal events marketing within the parish, and initiating a community marketing campaign for all events next year. The results of each fund-raising event will be tracked each month by the financial management team, and corrective actions carried out throughout the year, to ensure that the team's targets are met."

For each objective, note those that are interdependent, and how. Example: to execute a stewardship campaign, the financial management team needs to enlist 12 parish volunteers for the calling phase of the campaign, for 2 months. Those same volunteers will be needed by the congregation development team next year for their parishioner skills-and-passions inventory calling program. The financial management team will need to work closely with the congregation development team to ensure that the volunteer requirements of the two projects do not overlap. Or better yet, two project teams could integrate the calling phase of their two projects, so that all calls are made at the same time. Regardless, interdependencies such as these need to be documented in the plan, and consideration given to how they will be managed.

When the list of objectives is drawn up, inspect the objectives carefully. Are they realistic for the year? Can all the objectives be accomplished given the resources available to the team, the extra volunteers available in the parish, the parish's ability to absorb the changes proposed, and the parish budget available? Do any of the objectives depend on the successes of another program team? If so, are they in sync with yours?

It is better to drop objectives at the outset, and have the team meet a reduced set, than to overextend the team and have them fail. Remember, there is always next year. However, the team should always have objectives before them that "stretch" them—this is how teams grow and learn.

Here are some sample financial management objectives for the team's consideration:

1. To reduce the staff costs of the parish by 50% next year ($30,000), by using an ongoing volunteer team to do the corresponding work.

2. To reduce parish administration expenses by 30% next year ($10,000), by reducing the parish's stationery consumption, photocopy use, and postage costs through increased use of e-mails and better web site content: -$2,000; by switching from our current telephone provider to xxx and bundling all of our telephone services: -$3,000; and by replacing our leased photocopier with a purchase: -$5,000.

3. To reduce our financing costs by 10% next year ($12,000), by switching our line of credit to a mortgage, eliminating our banking fees, and reducing our float amount through better tracking of balances using the online banking service.

4. To reduce our secretary/bookkeeper's workhours by 500 ($5,000), by replacing the manual accounting ledger with QuickBooks.

Initiatives

List the program initiatives for the year that will address the objectives. For each, include

- **what** the initiative is, which objectives it will address, and a description of the development work required to complete it;
- **who** will be working on developing the initiative, including the number of volunteers needed in addition to the financial management team members;

- **when** the development work must be completed, related to when the initiative is to be provided to the parish; and
- **how** and **when** the program team will measure the initiative's success. (e.g., how and when the team will recalculate the staff costs, stationery costs, telephone costs, and so on, to confirm that the objectives were met).

Note any initiative prerequisites or assumptions, and any interdependencies of other program teams' initiatives.

Schedule

Two schedules are needed in the financial management plan:

1. A **schedule of upcoming financial management parish events** (fund-raisers, stewardship campaign launches, etc.), which should be reflected in the parish calendar, in the parish's service bulletins, newsletters, and web site, so that parishioners can plan their attendance/participation accordingly.

2. An **initiatives development schedule** that includes the resources and development time required for each parish event (e.g., stewardship campaign launches) or target milestones (e.g., "QuickBooks installed" or "term loan approved," etc.). This schedule will be used by the financial management team to ensure adequate preparation for the published parish events and planned milestones.

When the team meets each month, they should use the development schedule to determine if there are any problems with the planned development work and then take corrective action, if required (e.g., enlisting more people to help prepare, moving event dates, etc.).

Financials/Resources

Financials

With respect to the planned financial management initiatives, the team will need to summarize the costs of the program for the year ahead (capital costs for new office equipment/software, stewardship campaign promotional materials, fund-raising event costs, etc.) and indicate when the expenses will expect to be incurred. This way, the treasurer will be able to include these costs in the parish's budget for the upcoming year, under the appropriate expense lines. When approved by vestry, the budget line-items can be used by the financial management team, as needed.

In addition, the estimated additional annual parish income from the team's improvement initiatives (increased parish donations through the stewardship campaign, etc.) should be summarized, and the information passed to the treasurer for inclusion in the upcoming year's budget.

If the team discovers significant variances between the actual costs and income versus those planned in the parish budget (plus or minus), the team needs to advise the treasurer. A negative variance may be covered by a contingency budget line, or the treasurer may have to raise the matter with the wardens or advisory board for resolution.

Resources

The team should summarize the monthly volunteer resources and skills required (beyond those of the team) to support the financial management team. The parish's volunteer coordinator will use this information to recruit the appropriate volunteers.

When all parish program teams circulate their completed plans at the start of the year, the volunteer coordinator may advise the financial management team that the required resources may not be available in the numbers or at the time planned. In these cases, the team will need to revise the plan.

Program Management Process

The financial management plan needs to lay out how the team's progress will be monitored throughout the year. Some best practices for the team's consideration follow:

1. Team Meetings

The team should meet monthly (same time each month) to review planned activities, past and future. The team meeting should be chaired by the treasurer. Minutes are not necessary, but the treasurer will need to keep track of commitments made during the meeting, for follow-up purposes. The team should bring copies of their development schedule and events calendar with them to each meeting.

Team meetings should be issue-focused (e.g., issues with the development schedule/events calendar), not focused on brainstorming solutions. The meetings may then be conducted within one to one and a-half hours.

Here is a suggested agenda:

- How has the team been doing since the last meeting? Achievements should be celebrated. Problems should be learned from and used to modify subsequent events as appropriate, or used when preparing next year's plan.
- What's next? Who is working on what, according to the development schedule? How is it going? Will we be ready for the event(s)? If not, what needs to be done? Are there any cost variances?

- Are there any ideas for changes to the plan? Any new events needed but not included? If so, how might they be resourced? Are there any events that should be cancelled?

2. Program Reporting

The treasurer (or designate) should report the team's status to the wardens and advisory board each month, ideally following the team's own monthly meeting if possible. The treasurer may wish to schedule the team's monthly meetings to be a week or so ahead of the advisory board's meeting, so that the board receives up-to-date information.

Team reports may be quite brief (e.g., one-half to one page in length). The program update for the wardens and the advisory board should include events since the last update and results, upcoming development work and issues, and issues for the wardens' or board's action, if any.

The financial management report might be tabled only for the advisory board's information. Also, it is not necessary for the treasurer to attend the board's meeting, unless there are issues for the wardens' or board's action.

In addition to the advisory board's monthly report, the treasurer should prepare an annual financial management report for vestry that describes the work of the financial management team in the year ending, lessons learned, and plans for the upcoming year. The treasurer should attend, in case there are questions from the vestry on the program.

3. Parish Surveys

Before the team meets to develop their plan for the upcoming year, the team should ask the parish what they thought of the financial management work this year (expenses reduction, staffing costs reduction, stewardship campaign, etc.). What was good? What was not so good? What was missing?

The team should use the same guidelines in the parish survey (see chapter 4) when preparing a survey of the team's work (e.g., avoidance of tick boxes, use of pot-lucks, etc.).

The team should use the feedback to plan next year's program.

Key Financial Team Members

The parish secretary/bookkeeper's role often expands to include everything no one else wants to do, which is quite unfair: not only is it unrealistic to expect the incumbent to do everything for everyone, it becomes impossible for the incumbent to improve the processes and quality of the work done, or to be fairly assessed as to performance. To avoid this, parishes should document the secretary/bookkeeper's position description and make it clear to all who use the secretary/bookkeeper's services to keep their expectations (and requests) in line.

The following template may help in creating a position description for your secretary/bookkeeper. An electronic version may be found in Microsoft Word format on the enclosed CD (see sec.doc).

Position Description: Parish Secretary/Bookkeeper

Role

The role of the parish secretary/bookkeeper is twofold. The parish secretary acts as a day-to-day contact point for those phoning or e-mailing the parish for information and for message taking. The secretary also manages the parish office, its supplies, the mail, and filing systems. In addition, the secretary performs general clerical assistance as requested by parish officers.

The parish bookkeeper maintains the financial records of the parish, issues cheques for payments, produces financial reports for the parish officers, and reconciles the parish's financial records with those of the parish's bank.

Responsibilities

The responsibilities of the parish secretary/bookkeeper include

- pick-up and distribution of mail and faxes to the rector and wardens;
- answering the phone when in the office; leaving messages as necessary;
- ordering office supplies as requested by the rector and wardens;
- general filing;
- maintaining paper and toner supplies for the parish's photocopier(s), fax machine, and computer printer(s);
- contacting service people when office equipment breaks down;
- preparing and mailing cheques for payments to various payees (telephone company; water; electricity; etc.);
- updating the parish's financial records using the software package on the parish office computer;

- printing monthly financial reports from the system for the treasurer and wardens;
- reconciling the monthly bank and diocesan statements to the parish's financial records; and
- filing financial documents (invoices, cheque stubs, etc.).

Duration

The parish secretary/bookkeeper is appointed by the wardens or vestry for a term of one year, renewable each year following.

Skills Required

- Good telephone etiquette when answering the phone; a professional demeanour when taking messages;
- organizational skills, to sort out multiple assignments in order of priority;
- tact and professionalism, to deal with multiple requests at one time;
- understanding of filing systems, and appropriate filing sequences;
- operation of and primary troubleshooting for parish office equipment (computer, modem, printer, monitor, photocopier, fax machine);
- discipline to follow financial transaction procedures consistently, even when others attempt to short-cut the process;
- computer operations knowledge, including Windows, Microsoft Word, Microsoft Excel, telecommunications connection protocols, and the parish's financial accounting software system; and
- basic accounting knowledge, to track actual income and expenses to the monthly budget, and to report variances to the treasurer as required.

The parish treasurer acts as the chairperson of the financial management team, and as the financial advisor to the wardens. The treasurer is responsible for setting the parish's chart of accounts and income/expense categories, formatting the financial reportings and their frequencies, verification of the financial records of the parish, and the financing structure with the parish's bank. (All of these responsibilities are carried out in consultation with the wardens, who have delegated these responsibilities to the treasurer.)

The following sample position description for a parish treasurer may be found in Microsoft Word format on the enclosed CD (see treas.doc). The description assumes that the treasurer is a parish volunteer who does not serve as secretary/bookkeeper. In many parishes, the roles of treasurer and bookkeeper are combined. In these cases, the position descriptions provided here for secretary/bookkeeper and treasurer should be combined.

Position Description: Parish Treasurer

Role

The parish treasurer acts as the chief financial officer of the parish, setting up the financial records of the parish and ensuring that these are properly maintained. The treasurer sets the initial version of the parish's annual budget, adjusting it as necessary, based on approved changes from vestry. The treasurer monitors parish income and expenses to the approved parish budget, highlighting variances to the wardens, for resolution. The treasurer is the parish's representative to the parish's bank, ensuring that the services provided are as required by the parish.

The treasurer manages the work of the parish bookkeeper on a day-to-day basis, ensuring that the parish's financial records are properly maintained, and that the parish's financial procedures are being properly followed.

The treasurer verifies the records of the envelope secretary, ensuring that the donors ledger is properly maintained, and that the year-end tax receipts are issued properly.

Responsibilities

The parish treasurer reports to the church wardens and acts as the focal point in the parish for the tracking and reporting of all financial matters, including

- annual preparation of the parish's operating budget for approval by the wardens and vestry;
- monthly tracking of variances for the month between the budget's planned income and expenses versus actuals; reporting these to the wardens and the advisory board;
- monthly projection of the parish's year-end financial position based on variances to date;

- general supervision of the work of the parish bookkeeper, including the verification of proper financial recordkeeping throughout the year;
- monthly verification of the bank and diocesan accounts reconciliation carried out by the parish bookkeeper;
- general supervision of the work of the envelope secretary, including monthly verification of the donors ledger and verification of donor tax receipts at year-end;
- annual preparation of the treasurer's report to vestry, including income and expense totals for the year, along with closing balances;
- annual reporting to the Canada Revenue Agency for GST rebates; and
- annual assistance to the parish auditor in carrying out the parish's financial audit.

Duration

The parish treasurer is appointed by the wardens or voted from a roster of candidates at vestry. The treasurer is a voluntary position. The treasurer normally serves for one year, but the term can be extended in one-year increments by the wardens or vestry. The treasurer's term normally begins at the closing of the annual vestry meeting.

Skills Required

- Basic math and accounting skills, including the ability to prepare financial statements, understand banking, prepare an annual budget, and track actual variances to a budget;
- basic supervision skills (for the parish bookkeeper and envelope secretary). While the bookkeeper is responsible for all transaction-recording in the parish ledger, the treasurer ensures that the work is carried out properly. While the envelope secretary is responsible for all entries in the donors ledger and for the production of annual tax receipts, the treasurer ensures that the work is carried out properly;
- basic computer skills. Knowledge of the financial software package is not a requirement since the bookkeeper is the primary user of the system; and
- capacity to be highly responsible, ensuring that the parish stays on track to its approved budget, and that variances are properly dealt with.

Application to Your Parish

In all sizes of parishes, several basic financial management processes must be in place—if they are not, arrange to do so immediately:

1. The wardens should be on top of the financial situation of the parish; they should understand the actuals to date versus the budget, and the steps being taken to stay on track. If not, ensure that they get monthly reports to help them in this; schedule monthly meetings with the wardens, treasurer, and bookkeeper to ensure all are in sync.

2. No outstanding claims on, or rebates claimed by, the parish, should exist. If so, find out what is being done, who is responsible, and what are the due dates.

3. The financials of the parish are segregated—operating versus outreach versus capital versus cemetery (if applicable). If not, have these segregated. Consider separate bank accounts for each.

4. All financial transactions are processed using dual controls (i.e., two cheque signers, two payment authorizers, two collection counters). Consider using control forms such as the payment authorization form and the weekly collection form described in this chapter.

5. All payments have receipts. If not, they should not be paid.

6. Monthly bank and diocesan statement reconciliations are correct and up to date.

7. Monthly parish financial reporting is up to date versus the budget.

Once these critical financial management processes are in place, the parish can turn to more proactive financial management work:

8. Check to see if the parish is claiming all they can for GST rebates. (Many parishes do not, which means lost donor-based income). Make sure the returns are being prepared and sent properly, and that the Canada Revenue Agency is up to date with the parish's rebates.

9. Carry out an expense management program:

- ensure that office equipment is being serviced in the best (and least expensive) ways possible;
- look for ways to cut back on paper, postage, and photocopier use (through use of e-mails and the parish web site);
- look for ways to reduce the secretary/bookkeeper's workload (through volunteers, reassignment of work, automation, etc.);
- renegotiate the parish's telephone charges (through bundling with Internet access or choosing other suppliers);
- negotiate lower/no banking fees by leveraging the parish's overall relationship with the bank;
- consider renegotiating the parish's debt structures; and
- make sure that property expense management rests with the sexton and the assets management team. Check that they are being proactive in this regard. If not, offer to help them out.

10. If the parish does not yet have a computer, consider obtaining one, either as a donation or a secondhand purchase, especially if the parish's secretary/bookkeeper is a paid position—the computer will lower their workload and therefore, their remuneration. The computer will also enable the parish to take advantage of e-mail communication and to maintain a web site.

11. Regardless of parish size, potential to improve the level of stewardship will always exist. In small parishes, this may be done by word of mouth. In medium- to large-scale parishes, more planning will need to be carried out, due to the larger number of parishioners, and the potential levels of income involved. Consider having a stewardship campaign next year, following the tips in this chapter and those in chapters 8 (The Annual Outreach Campaign) and 9 (Capital Campaigns).

Medium- and Large-Scale Parishes

12. Review the parish's income and expense categories. Do they make sense to everyone? Are there enough, so that the underlying financial details can be analyzed for expense reduction opportunities or income improvement initiatives? Are there too many, or are they overly complex, and confusing to most people? How do they compare with the ones suggested in this chapter?

13. Have the responsibilities of parish treasurer been assigned to a volunteer other than the wardens? In medium- to large-scale parishes, usually wardens do not have time to act as parish treasurer in addition to their many other responsibilities. Consider making one of the deputy wardens the parish treasurer. For the deputy warden, this might be a training opportunity for when he/she becomes a warden.

14. Has the day-to-day payment process and bank reconciliation work been assigned to a parish bookkeeper (someone other than the parish treasurer)? Again, in medium- to large-scale parishes, the day-to-day work will overwhelm a parish treasurer, and will get them so deep in the forest, they won't be able to see the trees (e.g., analyzing the year-to-date trends to determine if the budget is still valid, etc.). Use the position description provided in this chapter (with parish-specific changes) to recruit the bookkeeper. Ensure that the bookkeeper is supported by the treasurer and wardens week by week. Provide motivation, clarification of the bookkeeping procedures, and protection to the incumbent from unreasonable demands by other parishioners.

15. If not already done, consider moving responsibility for reduction of property management expenses to the sexton and assets management team. They are in a far better position to get the necessary work done, and the parish treasurer will be too busy with other responsibilities to seriously look at these issues.

Chapter 12

Making It Happen

"Well, there's a lot to be done," you might be thinking. "Where do we start?"

Consider the evolution of your parish as a process of continuous improvement, flowing through four stages of development as outlined below—crisis avoidance, first aid, proactivity, and excellence. With respect to the following tasks in each stage, determine which stage your parish is at, and tackle only one stage's tasks at a time. When you have moved the parish through that stage, move on to the next.

Stage I—Crisis Avoidance

In this stage, the parish leadership team does not know if the parish has a crisis brewing or not. The idea is to find out where the parish stands on these "hot issues," and defuse them before they blow up. *These potential issues apply to all sizes of parishes:*

1. *Parish Leadership Team.* Is the team functioning well together and communicating well with the parish (refer to chapter 2)? If not, the parish is in crisis and will not progress much further than where it is now. Try team-building sessions facilitated by the diocese's consultants. Try widening the parish leadership team to include the two deputy wardens—often a team of five will operate with less personal stress than three. If these changes do not work, change the member(s) of the team.

2. *Property Inspection.* Does the parish know the condition of its buildings and lands? If not, there could be a significant problem that, if not attended to, could close the church building. Schedule an inspection and prioritize the findings for remediation. Make sure the parish has a copy of the deed and survey—there could be legal issues the parish is unaware of.

3. *Renters.* Does the parish's rental agreement have a liability and damages clause (see chapter 9)? If not, the parish could be sued by renters for accidents

occurring on church property, or renters could destroy parish assets without recourse by the parish. Make any necessary changes to the rental agreements, and have them re-signed.

4. *Financial Controls.* Are all cheques co-signed? Are all payments co-authorized? Is all cash dual counted? Are the bank accounts reconciled? Are operating funds segregated from capital and outreach? If not, have these procedural failures corrected, since they could lead to theft, fraud, and parish bankruptcy.

5. *Budget Tracking.* Are parish income and expenses being tracked to the year's budget? If not, the parish could be heading into account overdrafts and debt. Find out where the actuals are year-to-date, relative to the budget, and take any necessary corrective actions to get back on track. Or strike a new (balanced) budget, and call a special vestry to adopt it.

6. *Member Retention.* Do you know if the average Sunday attendance is stable, growing, or dropping? If you don't know, find out. If the parish is losing members at an unacceptable rate, find out why and take corrective action, or there may be no parish shortly.

Stage II—First Aid

Once the parish has moved beyond Stage I, it is necessary to look at causes for potential Stage I failures, and stop them at the source. ***Again, these issues apply to all sizes of parishes:***

7. *Capital Fund.* Does the parish have one, and if so, does it have a reasonable balance to cover contingencies (e.g., new furnace, computer, etc.)? If not, set up a capital fund, and initiate capital fund-raisers to get it in shape; otherwise a costly capital failure could cripple the parish. To be successful in this, the wardens will need to appoint a ***parish sexton*** to run with this initiative. In small parishes, one of the wardens could wear the sexton hat—however, this is not recommended, as both wardens usually have enough on their plates (even in the smallest parishes) without having to worry about capital fund-raising.

8. *Volunteer Burnout.* Are any key volunteers showing signs of burnout (see chapter 5)? If so, take corrective action, or the parish will soon lose them. In medium- to large-scale parishes, the wardens may need to appoint a ***volunteer coordinator*** to help recruit replacements.

9. *Advisory Board Atrophy.* Do the advisory board meetings drag on with no apparent purpose? Do the members feel underutilized or disenfranchised? If so, take corrective action immediately (see chapters 2, 5, and 6). Without a committed, valued, and active advisory board, the wardens will be working in a vacuum, and the parish could drift (back) into Stage I condition. Also, the board members will likely leave the parish, if they are not respected and listened to—the board members represent the future leaders of the parish.

10. *Financial Reporting.* Do the wardens receive complete and accurate monthly income and expense reports and trial balances (see chapter 11)? If not, take corrective action immediately—otherwise, the crisis avoidance you did in Stage I will only reoccur. To ensure that these reports are produced each month, the wardens will likely need to appoint a **parish treasurer** and a **parish bookkeeper**. In small parishes, one of the wardens could be wearing the treasurer's hat. However, they cannot efficiently carry out these two sets of duties and process the day-to-day financial transactions of the parish—a parish bookkeeper is needed in all sizes of parishes. If a small parish did appoint a treasurer, that person could also act as bookkeeper, although warden oversight would be needed in this situation to ensure dual controls are maintained.

11. *Rentals Collection.* Are there any rental payments outstanding? If so, follow up with the renters as soon as possible (see chapter 9). This is lost income for the parish.

12. *Cemetery Records.* Are they accurate and up to date? Is someone in the parish assigned to maintain them (e.g., sexton, parish secretary)? If not, follow up as soon as possible (see chapter 9), as future plot purchases could result in unforgettable problems.

13. *Staff Management.* Have the wardens reviewed the staff members' performance and morale lately (see chapter 10)? If not, do so immediately, otherwise, the parish could lose a valued paid volunteer or staff member. Or (the flip side) the parish may not be receiving the value they are paying for.

14. *Signage.* Are parish signs in good shape and well-lit (see chapter 4)? If not, follow up as soon as possible, as this is a direct reflection of the parish for passersby, newcomers, and current members.

15. *Expense Management.* Is the parish team working to reduce expenses (see

chapters 9 and 11)? If not, inflation and membership losses could combine to drive the parish's bank account into the red. In small parishes, the efforts of the sexton and treasurer might be sufficient to carry out any projects needed to reduce parish expenses (assets costs and administration costs). In medium- to large-scale parishes, an *assets management team* and a *financial management team* should help the sexton and treasurer, respectively, carry out the necessary projects. To create these teams, the parish's volunteer coordinator could recruit members.

16. *Absentee Parishioners.* Has anyone called the families on the parish list who have not been seen for some time (refer to chapter 4)? If not, get a calling program underway. It may not be too late to get these families back. In small parishes, this might be do-able by one of the wardens and a small team of volunteers. In medium- to large-scale parishes, it is best to appoint a *congregation development leader* and recruit a team. Again, the parish's volunteer coordinator could help with this.

Stage III—Proactivity

When the parish appears to be stable, look at ways to improve all aspects of the parish—financial growth, membership growth, quality of parish programs and worship, level and effectiveness of outreach, condition of buildings and property, relationship with the community, well-being of the parish family, etc. For small parishes, some of these steps may overtax the parish's human and financial resources. However, they should still be reviewed and adopted as possible:

17. *Parish Survey.* Have the members been asked what they are looking for in their parish—are they happy with things the way they are (see chapter 4)? If not, initiate a parish survey as soon as possible, or the parish will continue to lose members. In small parishes, the survey could be carried out by the wardens in a pot-luck event, assisted by some volunteer callers to interview absent members. Even with a small number of members, however, the wardens will need to give the survey questions some thought before asking for feedback.

In medium- to large-scale parishes, use the congregation development team to run with this initiative. They should consider additional help from the diocese to help facilitate the event. From the outcome of the survey, it is critical that the leadership team respond to the passions identified in the survey, to ensure that they are enabled through parish programs. In small parishes, the missing programs may need to be filled through partnerships with sister parishes, the diocese, or prepackaged adult education events. In medium- to large-scale parishes, the congregation development team should acquire program materials for groups wanting these, and initiate the formation of program teams where none exist.

18. *Worship Development Team.* Does the parish have a working worship development team, with lay members helping to develop the worship program for the parish (see chapter 7)? If not, get this underway as soon as possible to ensure that average Sunday attendance will rise.

19. *Pastoral Care Program.* Have shut-in members been visited in the last month? If not, get this underway immediately. In small parishes, the rector, wardens, and some volunteers could manage the visitation load. In medium- to large-scale parishes, assign this responsibility to the worship development team.

20. *Refinancing.* Has the parish approached its bank or the diocesan office to discuss better ways of managing the parish's debt (see chapter 11)? If not, the treasurer and wardens should schedule this immediately, as there may be ways of restructuring the parish's accounts and types of loans to save the parish banking fees and interest payments.

21. *Newcomers Focus.* Does the parish have greeters with welcome kits, who can identify and link up with newcomers as they arrive in the parish (see chapter 4)? Are there newcomers' events, so that newcomers are offered the opportunity to appreciate the programs available and meet the people who deliver them? If not, get this going as soon as possible, or the parish may become a revolving door to potential members. In small parishes, the wardens might take on the greeter role and do newcomer follow-ups, if the numbers are fairly small. In medium- to large-scale parishes, the congregation development team should be responsible for this. The parish's volunteer coordinator could recruit the greeters.

22. *Outreach Development Plan.* Does the parish have an annual outreach development plan that includes local needs assessments, community partnerships, and outreach programs integration (see chapter 8)? If not, follow up to get this going, or the parish's donors will be confused by all of the outreach appeals within and outside of the parish, and will not respond as well as they could. In small parishes, the appointment of an outreach coordinator will

probably suffice, with occasional help from volunteers during the outreach campaign (to handle phone calls, mailings, etc.). In medium- to large-scale parishes, the wardens should appoint an ***outreach development leader*** to lead an ***outreach development team***. The parish's volunteer coordinator could help recruit the team.

23. *Parish Web Site.* Does the parish have one (see chapters 4 and 7)? If not, initiate this as soon as possible. Several web-building kits are sold on the market, and often computer-savvy people in the congregation can do the building job for the parish on a volunteer basis. The web site will help advertise the parish to potential newcomers, advertise the availability of rental space to potential renters, include the service bulletin and sermon to reach out to shut-ins, improve communicating upcoming events to members, etc. Properly designed, the parish secretary could maintain the web site, with minimal training and effort.

24. *Accounting Automation.* If the parish has not already done so, consider the purchase of accounting software to assist the parish bookkeeper in managing the parish's financial records. If the bookkeeper is a paid position, this will save the parish some staff costs, and provide the financial reports that the wardens require.

Stage IV—Excellence in ParishWorks

With the parish on the road to continuous improvement, it is time to take stock. What attributes make your parish one of excellence in its ParishWorks, with its parishioners "stretching" themselves every day to be more than what anyone can ask or what they can imagine?:

25. *Volunteer Management.* All members of the parish are treated as a highly valued, passionate volunteer base (see chapters 4 and 5). The congregation development team and volunteer coordinator keep the volunteer profiles current by repeating the parish surveys each year or every other year. All key leadership positions have succession plans, with replacements in training. Formal volunteer appreciation services are held two or three times a year.

26. *Parish Mission Statement.* All parish initiatives are driven by the parish mission statement (see chapter 3). Its objectives are tangible and measurable. The parish measures itself each year to ensure that it continues to improve and grow.

27. *Parish Growth Plan*. The parish has an ongoing growth plan, which advertises the parish, leverages relationships with service partners in the community, and builds a reputation of excitement and depth in its program offerings (see chapters 4 and 6). The plan measures the growth in membership numbers, attendance, and volunteer rates, to feed a continuous improvement process.

28. *Outreach Programs*. The parish partners with other service organizations in the community to co-sponsor significant outreach programs and facilities for those in need locally. All members of the parish are donors and many are volunteers in these programs. ***The community looks to the parish as an anchor in building a caring community.***

29. *Stewardship Campaigns*. The parish runs annual stewardship campaigns, to remind its members of the callings of their faith, with annual targets that encourage members to grow in their gifts of time, talent, and treasure. These campaigns are held to educate newcomers and to celebrate existing members as they reach new heights.

30. *Three-Year Budgeting*. The parish maintains a rolling three-year budget, to help members see the bigger picture—where the parish is heading, and what needs to be done each year, to help get it there.

Templates

To help parishes improve, several resources in this book are included in Microsoft Word format and in rtf format on the enclosed CD. These templates may be copied onto the parish's computer and changed to reflect the parish's uniqueness. In this way, the templates can drive the parish to produce their own plans, forms, positions, etc. in a more complete way (also, many keystrokes will be eliminated). The files are listed by type, followed by their file name.

1. Parish Position Descriptions

Warden	(chapter 2)	warden.doc
Greeter	(chapter 4)	greeter.doc
Congregation Development Team Leader	(chapter 4)	congdevlead.doc
Volunteer Coordinator	(chapter 5)	volcoord.doc
Sexton	(chapter 9)	sexton.doc
Secretary/Bookkeeper	(chapter 11)	sec.doc
Treasurer	(chapter 11)	treas.doc

2. Parish Team Plans

Growth/Marketing	(chapter 4)	growth.doc
Congregation Development	(chapter 4)	congdevplan.doc
Outreach Development	(chapter 8)	outreach.doc
Assets Management	(chapter 9)	assetsplan.doc
Financial Management	(chapter 11)	finplan.doc

3. Forms and Checklists

ParishWorks Self-Assessment	(chapter 1)	selfassessment.doc
Parish Improvement Priorities	(chapter 1)	priorities.doc
Annual Parish Survey	(chapter 4)	survey.doc
Absentee Parishioner Calling Script	(chapter 4)	script.doc

Index

A

B

C

fund-raising, 18, 36, 44, 49, 113, 114, 124, 140, 150, 152, 154, 173, 212, 222, 223, 238

fund-raising costs, 178, 218, 225

G

grants, 126, 140, 146

greeters, 14, 18, 45, 46, **50**, 58, 59, 68, 241

groundskeeping, 122, 126, 128, 135, 154, 162, 176, 216

growth/marketing plan, 14, **38**

growth projects, 139

GST refundable, 188

GST refunds, 168

guest rectors, 16, 93

H

honorariums, 163, 164, 175, 215

I

income/expense categories, 171, 172, 183, 184, 231

income/expenses report, 193

inflation rate, 129, 210, 217

in-memoriums, 169, 172, 179, 212

inspections, 18, 22, **118**, 123, 142, 148, 152

insurance, 16, 22, 126, **129**, 131, 161, 177, 210, 217

interest income, 174, 179, 180, 182, 213, 219

Internet service provider, 199

internments, 134, 149, 170, 182

L

lay sermons 18

leading by example, 73

leasing, 177, 205

liabilities, 161

line of credit, 195, 218, 226

loan interest, 178, 218

M

N

O

P

Q

R

S

sub-ledgers, 169
Sunday school, 15, 18, 36, 41, 50, 82, 93, 94, 96, 114, 175, 215
suspense accounting, 170
synod, 182, 220

T

tax receipts, 125, 172, 185, 190, 192, 232, 233
team meetings, 64, 95, 109, 143, 150, 151, 158, 159, 199, 228
telecommunications software, 199
telephone charges, 235
term deposits, 169, 170, 174, 179, 196
time-keeping, 165
time-out password, 200
treasurer, 16, 24, 63, 84, 87, 108, 118, 124, 130, 137, 154, 167, 171, 183, 184, 190, 193, 195, 200, 205, 210, 221, 222, 224, 229, **232**, 234, 239, 240
trial balance report, 195

U

utilities, 126, 135, 137, 156, 157, 183

V

variance management, 221
variance reporting, 23, 202
vestry, 23, 57, 63, 79, 86, 90, 108, 118, 130, 142, 150, 154, 195, 196, 210, 221, 224, 232, 238
visitations, 18, 24, 43, 61
volunteer appreciation events, 14, 78
volunteer burnout, 18, **75**, 79, 80, 160, 238
volunteer coordinator, 33, 56, 59, 66, 77, 80, 108, 128, 158, 228, 238, 240, 242
volunteer inventory, 19, 79
volunteer management, 18, 25, 60, **72**, 77, 242
volunteer recruiting, 74

W

web site, 15, 25, 28, 41, 54, 58, 62, 67, 82, 83, 85, 95, 133, 147, 157, 175, 177, 198, 205, 215, 217, 223, 235, 242

Ward McCance is available on a consulting basis to help kick-start or evaluate your ParishWorks and program(s). He can be contacted through e-mail (parishworks@sympatico.ca).